Commitment to Musical Excellence

# Commitment to Musical Excellence:
# A 75 Year History of the Gustavus Choir

By

David Holdhusen

Commitment to Musical Excellence:
A 75 Year History of the Gustavus Choir,
by David Holdhusen

This book first published 2011

Cambridge Scholars Publishing

12 Back Chapman Street, Newcastle upon Tyne, NE6 2XX, UK

British Library Cataloguing in Publication Data
A catalogue record for this book is available from the British Library

Copyright © 2011 by David Holdhusen

All rights for this book reserved. No part of this book may be reproduced, stored in a retrieval system, or transmitted, in any form or by any means, electronic, mechanical, photocopying, recording or otherwise, without the prior permission of the copyright owner.

ISBN (10): 1-4438-2670-7, ISBN (13): 978-1-4438-2670-9

Dedicated to:
Deedra, Annika, Eleanor,
and all those who supported and mentored me

# Table of Contents

List of Illustrations .................................................................................. ix

Foreword .................................................................................................. xv
Dr. Gregory Aune

Chapter One .............................................................................................. 1
Introduction
    Gustavus Adolphus College
    The F. Melius Christiansen Legacy

Chapter Two ............................................................................................. 7
Choral Music Activities at Gustavus Adolphus College Prior
to and Including the Formation of the Gustavus Choir
    G. Adolph Nelson
    The Gustavus Choir is Founded

Chapter Three ......................................................................................... 33
The Rebirth of the Gustavus Choir from 1945-1954: The Wilbur
Swanson and Eugene Casselman Years
    Wilbur Swanson
    The Gustavus Choir is Reborn
    The Eugene Casselman Years

Chapter Four ........................................................................................... 47
The Gustavus Choir from 1954 to 1980: The Philip Knautz Years
    Philip Knautz's Choral Approach
    The Philip Knautz Era
    Christ Chapel
    The Continued Contributions of Philip Knautz
    Christmas in Christ Chapel
    The Final Years of the Phil Knautz Tenure

Chapter Five .................................................................................................. 77
The Gustavus Choir from 1980 to 1994: The Karle Erickson Years
    Karle Erickson's Choral Approach
    The Karle Erickson Era

Chapter Six ................................................................................................. 101
The Gustavus Choir from 1995 to 2007: The Contributions
of Gregory Aune
    Gregory Aune Becomes Gustavus Choir Director
    Gregory Aune's Choral Approach
    The Gregory Aune Era

Chapter Seven............................................................................................ 125
Conclusion

Appendix A ................................................................................................ 127
Repertoire Performed by the Gustavus Choir on its Extended Concert
Tours

Appendix B................................................................................................ 197
Concert Locations for the Gustavus Choir on its Extended Concert Tours

Appendix C................................................................................................ 229
Christmas in Christ Chapter Themes

Bibliography ............................................................................................. 231

Index ......................................................................................................... 245

# LIST OF ILLUSTRATIONS

Fig. 2-1 ............................................................................................................... 9
Lyric Quarter in 1891, Gustavus Adolphus College Photograph Collection, 1855-Ongoing. GACA Collection 162.
Gustavus Adolphus College Archives, St. Peter, Minnesota. P-2630.

Fig. 2-2 ............................................................................................................. 13
Schuman/Lyric Tour 1919. Gustavus Adolphus College Photograph Collection, 1855-Ongoing. GACA Collection 162. Gustavus Adolphus College Archives, St. Peter, Minnesota. P-5259.

Fig. 2-3 ............................................................................................................. 14
A Cappella Choir with Director Matthew Lundquist. Gustavus Adolphus College Photograph Collection, 1855-Ongoing. GACA Collection 162. Gustavus Adolphus College Archives, St. Peter, Minnesota. P-2689.

Fig. 2-4 ............................................................................................................. 17
G. Adolph Nelson. Gustavus Adolphus College Photograph Collection, 1855-Ongoing. GACA Collection 162. Gustavus Adolphus College Archives, St. Peter, Minnesota. P-1074.

Fig. 2-5 ............................................................................................................. 21
G. Adolph Nelson with an Early Gustavus A Cappella Choir. Gustavus Adolphus College Photograph Collection, 1855-Ongoing. GACA Collection 162. Gustavus Adolphus College Archives, St. Peter, Minnesota. P-2729.

Fig. 2-6 ............................................................................................................. 25
Choir as part of the May Festival 1935. Gustavus Adolphus College Photograph Collection, 1855-Ongoing. GACA Collection 162. Gustavus Adolphus College Archives, St. Peter, Minnesota. P-5398.

Fig. 2-7 ............................................................................................................. 28
Loading the Bus for the Tour of 1939. Gustavus Adolphus College Photograph Collection, 1855-Ongoing. GACA Collection 162. Gustavus Adolphus College Archives, St. Peter, Minnesota. P-2726.

Fig. 2-8 ............................................................................................................. 30
Percy Grainger Greets People at Gustavus. Gustavus Adolphus College Photograph Collection, 1855-Ongoing. GACA Collection 162. Gustavus Adolphus College Archives, St. Peter, Minnesota. P-4521.

List of Illustrations

Fig. 3-1 .................................................................................................... 34
Wilbur Swanson. Gustavus Adolphus College Photograph Collection, 1855-Ongoing. GACA Collection 162. Gustavus Adolphus College Archives, St. Peter, Minnesota. P-1433.

Fig. 3-2 .................................................................................................... 41
Eugene Casselman with the Choir. Gustavus Adolphus College Photograph Collection, 1855-Ongoing. GACA Collection 162. Gustavus Adolphus College Archives, St. Peter, Minnesota. P-2717.

Fig. 4-1 .................................................................................................... 48
Philip Knautz at Piano. Gustavus Adolphus College Photograph Collection, 1855-Ongoing. GACA Collection 162. Gustavus Adolphus College Archives, St. Peter, Minnesota. P-2645.

Fig. 4-2 .................................................................................................... 53
Gustavus Choir in Robes with Conductor Philip Knautz. Gustavus Adolphus College Photograph Collection, 1855-Ongoing. GACA Collection 162. Gustavus Adolphus College Archives, St. Peter, Minnesota. P-2500.

Fig. 4-3 .................................................................................................... 55
Congressman O'Hara with the Choir in 1957. Gustavus Adolphus College Photograph Collection, 1855-Ongoing. GACA Collection 162. Gustavus Adolphus College Archives, St. Peter, Minnesota. P-2724.

Fig. 4-4 .................................................................................................... 60
Christ Chaple Dedication. Gustavus Adolphus College Photograph Collection, 1855-Ongoing. GACA Collection 162. Gustavus Adolphus College Archives, St. Peter, Minnesota. P-2364-02.

Fig. 4-5 .................................................................................................... 61
Christ Chapel Construction. Gustavus Adolphus College Photograph Collection, 1855-Ongoing. GACA Collection 162. Gustavus Adolphus College Archives, St. Peter, Minnesota. P-2362-02 & P-2362-06.

Fig. 4-6 .................................................................................................... 62
Christ Chapel Inside. Gustavus Adolphus College Photograph Collection, 1855-Ongoing. GACA Collection 162. Gustavus Adolphus College Archives, St. Peter, Minnesota. P-2403.

Fig. 4-7 .................................................................................................... 63
Knautz Rehearsing in Chapel. Gustavus Adolphus College Photograph Collection, 1855-Ongoing. GACA Collection 162. Gustavus Adolphus College Archives, St. Peter, Minnesota. P-2709.

Fig. 4-8 .......................................................................................................... 65
King Gustav Adolph VI with Choir 1967. Gustavus Adolphus College Photograph Collection, 1855-Ongoing. GACA Collection 162. Gustavus Adolphus College Archives, St. Peter, Minnesota. P-2505.

Fig. 4-9 .......................................................................................................... 67
Fine Arts Building Completed in 1971. Gustavus Adolphus College Photograph Collection, 1855-Ongoing. GACA Collection 162. Gustavus Adolphus College Archives, St. Peter, Minnesota. P-2476-03.

Fig. 4-10 ........................................................................................................ 68
Paul Allwardt at Christ Chapel Organ. Gustavus Adolphus College Photograph Collection, 1855-Ongoing. GACA Collection 162. Gustavus Adolphus College Archives, St. Peter, Minnesota. P-2476-03.

Fig. 4-11 ........................................................................................................ 70
Christmas in Christ Chapel from the 1980s. Gustavus Adolphus College Photograph Collection, 1855-Ongoing. GACA Collection 162. Gustavus Adolphus College Archives, St. Peter, Minnesota. P-2692.

Fig. 4-12 ........................................................................................................ 71
O Come All Ye Faithful with Herald Trumpets at Christmas in Christ Chapel in 2005. Photo courtesy Gustavus Adolphus College Public Relations Office.

Fig. 4-13 ........................................................................................................ 76
Philip Knautz Conducts the Gustavus Choir. Gustavus Adolphus College Photograph Collection, 1855-Ongoing. GACA Collection 162.
Gustavus Adolphus College Archives, St. Peter, Minnesota. P-2649.

Fig. 5-1 .......................................................................................................... 78
Karle Erickson. Photo courtesy Karle Erickson

Fig. 5-2 .......................................................................................................... 82
Gustavus Choir in Velvet Robes. Gustavus Adolphus College Photograph Collection, 1855-Ongoing. GACA Collection 162. Gustavus Adolphus College Archives, St. Peter, Minnesota. P-4487.

Fig. 5-3 .......................................................................................................... 86
King and Queen of Sweden Greet Gustavus Choir Members. Gustavus Adolphus College Photograph Collection, 1855-Ongoing. GACA Collection 162. Gustavus Adolphus College Archives, St. Peter, Minnesota. P-2519.

Fig. 5-4 .......................................................................................................... 91
The Gustavus Choir Performs in Poland. Gustavus Adolphus College Photograph Collection, 1855-Ongoing. GACA Collection 162. Gustavus Adolphus College Archives, St. Peter, Minnesota. P-2523-03.

List of Illustrations

Fig. 5-5 .................................................................................................... 92
Erickson Rehearses the Choir for the 125$^{th}$ Anniversary Celebration. Gustavus Adolphus College Photograph Collection, 1855-Ongoing. GACA Collection 162. Gustavus Adolphus College Archives, St. Peter, Minnesota. P-2524-21.

Fig. 5-6 .................................................................................................... 93
Cast of St. Erik's Crown. Gustavus Adolphus College Photograph Collection, 1855-Ongoing. GACA Collection 162. Gustavus Adolphus College Archives, St. Peter, Minnesota. P-2535.

Fig. 5-7 .................................................................................................... 96
Choir Members Touring China. Gustavus Adolphus College Photograph Collection, 1855-Ongoing. GACA Collection 162. Gustavus Adolphus College Archives, St. Peter, Minnesota. P-2685-18.

Fig. 5-8 .................................................................................................... 97
Film Crew Catches Choir Performance. Gustavus Adolphus College Photograph Collection, 1855-Ongoing. GACA Collection 162. Gustavus Adolphus College Archives, St. Peter, Minnesota. P-2685-12.

Fig. 5-9 .................................................................................................. 100
Karle Erickson Conducts the Gustavus Choir at Christmas in Christ Chapel. Gustavus Adolphus College Photograph Collection, 1855-Ongoing. GACA Collection 162. Gustavus Adolphus College Archives, St. Peter, Minnesota. P-5401.

Fig. 6-1 .................................................................................................. 102
Kenneth and Carolyn Jennings with Gustavus President and First Lady on Tour. Photo provided by the author.

Fig. 6-2 .................................................................................................. 105
Gregory Aune. Photo courtesy Gregory Aune.

Fig. 6-3 .................................................................................................. 110
Aune Conducts the Gustavus Choir. Photo courtesy Gregory Aune.

Fig. 6-4 .................................................................................................. 113
Christ Chapel is Damaged by the Tornado. Photo courtesy Gustavus Adolphus College.

Fig. 6-5 .................................................................................................. 115
Aune Talks Music with People in South Africa. The Gustavus Quarterly, 55: 3 (Spring 1999).

Fig. 6-6 ............................................................................................................ 116
Gustavus Choir Performs with South African Dancers. The Gustavus Quarterly, 55: 3 (Spring 1999).

Fig. 6-7 ............................................................................................................ 122
The Gustavus Choir Performs in Spain. The Gustavus Quarterly, 63: 3 (Spring 2007).

Fig. 6-8 ............................................................................................................ 123
75th Anniversary Reunion Choir. The Gustavus Quarterly, 64: 1 (Winter 2007-2008).

# Foreword

## Dr. Gregory Aune
### Director of the Gustavus Choir

In his foreword to the book "Face to Face With An Orchestra", the late Robert Shaw observed that one of the most remarkable developments in the musical world of this century has been the transformation of choral performance from a social and recreational pastime to a level in which the technical and artistic standards rival that of the instrumental and orchestral genres. The catalyst for this phenomenon can justly be attributed to the vision of F. Melius Christiansen and his work with the St. Olaf Choir. In short order, similar choral programs were developed by the other Lutheran Colleges in the Midwest, among them Gustavus Adolphus College. Long noted for their technical and musical accomplishments, rigorous discipline, and professionally managed concert touring, these choirs also function within the greater mission of these church related colleges. This aspect of their identity is somewhat less tangible, one might say philosophical in nature, but viewed as an equally important, underlying core of these ensembles.

After sixteen years of teaching and conducting the Gustavus Choir, my personal reflections affirm the ensemble's place within the Christiansen legacy and philosophy. The singers in the Gustavus Choir eagerly accept and embrace the rigorous daily rehearsal regimen that is recognized as part of our tradition. Each day, these students have congregated in the hallway outside my office door prior to our 4:30 p.m. rehearsal, permeating the space with their energy and enthusiasm, eager to invest in an endeavor that they view as an important and meaningful part of their daily routine. Over the years many singers in the Gustavus Choir have expressed to me how the process of achieving technical mastery of the music we study has enhanced their personal and spiritual growth, and has defined their overall experience at Gustavus. I have also observed that as a result of this communal and intensely creative - aesthetically rewarding experience, a deep and lasting bond is forged among the members of the choir. It should be clearly stated that the choirs from this tradition do not have a monopoly, as it were, on fostering the spiritual/emotive side of the individual. However, because of the liberal arts milieu that these institutions embrace, the high value placed upon music for both the major and non- major in the academic curriculum, and the tradition within which we exist, it is accurate to state that this aspect of the student musician's development is deliberately fostered and nourished. Students that have sung in the Gustavus Choir have been given the rare opportunity to learn discipline for the sake of creating art, imbued with a very real and valued sense of mission in which they engage a wide spectrum of people in a noble and meaningful way. Certainly this book documents and affirms the place of the Gustavus Choir in this long and important Lutheran choral tradition, a tradition that uniquely exemplifies the power of music.

immigrants began to settle in Minnesota. In 1858 the Lutheran Minnesota Conference was organized and two years later the conference became the largest part of the Augustana Synod. The congregations that made up these organizations believed in the importance of a Christian education. In 1860, the Synod formed Augustana College and Theological Seminary in Chicago to train teachers and pastors for this area. The people of Minnesota believed this school to be too great a distance away to serve its needs.[8]

In 1862, the idea for a school emerged from a meeting of the Minnesota Conference. Later that year, Erik Norelius united eleven "older students," who traveled to Red Wing, Minnesota, with the children of the Red Wing congregation to form a school, for which he served as its only teacher.[9] The following year, the Minnesota Conference adopted the school and voted to establish its permanent location in the settlement of East Union in Carver County. At this time it received its first name from the synod, the Minnesota Elementary School. The name was later changed to St. Ansgar's Academy in 1865 to commemorate the 1000th anniversary of St. Ansgar's death.

When the school opened in East Union in 1863 it was housed in a small church. As land and money were acquired, several renovations took place to expand the building and the campus.[10] Throughout the period that the school was located in Carver County, the subjects taught were the same as at Norelius' original school in Red Wing. Students received an education in Christianity, Swedish, English, history, geography, arithmetic, writing, and singing. The total enrollment for the school during the East Union days, 1863-1876, numbered approximately 700 students, the largest class being 68.[11]

Throughout the college's early existence, debate on educational philosophy raged within the Synod between those who wanted centralization, and those who wanted to strengthen the conferences. Finally, a compromise was reached which allowed individual conferences to establish colleges, but kept Augustana as the primary institution for the entire Synod and was to be the only theological seminary.[12] As the population of Minnesota grew and high schools developed throughout the state, Erik Norelius, now a leader in the Conference, recognized the need for a college. He began to search for a location for the institution. In

---

[8] Peterson 9.
[9] Lund 13.
[10] Peterson 19.
[11] Lund 26.
[12] Peterson 27-28.

1873, a board of directors was chosen and the name Gustavus Adolphus Literary and Theological Institute was chosen to replace St. Ansgar. After failing to raise the funds necessary to move to East Minneapolis and partner with the University of Minnesota, the small town of St. Peter promised $10,000 and 10 acres of land in order to persuade the college to be built in its current location. In May of 1874, ministers of the conference, forming the first Board of Education, signed the charter of Gustavus Adolphus College, named to honor Swedish King Gustav Adolf II, who defended Protestantism during the Thirty Years War. Two years later, the construction of Old Main was complete and the first classes were offered.[13]

Since its founding, academic institutions have recognized Gustavus Adolphus College as having a distinguished reputation. It has been identified in numerous publications as one of the top colleges in the United States.[14] The college offers more than 50 majors and 15 pre-professional programs and prides itself on providing a rich learning environment for its students. In addition to seeking a balanced educational tradition, the mission statement also emphasizes the ideals of the Christian faith. The school was founded by the Lutheran Church and the Church continues to play an important role in the life of the college. Gustavus Adolphus College is firmly rooted in its Swedish and Lutheran heritage. It is this legacy from which the institution's mission is derived.[15]

## The F. Melius Christiansen Legacy

As a Lutheran college, situated in the heartland of America, the connection between the Gustavus Choir and the F. Melius Christiansen choral heritage is easily drawn. Gustavus Adolphus College music faculty members agree that this choral tradition is simply part of the culture of the school and is a legacy that is willingly embraced.[16] The Christiansen heritage was clearly evident to former Gustavus Choir director, Karle

---

[13] Lund 33-35, Peterson 30.
[14] Gustavus Adolphus College, *The Gustavus Choir in Concert, 1993*, Program Notes, 1993.
[15] Gustavus Adolphus College, *Gustavus Adolphus College academic catalog, 2006-2007*, (St. Peter, MN: Gustavus Adolphus College, 2006).
[16] David Fienen, interview by author, 12 June 2006, St. Peter, MN, Tape Recording, Gustavus Adolphus College, St. Peter, MN, and Michael Jorgensen, interview by author, 12 June 2006, St. Peter, MN, Tape Recording, Gustavus Adolphus College, St. Peter, MN, and Doug Nimmo, interview by author, 14 June 2006, St. Peter, MN, Tape Recording, Gustavus Adolphus College, St. Peter, MN.

This tradition has been fully embraced throughout the history of the Gustavus Choir.

Since its initial concert tour in 1932, the Gustavus Choir has consistently earned acclaim throughout the world, from audiences and critics alike, for its artistry in performance.[5] The tradition of the extended concert tour showcases the best of the on campus students, while providing an outreach opportunity for the college. Touring aids in attracting prospective students to the college, allows a time for touching base with the alumni, and provides a venue for fundraising. Most importantly, the extended concert tour allows the students to delve more deeply into the literature and grow as musicians with each performance. By performing the same music numerous times in widely varying venues, the choir comes together learning to adapt and develop the discipline needed for consistent artistry.[6] Throughout its history, the Gustavus Choir has gained an international reputation as a quality performing ensemble. It is widely recognized for its performance excellence, as a result of annual tours throughout the United States, Europe, Asia, and Africa. These tours, presented mostly in churches, have served to promote choral music and Gustavus Adolphus College in numerous communities. They have enhanced the artistic understanding of the students in the choir by providing opportunities for them to perform in a variety of venues and locations, while at the same time promoting Gustavus Adolphus College and it mission.

The Gustavus Choir has long stood as the premiere choral ensemble on the campus of Gustavus Adolphus College. It is a tradition rich group that binds its members across generations. Whether it be singing "Praise to the Lord," or touring across the country, the choir has developed a lasting place on the choral landscape. Throughout its history one common element has been a constant for the Gustavus Choir; the ensemble's commitment to musical excellence.

## Gustavus Adolphus College

Gustavus Adolphus College is a small private, liberal arts college located in St. Peter, Minnesota and affiliated with the Evangelical Lutheran Church of America.[7] The roots of the college can be traced back to the mid-nineteenth century when the first significant wave of Swedish

---

[5] Gustavus Adolphus College. *The Gustavus Choir in Concert*. Concert Program Notes. 2006.

[6] Wahlund, interview

[7] Gustavus Adolphus College, *Gustavus Music Showcase*, Program Notes, March 20, 2005.

# CHAPTER ONE

# INTRODUCTION

For seventy-five years, The Gustavus Choir has been an indispensable contributor to the educational environment of Gustavus Adolphus College. The ensemble provides the campus, and the community of St. Peter, Minnesota, as well as areas beyond, with outstanding choral music deeply rooted in the traditions of the Lutheran Choral School, established by F. Melius Christiansen and the a cappella choral movement. From the earliest choir activities on the Gustavus campus to the choir's current mission and philosophies, this stance has been firm. Of the six men who have conducted the ensemble, four of them have some direct tie to the Christiansen family legacy.

The literature performed by the choir reveals information about the philosophies and traditions of the group, as well as insight into its evolution.[1] The traditional programming for the Gustavus Choirs has been music that is primarily unaccompanied and of a sacred nature. F. Melius Christiansen is greatly responsible for the rebirth of a cappella sacred choral music in the colleges of the United States by bringing this style back to the concert halls.[2] The earliest collegiate choral ensembles, like those at Gustavus Adolphus College, were generally glee clubs, which were more socially oriented. These organizations sang mostly "good old college songs" and usually did not perform them at a high quality.[3] Christiansen believed that a cappella choral music could be interpreted in a more refined manner and that there was more of a natural connection between the music and text. He believed that singing unaccompanied also improved the technique of the individual singers. These factors, combined with the age of his singers and the relative ease of touring without the burden of instruments, led to the tradition of a cappella programming.[4]

---

[1] Fenton, 169.
[2] Armstrong, 11.
[3] Van Camp, 11.
[4] Armstrong, 11-12.

Erickson, when he chose the F. Melius Christiansen arrangement of "Praise to the Lord" to serve as the choir's signature selection. Erickson chose this piece primarily because it was composed by Christiansen. It was his hope that the composition would impact the members of Gustavus Choir as "Beautiful Savior" had impacted those from St. Olaf.[17]

The legacy of the Christiansen family is an important factor in the development of the Gustavus Choir and one that has influenced the history of choral music in the United States. The book, *Choral Conducting Symposium*, lists the ideology of F. Melius Christiansen as one of the "six schools of thought that in theory and practice have greatly influenced choral singing in America."[18] In 1963, Leonard Van Camp distributed a questionnaire to choral directors in the United States asking them to indicate those people who influenced their decision to enter the choral music profession. More than 200 names were submitted by respondents, from school teachers, parents, and church choir directors, to professional conductors. More than ten percent of those who responded, by far the highest percentage, designated F. Melius Christiansen, or one of his two sons, Paul or Olaf, as that person of influence. Robert Shaw was the only non-Christiansen named in the top four.[19]

The Christiansen legacy was born in 1907 when, after returning to St. Olaf College following an extended period of study in Leipzig, F. Melius Christiansen organized a mixed octet that would tour in the summer of 1908 to sing primarily his newly composed chorale settings. These chorale arrangements became very popular with the students, who enjoyed the challenging nature of the compositions. Soon after, the students joined with the members of the choir from St. John's Lutheran Church, where Christiansen served as choir director and organist. This ensemble's collaboration with St. Olaf College President J. N. Kildahl in the song services of St. John revitalized the Lutheran tradition of chorale singing.[20] By 1911, the members of the choir were almost entirely connected to St. Olaf College either as students or faculty members. The following year the invitation came for the choir to travel to Eau Claire, Wisconsin, which

---

[17] Karle Erickson, interview by author, 13 June 2006, St. Peter, MN, Tape Recording, Erickson Home, Eden Prarie, MN.
[18] Howard Swan, "The Development of a Choral Instrument" in *Choral Conducting Symposium*. (Upper Saddle River, NJ: Prentice Hall, 1998). 11.
[19] Leonard Van Camp, "The Development and Present Status of A Cappella Singing in the United States Colleges and Universities" (D.M.A. diss., University of Missouri-Kansas City, 1964), 115.
[20] Anton Armstrong, "The Musical Legacy of F. Melius Christiansen," *Choral Journal* 37, no. 4 (1996): 9.

began the tradition of extensive tours. It was for this tour that the name was changed from St. John's Church Choir to St. Olaf Lutheran Choir, which eventually became the St. Olaf Choir.[21] It is this organization that continues to serve as the model for the traditional collegiate a cappella choir in the United States. That is, an ensemble that tours extensively throughout the world, performs primarily music of a sacred nature, pays particular attention to intonation and choral blend, and demonstrates a discipline and control in both rehearsal and performance.[22]

The F. Melius Christiansen School of choral singing continues to influence singers and conductors throughout the world. It also has provided a foundation around which many choral ensembles have been shaped, especially in the church related colleges and those within the Lutheran tradition.[23] Many quality choirs subscribe to the philosophy of precision that this school represents.[24] The Gustavus Choir was born into the Christiansen heritage and has developed a legacy of choral singing that is firmly ensconced in its traditions.

---

[21] Albert Rykken Johnson. "The Christiansen Choral Tradition: F. Melius Christiansen, Olaf C. Christiansen, and Paul J. Chirstiansen" (Ph.D. diss., University of Iowa, 1973), 2.
[22] Gregory J. Aune, "The Choral Methodology and Philosophy of F. Melius Christiansen: A Tradition Continues," *Choral Journal* 37, no. 4 (1996): 15-17. and Van Camp 22.
[23] Armstrong 14.
[24] Swan 131.

# Chapter Two

# Choral Music Activities at Gustavus Adolphus College Prior to and Including the Formation of the Gustavus Choir

From its founding in 1862, Gustavus Adolphus College has included vocal music as a vital part of its curriculum. In its earliest days in Red Wing and Carver County, Minnesota, singing was listed alongside writing, arithmetic, Swedish, Christianity, and others, as subjects to be taught.[1] These initial vocal music classes focused primarily on the foundations of singing. Participation in vocal music was obligatory. Students met with professors of the Music Department twice a week to practice. The "do-re-mi-system" or "sol-fa-system" was used to teach reading skills that included singing the major and minor scales in sharps and flats, as well as chromatic tones. In addition to these exercises in vocal technique, the students practiced hymns, anthems, and choruses as a part of their vocal training. The college sought to prepare its students to become music teachers and organists in order to take the musical traditions into area congregations.[2]

Choral ensembles did not officially exist as recognized societies until the 1880s. However, choral singing as part of a student's vocal training did produce choirs that performed at campus events prior to this. This "Choir" played a significant role in commencement exercises each year

---

[1] Lund 27.
[2] *Tenth annual catalogue of Gustavus Adolphus College at St. Peter, Minnesota, for 1885*-1886, (Rock Island, IL: Augustana Book Concern, 1886), 18 and *Catalogue of Gustavus Adolphus College, at St. Peter, Minnesota, for 1889-1890*, (St. Peter, MN: The Herald Book Print, 1890), 29.

during the 1880s, singing various numbers on each occasion.[3] In May of 1885, the "College Choir" performed as part of the Jubilee Festival of Gustavus Adolphus College at Swedish Lutheran Church in St. Peter, Minnesota.[4]

The first official choral ensembles associated with the college were formed in the early 1880s; an exact date of formation is unclear. These organizations were the Caliope, a male quartet, the Thalia, a mixed quartet. Later in the decade, another mixed quartet, the Sappho, was established. Several unrecognized organizations may have existed prior to the formation of these ensembles, but do not appear in official college records.[5] The *Catalogue of Gustavus Adolphus College* first listed choral groups during the 1887-1888 school year. The Male Chorus under the direction of O. A. Allen consisted of sixteen voices. The Polyhymnian Octette, an eight member mixed ensemble that established a reputation as a concert company, was directed by a young Carl Seashore. A student at the time, Seashore went on to become a noted music psychologist and was the author of the *Seashore Measures of Musical Talent*, the first standardized musical aptitude test.

The following year the band director, Dr. Reinhold Lagerstrom, assumed the responsibility of leading the Male Chorus, which would later become the Lyric Quartette. It was at this time that the tradition of touring began at Gustavus Adolphus College as the Male Chorus joined with the college band on a concert tour through central Minnesota during the Christmas break.[6] The traveling tradition would become a hallmark of the ensemble and later the Gustavus Choir.

The Lyric Quartette began as a nine voice male, a cappella ensemble that included its director, Dr. Lagerstrom, as one of its second basses. The Quartette performed primarily folk music from the United States and Sweden. The group quickly became the most visible vocal ensemble on

---

[3] *Commencement Program*, (St. Peter, MN: Gustavus Adolphus College, 1883) and *Commencement Program*, St. Peter, MN: Gustavus Adolphus College, 1885) and *Commencement Program*, St. Peter, MN: Gustavus Adolphus College, 1887) and *Commencement Program*, St. Peter, MN: Gustavus Adolphus College, 1888).

[4] Programme of Jubilee Festival of Gustavus Adolphus College at Swedish Lutheran Church, St. Peter, Minn, (St. Peter, MN: Gustavus Adolphus College, 1885).

[5] "Conservatory of Music," In *Breidablick*, (St. Peter, MN: Gustavus Adolphus College, 1912), 124.

[6] Catalogue of Gustavus Adolphus College at St. Peter, Minnesota, for 1887-1888, (Rock Island, IL: Augustana Book Concern, 1888), 36 and Catalogue of Gustavus Adolphus College, at St. Peter, Minnesota, for 1888-1889, (St. Peter, MN: Tribune Steam Print, 1889), 40.

the Gustavus campus. Known for its precision and harmonic mastery, its tours throughout the state of Minnesota were very well received by audiences and critics alike.[7]

Fig. 2-1 Lyric Quartet in 1891
Photo courtesy Gustavus Adolphus College Archives, GACA Collection 162, P-2630.

The success of the Lyric Quartette opened the door for an influx of new choral ensembles at Gustavus Adolphus College. During the 1892-1893 school year, the Conservatory Chorus, a fifty voice mixed ensemble, was assembled for the purpose of performing sacred and secular music by master composers. This group was also under the direction of Reinhold Lagerstrom.[8] The first known performance of the choir was in the spring of 1893 when it appeared in The Pipe Organ Concert at the Swedish Lutheran Church in St. Peter, Minnesota. The literature performed by this

---

[7] *The Lyric Concert Co. The Lyric Quartette,* (St. Peter, MN: Gustavus Adolphus College Archives, 1893).
[8] *Gustavus Adolphus College Catalogue for the year 1892-1893,* (St. Peter, MN: Herald Power Print, 1893), 47.

choral organization strayed from the a cappella establishment in favor of larger scale works and was usually accompanied by the organ.

In addition to the Conservatory Chorus, the Pipe Organ Concert also featured the Lyric Quartette, and a women's choir. The Ladies Octette sang "Be Still," by Möhring, marking the first time a strictly women's ensemble performed at a Gustavus Adolphus College event.[9] The following year, this ensemble, now known as The Gounod Ladies Quartet, first appeared in the college catalog. By 1895 the Quartet began sharing concerts with the already established Lyric Male Quartet. These concerts featured performances by each group individually, but also included the performance of one selection as a mixed choir.[10]

Over the next several years, the college saw the formation and disbandment of numerous choral organizations, made up of all combinations of singers. The Gounod Ladies Quartet ceased to exist, but other women's ensembles continued the traditions of treble singing that it had established. The Conservatory Chorus and The Lyric Quartet became the staples of the growing and evolving choral department at Gustavus. The Lyric Quartet continued its tradition of touring, branching out beyond Minnesota by bringing concerts into the surrounding states. In May of 1898, the Conservatory Chorus performed *The Holy City*, an oratorio composed by Alfred Robert Gaul, at the Swedish Lutheran Church in St. Peter, Minnesota.[11] This marked the first of what would become an annual tradition of oratorio performance by this ensemble. The popularity of this ensemble and its mission to perform large accompanied literature were typical of collegiate organizations of the time. By the turn of the century, the Conservatory Chorus had joined the college band and Mozart Orchestra as the permanent musical organizations of Gustavus Adolphus College open to all students at no fee. The Lyric Quartet expanded its membership and became the Lyric, and continued as an ancillary musical

---

[9] *Program for the Pipe Organ Concert, in the Swedish Lutheran Church*, (St. Peter, MN, Gustavus Adolphus College, 1983).
[10] *Gustavus Adolphus College Catalogue for the Year 1894-1895*, (St. Peter, MN: Herald Power Print, 1895), 54-55 and *The Lyric Male Quartet and The Gounod Ladies Quartet Assisted by Mr. Leonard N. Pehrson, the Popular Trombone Soloist, Will Give a Select Concert*, (St. Peter, MN: Gustavus Adolphus College, 1895).
[11] *The Holy* City, Concert Program. (St. Peter, MN: Gustavus Adolphus College, 1898).

group while all other choral ensembles existed in connection with the literary societies.[12]

In 1905, Reinhold Lagerstrom relinquished control of Lyric to C. J. Knock and the Conservatory Chorus to J. Victor Bergquist. Following the 1906-1907 school year, Lagerstrom resigned his professorship, ending a nineteen-year service to the music department at Gustavus.[13] Knock and Berquist continued the many traditions previously ensconced in these ensembles. During this time, the Conservatory Chorus swelled to more than 100 members and became exclusively the performers of classical sacred cantatas, anthems, and oratorios. In 1909, both of these organizations became the responsibility of Per Olson for one year before he surrendered leadership. A. Waldemar Anderson became the next music faculty member to assume the responsibilities of the college band and orchestra, as well as the Conservatory Chorus and the Lyric organization.[14]

During this era of music professor transition, Gustavus Adolphus College saw the formation of a new choral ensemble, the Echoes Ladies' Chorus, a twenty member female choir, which was the same size as the well-established male ensemble, The Lyric. This ensemble, founded in 1905 by Carl Knock, quickly became a part of the Gustavus Adolphus College musical landscape as a group to rival the Lyric in popularity on campus. Soon the Echoes joined the Lyric as a music organization no longer under the umbrella of the literary societies. In 1913, Professor Anderson took over directorship of this ensemble. The group changed its name to the Schumann Ladies Chorus and began a long and distinguished run as a quality college women's glee club. It was also at this time that the organization began its own tradition of touring by traveling through the state of Minnesota.[15]

---

[12] *Catalogue of Gustavus Adolphus College for the Academic Year 1900-1901*, (St. Peter, MN: Gustavus Adolphus College, 1901), 17-18 and *Catalogue of Gustavus Adolphus College for the academic year 1901-1902*, (St. Peter, MN: Gustavus Adolphus College, 1902), 17.

[13] Lund 87.

[14] "Conservatory of Music," in *Breidablick* (St. Peter, MN: Gustavus Adolphus College, 1912), 126. and "The Lyric," in *Breidablick* (St. Peter, MN: Gustavus Adolphus College, 1912), 134.

[15] *Gustavus Adolphus College Catalog of the academic year 1910-1911*, (St. Peter, MN: Gustavus Adolphus College, 1911), 18 and *Gustavus Adolphus College Catalog for the academic year 1912-1913*, (St. Peter, MN: Gustavus Adolphus College, 1913), 40 and *Gustavus Adolphus College Catalog for the academic year 1913-1914*, (St. Peter, MN: Gustavus Adolphus College, 1914), 37 and *Gustavus Adolphus College Catalog for the academic year 1914-1915*, (St. Peter, MN: Gustavus Adolphus College, 1915), 17-18.

By 1916, the Schumann had joined with the Lyric to present a "Home Concert" in the spring of each year. These concerts included individual performances by each chorus, featured soloists and small groups from the ensembles, and combined the two organizations to perform a selection as a mixed choir.[16] In the spring of 1919, these two choruses completed a successful joint tour marking the first time these organizations traveled as one entity.[17] While the joint Schumann–Lyric tour did not become an annual event, it did solidify the Schumann's standing as a musical organization on campus and hinted, for the first time, at the possibility of a touring mixed choir affiliated with Gustavus Adolphus College.

As the Schumann and Lyric organizations were evolving and continuing to make a name for themselves and the college, the Conservatory Chorus was also beginning to shift its ideology. The choir's membership continued to swell, with enrollment pushing well beyond 150 musicians, including both campus students and city residents. As the group grew, the oratorio became the exclusive performance genre for the ensemble, with the performance of G. F. Handel's, *Messiah*, becoming a frequent occurrence. In 1917, the group changed its name to the Oratorio Chorus to reflect this transition in performance thought.[18]

The fall of 1921 brought a change of leadership to the choirs at Gustavus Adolphus College. Dr. Matthew Lundquist assumed the directorship. Under his guidance, the Oratorio Chorus's performance of *Messiah* became an annual commencement event. The Schumann and Lyric organizations further contributed strongly to the institution with each group continuing its tradition of annual concert tours.[19] Dr. Lundquist's greatest contribution to the musical landscape at Gustavus came in the fall of 1922, when he proposed the formation of an a cappella chorus.

---

[16] *Schumann – Lyric Home Concert*, Concert Program, (St. Peter, MN: Gustavus Adolphus College, 1916) and *Schumann – Lyric Home Concert*, Concert Program, (St. Peter, MN: Gustavus Adolphus College Archives, 1917).
[17] "The Past, Present and Future," In *The Gustavian*. St. Peter, MN: Gustavus Adolphus College, 1920), 80-81.
[18] *Gustavus Adolphus College Catalog for the Academic Year 1916-1917*, (St. Peter, MN: Gustavus Adolphus College, 1917), 17 and "Musical organizations," in *The Gustavian*. (St. Peter, MN: Gustavus Adolphus College, 1917) 165.
[19] *Gustavus Adolphus College Catalog for the Academic Year 1920-1921*, (St. Peter, MN: Gustavus Adolphus College, 1921), 19-20.

Choral Music Activities at Gustavus Adolphus College          13

Fig. 2-2  Schuman/Lyric Tour 1919
Photo courtesy Gustavus Adolphus College Archives, GACA Collection 162, P-5259.

At a joint meeting of the Lyric and Schumann organizations on September 28, 1922, Dr. Lundquist presented the suggestion for a Gustavian Choir, a mixed a cappella chorus. He noted that, "if this idea goes through as I have planned it, we will be pioneers of an entirely new field of music." The intention of the proposed choir was to sing primarily the music of the Swedish Lutheran Church. Lundquist believed that the hymns of the church would provide the foundation for the music to be performed. He noted:

> Our psalm book is a rich goldmine from which untold riches can be obtained with proper handling. Our ancient, mighty chorales are masterpieces of pure religious music. With correct harmonization they can be made into something tremendous if interpreted feelingly by a well-trained chorus.[20]

Dr. O. J. Johnson, President of Gustavus Adolphus College, was also present at this meeting of the choruses and heartily endorsed the formation of this new group, noting that students would be missionaries. "You have an opportunity that cannot be overestimated in presenting this religious

---

[20] "Dr. Lundquist Proposes Occopello Chorus," *The Gustavian Weekly*, 3 October 1922: 1.

music to our people." It was his belief that there was no reason the Gustavian Choir would fail.[21]

Both the Lyric and Schumann Choruses responded enthusiastically to the proposal. After a brief discussion, it was unanimously decided to adopt the plan and form the Gustavian Choir for at least that year. The Schumann and Lyric organizations would remain intact and exist as separate performance groups. By combining the members of these two ensembles the new choir would take shape.

The newly formed a cappella choir soon began rehearsing. In January of 1923, a tour was proposed that would take the ensemble through southern Minnesota and parts of Iowa, Nebraska, and South Dakota. The planned tour was to begin at the end of April and extend into the early part of May. As the prospects for this tour strengthened, a rehearsal was added bringing the total number of practice times per week to three.[22]

Fig. 2-3  A Cappella Choir with director Matthew Lundquist
Photo courtesy Gustavus Adolphus College Archives, GACA Collection 162, P-2689.

Throughout the spring semester, in preparation for the tour, the choir performed at various campus and local events. One such performance included Cap and Gown Day at Gustavus. At this service the choir performed two numbers by F. Melius Christiansen, including "Praise to the Lord," a piece that would become the signature selection of the Gustavus Choir 58 years later. In addition to these Christiansen pieces, this first edition of the Gustavian Choir performed other musical standards of the a cappella tradition including Richard Wagner's *Pilgrims Chorus* and a chorale by J. S. Bach. At the end of April, 1923, the choir took these

---

[21] Ibid. 2.
[22] "Tour Prospects for College Singers Very Encouraging," *The Gustavian Weekly*, 13 February 1923, 1.

selections and others by both the full choir and the Schumann and Lyric individually on a successful concert tour.[23]

The following year changes were made to accommodate and support the choir. The faculty decided to award one credit per semester for work that was done in the ensemble. Arrangements were also made to hold additional part practice outside the regularly scheduled two rehearsals per week.[24] Despite the support of the college, new director, Waldo Nielsen, was unable to build on the success of the initial Gustavian Choir. The need for voices and rehearsal time was too great and the choir faded into the background of the musical organizations on campus. The Lyric and Schumann continued to thrive during this time with each group touring individually over the next few years. According to Gustavus Adolphus College catalogs, these two choruses did occasionally unite to perform mixed choir music, but the Gustavian Choir was dormant until 1926.

In the fall of 1926, Albin O. Peterson, who had joined the faculty as director of the school of music in 1925, announced the organization of the A Cappella Choir and set tryouts for the afternoon of September 28. The choir was established as a mixed chorus to render classical sacred music. Peterson noted this was not a new organization to take the place of the Oratorio Chorus, but instead a revival of the Gustavian Choir under a new name. It was his hope that this renewal would be the first step toward further activity for the organization.[25]

This choir, unlike its predecessor, was chosen through competitive audition from the entire student body, not simply by combining the Schumann and Lyric choruses. Forty members were to be selected with ten people on each voice part. The choir members were selected over several weeks of auditions. The entire Schumann chorus entered in whole, while only a very few members of Lyric responded, leaving a need for male singers, especially in the first tenor section. Music was selected for a concert tour to include a repertoire of a cappella standards. This program was to include compositions by Bach, Mendelssohn, and Rachmaninoff as well as "Beautiful Savior," "Hosanna," and "Praise to the Lord," by F.

---

[23] "Senior Class Observes Cap and Gown Day in Presence of Board," *The Gustavian Weekly*, 10 April 1923, 1 and "Acapella Chorus Sings," *The Gustavian Weekly*, 27 February 1923, 2.
[24] "Intensive Drill for the Gustavian Choir," *The Gustavian Weekly*, 25 September 1923, 1.
[25] "Music Head Plans Organization of A Capella Choir," (1926). *The Gustavian Weekly*, 25 September 1926, 1.

Melius Christiansen.[26] Despite the best efforts of Professor Peterson, the A Cappella Choir again failed to take hold on the Gustavus Adolphus campus. The tour never materialized and the organization again faded from the landscape and eventually ceased to exist as a musical organization.

Regardless of the continued failure of the a cappella mixed choir at Gustavus, the choral program continued to flourish. The Oratorio Chorus of well over one hundred singers continued its annual spring presentation of *Messiah*. In addition, this ensemble also strived to perform another oratorio of a master composer each fall. The Lyric and Schumann organizations continued to be the face of choral music at Gustavus. The Ladies Chorus became so popular at the college that the group was divided into an A and B section in 1929 to accommodate the number of interested women. These groups continued to perform regularly on and off campus with each ensemble participating in an annual concert tour.[27]

From its founding, Gustavus Adolphus College supported and encouraged vocal music on its campus. Singing was perceived as a way the students could extend beyond the school and bring their heritage into the Lutheran community. As the choirs developed, they became an important face for the school. It was through the foundation of excellence laid out by the Lyric, Schumann, and Oratorio Choruses that determined the future successes of the Gustavus Choir. As the 1920s came to a close, Professor Albin Peterson left the faculty of Gustavus Adolphus College and G. Adolph Nelson became the next head of the school of music. Professor Nelson's arrival brought with him the dawning of a new era of vocal music at Gustavus.

## G. Adolph Nelson

Gustav Adolph Nelson began his musical studies while growing up in his native Michigan. His first musical encounters were under the tutelage of his mother at a very young age. During this time Nelson began to study and hone his keyboard skills, becoming an accomplished pianist and organist. At age seventeen, he became the organist for a prominent church in Duluth, Minnesota. Over the next few years, Nelson continued his musical training earning both a Bachelor of Arts and an A. J. O. degree in music.[28]

---

[26] "A Capella Tryouts are Completed Today," *The Gustavian Weekly*, 12 October 1926, 1.
[27] *Gustavus Adolphus College Catalog for the Academic Year 1928-1929*, (St. Peter, MN: Gustavus Adolphus College, 1929), 86-87.
[28] "Gustav Adolph Nelson, " *St. Peter Herald*, 17 May 1979.

Nelson then spent several years in New York studying with A. M. Richardson and George Boyle. He returned to Minnesota and joined the faculty of the MacPhail School of Music in Minneapolis where he had also studied. In 1930, G. Adolph Nelson assumed the responsibilities as head of the music department at Gustavus Adolphus College. His duties at the college included the director of the choirs and orchestra, instructor and performer on organ and piano, as well as administrative tasks.[29]

Fig. 2-4   G. Adolph Nelson
Photo courtesy Gustavus Adolphus College Archives, GACA Collection 162, P-1074.

## The Gustavus Choir is Founded

In November of 1930 Professor G. Adolph Nelson united the two Schumann choruses and Lyric for the purpose of forming a mixed choral organization to sing the music of the church. By combining these ensembles, this new chorus would provide the opportunity to perform a wider range of literature due to the existence of more sacred music written for mixed voices. It was Nelson's belief that Gustavus Adolphus College was lacking in a chorus of this nature and the formation of this ensemble

---

[29] "Music Panorama of 800 Years: A Choral Achievement," *The Lutheran Companion*, 5 February 1942, 172 and "Prof. Nelson Leads Busy Life Guiding Music Dept.," *The Gustavian Weekly*, 3 19 1940, 3.

would revitalize the interest in choral singing. His hope was to establish an ensemble similar to those at other Lutheran Colleges in the area. The Schumann and Lyric choruses would continue to exist as individual organizations maintaining busy performance and touring schedules. This newly formed ensemble, which numbered about sixty voices, would also supplement the Oratorio Chorus, practicing with the group at alternating rehearsals. This organization would be called the A Cappella Chorus and feature the performance of unaccompanied music that would be memorized by the choir.

Nelson planned the first performances of the A Cappella Chorus to be in the spring of 1931. Rehearsals began on the afternoon of Wednesday, November 19, 1930 and continued once a week on Wednesday afternoons throughout the year. In addition, the choir supplemented these rehearsals with part practice outside the scheduled time. Paul Noren was elected president of the organization and the chorus under Nelson's leadership began.[30]

The group started working on literature that would become standards of the repertoire, both for the Gustavus Choir and the A Cappella Choral Movement. The ensemble prepared music that was similar to the earlier editions of a cappella choirs attempted at Gustavus. Composers such as J. S. Bach, Gretchaninoff, and three pieces by F. Melius Christiansen were again represented, including "Praise to the Lord," later the choir's signature selection.[31]

The first performance of the A Cappella Chorus occurred on Sunday, February 15, 1931 at a communion service in connection with the meeting of the Minnesota Conference. The group performed Gretchaninoff's, "O, Lord, Hear My Prayer." Approximately one month later, the choir again sang this selection, for a student chapel service on campus.[32]

As the spring semester continued, the A Cappella Chorus lost momentum. The individual performances of the Schumann and Lyric organizations become a higher priority. The Lyric Male Chorus embarked on a three state concert tour in late March under the direction of Walter Scott Johnson. Adolph Nelson led the Schumann Ladies Chorus on a separate ten-day tour through northern Minnesota. These individual concert tours were very well received. The high level of success for both

---

[30] "A Capella Choir is Organized at Meet," *The Gustavian Weekly*, 13 January 1931, 1.
[31] "Schumann, Lyric Groups Unite in Acapella Chorus," *The Gustavian Weekly*, 18 November 1930, 1.
[32] "A Cappella Appears on Chapel Program," *The Gustavian Weekly*, 24 March 1931, 1.

the Schumann and Lyric choruses, in combination with additional scheduling conflicts on campus, again rendered the A Cappella Chorus inactive at Gustavus Adolphus College by the end of the year 1931.[33]

In the fall of 1932 an a cappella choir at Gustavus Adolphus College finally took permanent hold. In its announcements for the 1932-1933 school year, the college catalog listed "The College Choir" for the first time as a course within the Conservatory of Music. The purpose of this organization, led by G. Adolph Nelson, was again to perform the best of unaccompanied music, this time encompassing both the sacred and secular realms.[34] However, the choice of literature tended to be of a sacred nature.

Again, the choir began as the combination of the Schumann and Lyric organizations. This time, however, the independent nature of these ensembles was somewhat stripped away in order to focus primarily on the mixed chorus. Adolph Nelson had assumed the leadership of Lyric Male Chorus giving him complete control over the choral organizations. The a cappella choir sang throughout the fall semester, including performances at homecoming and for regular chapel services. While these performances started to build the ensemble's reputation, it was the plans being made for the spring of 1933 that would ensure the lasting success of the Gustavus Adolphus College Choir.

The first full concert performance of the Gustavus Adolphus A Cappella Choir took place on March 15, 1933, at Calvary Lutheran Church in Minneapolis, Minnesota. The choir sang as part of a program sponsored by the Gustavus Alumni Association at the Minnesota Conference meeting. This concert, which featured the standards of Bach, Gretchaninoff, and F. Melius Christiansen, established the A Cappella Chorus as the featured ensemble representing the college. While individual performances by the Schumann and Lyric organizations were also included as sections within the concert program, the A Cappella Choir was the featured ensemble and provided the bulk of the repertoire performed.[35]

The further establishment of the A Cappella Choir's role within the choral department continued just two weeks later when the ensemble set out on its first annual concert tour. The itinerary took the choir to northern

---

[33] "The A Capella Chorus," in *The Gustavian*, 146, St. Peter, MN: Gustavus Adolphus College, 1932 and "Lyric Male Chorus," in *The Gustavian*, 142, St. Peter, MN: Gustavus Adolphus College and "Schumann Laides Chorus," in *The Gustavian*, 143, St. Peter, MN: Gustavus Adolphus College.

[34] *Gustavus Adolphus College Catalog for the academic year 1931-1932,* (St. Peter, MN: Gustavus Adolphus College, 1932), 81.

[35] "A Capella Concert Given at Minnesota Conference Meeting," *The Gustavian Weekly*, 21 March 1933, 1.

and central Minnesota for nine performances in churches throughout the synod. The concerts were well received by audiences and the choir earned stellar reviews. The musicianship with which they sang prompted Walter Buszin of the Mankato Free Press to pen, "This Choir rendered a program which would do honor to a reputable veteran choir. The fact that Gustavus Adolphus Choir is but one year old adds to the credit it deserves."[36]

The tour concluded with a "Home Concert" presented on April 11, 1933, in the auditorium on the Gustavus campus. The program for the tour featured the same musical selections performed at the Minnesota Conference meeting. While this tour was not the first to feature the combined Lyric and Schumann organizations, it was the first which placed its emphasis on the A Cappella Choir. The individual performances of the men's and women's ensembles played only a minor role in the entire program.[37]

The school year concluded with performances as part of the commencement activities for the college. The choir presented an encore performance of its tour program on the Saturday evening prior to graduation to an appreciative audience. The final appearance of the ensemble was made as the representative of choral department at the annual commencement ceremony on June 6.[38]

Throughout the course of the 1932-1933 school year, the Gustavus Adolphus College A Cappella Choir became the choral organization most associated with the college. By establishing the College Choir as the premiere ensemble for the choral department, using the Lyric and Schumann groups as ancillary ensembles, Nelson ensured the a cappella choral tradition at the college would endure.

The following year tryouts for the A Cappella Chorus were held early in the fall. Believing that the prospects for the success of the choir were the brightest in many years, Nelson actively recruited students of all abilities to try out. He auditioned the singers specifically for the mixed ensemble and stated that the division of the men and women of the college choir would then form the Schumann and Lyric organizations. This marked the first time these ensembles were not selected through independent auditions, instead as part of a larger choir.[39]

---

[36] "A Capella Choir to Begin Concert Tour Sunday Afternoon," *The Gustavian Weekly*, 28 March 1933, 1.
[37] Ibid.
[38] "A Capella Chorus Presents Concert Saturday Evening," *The Gustavian Weekly*, 6 June 1933, 1.
[39] "Choir Organization by Prof G. A. Nelson to Begin this Week," *The Gustavian Weekly*, 19 September 1933, 1.

Auditions took place over a four-day period during which Nelson heard approximately seventy voices. From the interest shown by the students, it was clear that the A Cappella Chorus was growing in popularity and had clearly established itself as the flagship for the choral program. Nelson selected forty-one singers to make up the 1933-1934 choir. Due to the abundance of students interested in singing, he even suggested the formation of a second a cappella choir at Gustavus, but this idea was not acted upon and the choir never materialized.[40]

The choir was active during the year, performing at various campus events, chapel services, and serving as the Gustavus representative at the Minnesota Conference convention. In December of 1933, the ensemble hosted a Christmas party for the college for the purpose of raising funds to purchase robes for the choir. Nelson featured a performance by the choir and several other student presentations that depicted Christmas traditions from countries around the world. Following the program, members of the choir planned a "gala funfest of games and merriment, supplemented with generous refreshments" for the student body.[41] The party proved to be a successful endeavor and the choir was completely outfitted in robes of black and white for the spring concert tour. This marked the start of the Gustavus Choir tradition of wearing robes as concert attire.

Fig. 2-5　G. Adolph Nelson with an early Gustavus A Cappella Choir
Photo courtesy Gustavus Adolphus College Archives, GACA Collection 162, P-2729.

---

[40] "Seventy Voices Try Out for A Capella," *The Gustavian Weekly*, 26 September 1933, 1 and "College Choir of 41 Voices Begins Work," *The Gustavian Weekly*, 3 October 1933, 1.
[41] "Choir Will Sponsor Big Christmas Party," *The Gustavian Weekly*, 21 November 1933, 1.

In 1934, Nelson organized his most ambitious spring concert tour. On April 8 the choir, now consisting of forty-two members, set out on a Greyhound bus for a sixteen-day tour that would encompass 1500 miles and five states, Illinois, Iowa, Minnesota, Nebraska, and South Dakota. His plans included the choir's first radio appearance from the Moody Bible College in Chicago. The choir presented a thirty-minute musical program that was broadcast over the airwaves of WEMB radio on April 16.[42]

While the tour did provide many challenges, including traveling through a severe dirt storm in southeastern South Dakota, it proved to be a successful venture for the choir, its audiences, and the college. The choir performed for churches filled to capacity throughout the tour making for a financially profitable undertaking. This was a particularly encouraging aspect of the tour because the more established St. Olaf Choir, from Northfield, Minnesota, often preceded the Gustavus Choir by just a few days, at many stops.[43]

Upon the conclusion of the tour, the choir presented a homecoming concert as part of the first Festival of Sacred Music on the Gustavus campus. The concert was attended by more than 500 pastors, church choir directors, and congregates who had participated in the music festival. The program featured several a cappella pieces that had been performed on its extended tour. In all, the choir presented 25 concerts during the 1933-34 school year, not including local appearances and chapel services. The continued improvement and accomplishments of the choir in its short existence further enhanced the reputation of the group.[44]

By the fall of 1934 this choral organization, now officially named "The Gustavus Adolphus Choir" in the college catalog, was running like clockwork. Nelson selected a forty-seven voice ensemble that proceeded through another ambitious and successful year.[45]

In December of 1934 the Choral Department strayed from its traditional rendering of G. F. Handel's *Messiah*. Instead, the Gustavus Choir presented "The Story of Christmas," a pageant of music revolving around

---

[42] "College Choir Begins Tour of Five States," *The Gustavian Weekly*, 10 April 1934, 1.
[43] "G. A. Choir Meets with Big Welcome," *The Gustavian Weekly*, 17 April 1934, 1 and "Choir Returns from Sixteen Day Schedule," *The Gustavian Weekly*, 24 April 1934, 1.
[44] "500 applaud A Capella Choir in Homecoming Concert Sunday," *The Gustavian Weekly*, 8 May 1934, 1.
[45] "Personnel of College Choir Includes 47," *The Gustavian Weekly*, 9 October 1934, 1.

the birth of Christ. The program was a combination of speaking roles, solos, duets, quartets and performances by the entire choir. The pageant opened with the Schumann Chorus and progressed through the well-known portions of the Christmas story with the Gustavus Choir playing the major role. Following the final tableau centered at the Christmas altar, the choir assembled on the stage with lighted candles to perform, "The Earth Has Grown Old," before concluding the evening by singing "Adeste Fideles" with the audience.[46] An arrangement of "Adeste Fideles," or "O Come All Ye Faithful," would become the annual closing hymn for the Christmas Program in Christ Chapel during the 1970s.

The second half of the school year included many regular campus performances and rehearsals leading up to the spring concert tour. In addition to these preparations, the choir combined with the Choral Club, formerly the Oratorio Chorus, to present a program in commemoration of the 250$^{th}$ birthday of J. S. Bach. The event showcased the compositional excellence of Bach, but also brought to light the religious nature of his work, which has been utilized extensively in Lutheran worship. The concert included several numbers by the Choral Club, historical and religious presentations by Gustavus faculty, and showcased Adolph Nelson's stellar keyboard performance skills with a set of organ selections. The Gustavus Choir concluded the program with the Bach motet, "Sing Ye to the Lord," a piece they were preparing to open their tour program, which would begin the following month.[47]

Despite a severe bout of influenza that kept Nelson away from campus for ten days, the third annual concert tour began in March of 1935. In the two weeks leading up to the departure, student director, Ralph Erickson, lead the ensemble in rehearsal and also conducted the choir for a concert in Mankato. This tour included the use of a new staging platform purchased by the choir that was designed to be more durable and easily erected. In addition, this platform was covered in rubber matting making it more comfortable for the choir members to stand for the duration of the concert. This coating also made individual movement by the singers less audible to the audience.[48] The concert program continued to feature a set of selections performed by the Schumann Chorus, but for the first time did not include any performances by the men of the choir. While the Lyric

---

[46] "College Choir Sings Story of Christmas," *The Gustavian Weekly*, 11 December 1934, 1.
[47] "Bach's Birthday Commemorated by Singers, Organist," *The Gustavian Weekly*, 26 February 1935, 1.
[48] "Mankato concert postponed because of director's illness." *The Gustavian Weekly*, 12 March 1935, 1.

Chorus did continue to exist, performances were scarce and the ensemble eventually faded from the choral landscape.

On March 24, the choir set out on a twenty-day tour that took them to nine states and featured twenty performances. For the first time, the ensemble chartered two buses giving choir members room to spread out during the long travel days. They began with two capacity crowd performances in Minneapolis, then traveled as far east as Jamestown, New York presenting concerts in Wisconsin, Michigan, and Ohio before making the return trip through Pennsylvania, Indiana and Illinois. Performances throughout the tour were extremely well attended and proved to be financially successful.[49] Audiences all along the eastern United States praised the choir's concerts, including one critic from St. Ignace, Michigan writing:

> All who heard this concert shall long cherish the beautiful memories of this superb choir. The Gustavus Choir has won a place in the hearts of the people of the eastern end of the Upper Peninsula and we await with the highest joy another appearance of the singers under Prof. Nelson's capable direction.[50]

The choir concluded its year by presenting its home concert for 1935 on May 5 as the climax to the second annual Music Festival at Gustavus.

The fall of 1935 brought about the start of a new school year and the selection of a new forty-seven voice choir. In October, Nelson established a tradition that would continue into the 1950s. As part of the homecoming festivities, the choir hosted a reunion of past Gustavus Choir members. In 1935, about fifty former singers came together to perform three pieces for a special chapel service on the Saturday of homecoming. Sunday included a lunch in the college cafeteria, featuring speeches and entertainment by the choir alumni.[51]

In December, the choir again presented a yuletide program; this time entitled "Vespers of Christmas." The program presented the traditional Lutheran service of Lessons and Carols in which the choir, as well as soloists, provided choral responses to the reading of Christmas related

---

[49] "Large Crowds Hear Choir in the Twin Cities," *The Gustavian Weekly*, 26 March 1935, 1 and "Choir Leaves Sunday on Tour of Eastern United States," *The Gustavian* Weekly, 19 March 1935, 1.
[50] "Choir Winds Up Successful Tour of Twenty Days," *The Gustavian* Weekly, 16 April 1935, 1.
[51] "First Choir Reunion Attracts Many Alumni," *The Gustavian Weekly*, 8 October 1935, 3.

Scripture lessons. As each carol was sung, a tableau was presented depicting the various events of the Christmas story. Again, the recessional hymn "Adeste Fideles" brought the service to a close.[52] This marked the final staging of such a Christmas event during Nelson's tenure. In the years that followed, the choir returned to the tradition of joining the Choral Club in presenting Handel's *Messiah*.

Fig. 2-6 Choir as part of the May Festival 1935
Photo courtesy Gustavus Adolphus College Archives, GACA Collection 162, P-5398.

The tour of 1936 took the choir throughout Minnesota and into parts of North and South Dakota, Iowa and Nebraska during its sixteen-day trip. In addition to the twenty concerts performed during the journey, the choir was also broadcast over KSTP and WNAX radio. The choir was again met very enthusiastically by capacity audiences throughout the tour, which illustrated the popularity of the a cappella choir. The home concert concluded the year as the final event at Gustavus's annual Music Festival.[53] The financial success of the concert tour combined with the money raised by hosting the St. Olaf Choir's first St. Peter appearance in May of 1936 allowed the choir to purchase a new piano for the chapel on campus.[54]

Over the next five years the students who audition for the choir continued to increase in both number and quality. The choir increased its

---

[52] "Choir Opens Yuletide Season with 'Vespers of Christmas,'" *The Gustavian Weekly*, 17 December 1935, 1.
[53] "Success Crowns Choir Concerts on Annual Tour," *The Gustavian Weekly*, 24 March 1936, 1.
[54] "St. Olaf Choir Will Sing Here Friday Evening," *The Gustavian Weekly*, 12 May 1936, 1.

membership to more than fifty singers. Now rehearsing four days per week, the choir had earned an esteemed reputation on campus as the most significant musical ensemble. The college yearbook, *The Gustavian* 1936-37, reads, the "most influential among the musical groups in gaining recognition for the college, most noted for the quality of its entertainment, and most respected for its high aspirations is the Gustavus Choir."[55] As the choir continued to evolve and grow in popularity, its tours became increasingly extensive and the demand for musical excellence increased. As the focus on the a cappella choir intensified, the Schumann Chorus continued as a vital portion of the tour program. However, performances by this ensemble outside of choir tour began to dwindle.

The annual spring tour of the a cappella choir was now the priority for each school year. Due to the touring success of the Gustavus Choir, both musically and financially, a faculty member was named as the organization's business manager in 1936, when Professor Ove Olson, of the education department, assumed the position and also sang in the choir's bass section. The following year, this job became that of Florence Myrum who took over the responsibilities as her only appointment at the college.[56] The naming of a business manager took the day-to-day planning of tours away from director Adolph Nelson allowing him to focus more completely on preparing the choir for performance.

Live campus and area concerts for the ensemble were cut back during this period in order to allow adequate rehearsal time for the choir. However, during this period, Nelson established a tradition for the choir of presenting a half hour program for broadcast over KYSM on the first Sunday of each month.[57] Professor Nelson also stepped up the intensity for the ensemble by demanding greater musicianship and accountability. He pushed singers by requiring vocal examinations, where he would listen to individual members sing in quartets. During the first semester Nelson listened to each group individually perform the entire tour program from memory. He believed this process gave "the public the best choir which has ever been sent out by Gustavus."[58]

In 1937, the choir again traveled eastward, this time extending all the way to the Atlantic coast. During this, its fifth anniversary tour, and for

---

[55] "The A Capella Choir," in *The Gustavian* (St. Peter, MN: Gustavus Adolphus College, 1936), 148.
[56] "Mrs. Myrum starts new choir duties," *The Gustavian Weekly*, 5 October 1937, 1.
[57] "Nelson Selects Forty-Five for A Cappella Choir," *The Gustavian Weekly*, 26 September 1939, 3.
[58] "Olson Books Three State Appearances for the College Choir," *The Gustavian Weekly*, 8 December 1936, 1.

the next three years, the choir would be known as the Cathedral Choir of the Augustana Synod. The renaming was used to publicize the choir and draw attention to the entire synod, but in concert programs the ensemble remained the Gustavus Adolphus College Choir. The east coast tour proved to be very taxing on the ensemble members. The demanding schedule, which included concerts at many of the largest cities on the east coast, including New York and Boston, did not allow them any time to explore the sights in these areas, which caused the choir to coin the slogan, "When better sights are to be seen, the choir will miss them."[59] The tour, which took the choir over 4000 miles and featured more than twenty performances over the three-week period, was a critical success. One critic from Ohio said of the ensemble, "This a cappella choir sang exceptionally well; in fact technically its work was superior to many of the several dozen similar organizations that are touring the country."[60]

The critics continued to laud the choir's performances during its Midwestern tours of 1938 and 1939. The program continued to highlight the masters of a cappella composition, but also began to include the music of Sweden in an attempt reconnect to the heritage of the college. The reputation of the choir soared, drawing favorable comparisons to its counterpart at St. Olaf. Roy Copperud wrote in the Duluth Herald Tribune:

> For many years in this state, the most complimentary references were justly reserved to one choir – that of Dr. F. Melius Christiansen at St. Olaf's college. Now it appears that a creditable contender for honor in this field has come upon the scene.[61]

As the status of the Gustavus Choir grew, its performances within the state of Minnesota, and beyond, became more widely attended and more prestigious in nature. In Minneapolis, the choir was featured in a concert dedicated to the tercentennial celebration of the Swedish colony in Delaware. The performance took place in the Northrup Auditorium at the University of Minnesota before more than 4500 people in 1938. The following year the choir presented the opening concert before the delegates of the Minnesota Conference and featured Gustavus band

---

[59] "Choristers Finally Return: Now They Reveal Hardships," *The Gustavian Weekly*, 20 April 1937, 1.
[60] "Press Comment Cites Concerts of A Cappella," *The Gustavian Weekly*, 11 May 1937, 1.
[61] "Gustavus Choir Returns After Concert Tour Acclaimed Most Successful in History," *The Gustavian Weekly*, 5 April 1938, 1.

director Professor Frederic Hilary on violin. These Midwestern tours also included a stop in Chicago that featured performances each year at Orchestra Hall before a capacity audience and, in 1939, the city originated the choir's first nationwide broadcast on NBC radio.[62]

Fig. 2-7 Loading the Bus for the Tour of 1939
Photo courtesy Gustavus Adolphus College Archives, GACA Collection 162, P-2726.

During the tours of 1940 and 1941 the choir traveled through the heart of its constituents by performing throughout the state of Minnesota. Nelson experimented with the repertoire he programmed for these tours. He called the distinctive programs a combination of, "old and new with the conventional and unusual." The choir performed pieces with a Russian undercurrent and branched out to the more modern and dramatic music;

---

[62] "Choir Season Climaxed by Midwest Appearances on Extensive Tour," *The Gustavian Weekly*, 7 June 1938, 5; and "College Choir Acclaimed During Annual Concert Tour," *The Gustavian Weekly*, 6 June 1939, 5.

departing from its more conventional programs of four sets of pieces by classical composers.[63]

The experimentation of programming continued in 1942 when composer Percy Grainger selected the Gustavus Choir to perform his *Kipling Jungle Book Cycle* as a complete work for the first time anywhere. The relationship with the composer had been fostered by band director Frederic Hilary over the previous two years, during which Grainger traveled on numerous occasions to the Gustavus campus and toured as a soloist with the Gustavus Band. The tenth annual concert tour for the choir featured Grainger conducting the performances of this newly completed piece for choir and orchestra as well as an arrangement of *Song of the Vermeland* he specially composed for the choir.[64] The program also presented Grainger at the piano in a duet with Nelson and as a soloist in the performance of his *Tribute to Foster*, which also included choir, vocal soloists and the playing of musical glasses.[65]

Nelson believed that the choir's work with Percy Grainger and the innovative programming would educate audiences because the music represented "800 Years of Music." Nelson was attempting to present a survey of the development of choral music from the thirteenth century to the present day. The program also showcased Nelson's new idea of the meaning of the term a cappella, which some musicologists of the time identified as, "with the full force of the chapel." With this idea firmly in mind, the choir's programs included the use of organ and string orchestra.[66] To Nelson, the 1941-1942 school year marked a definite change in the character of the choir, which he hoped would establish the Gustavus Choir as a center for musical thought in America.[67]

The Gustavus Board of Administration determined that the choir would be allowed to tour outside of the Minnesota Conference for its 1942 concert tour due to the unique nature of the program. With the consent of the administration, Eddie Johnson, the choir's manager, began the task of arranging the tour. Within a month, dates and locations had been determined for a six state Midwestern tour that encompassed two-weeks,

---

[63] "Choir Director Prepares Singers for Spring Tour," *The Gustavian Weekly*, 12 March 1940, 1.
[64] "Famous Composers Tour with Band and Choir," *The Gustavian Weekly*, 23 September 1941, 5.
[65] Gustavus Adolphus College, *Gustavus Adolphus College Choir 10th Annual Concert Tour*, Concert Program, 1942.
[66] "Famous Composers Tour with Band and Choir," 5.
[67] "Choir Sings Bach's Cantata in Broadcasts," *The Gustavian Weekly*, 4 November 1941, 3.

a time period longer than the previous two years.[68] With the tour now set, the choir and orchestra turned to rehearsal. Grainger spent time on campus preparing to direct the ensemble on the tour. The students took well to the composer and embraced his unique personality. Grainger, in turn, complimented the students and as the tour approached he was very pleased with their efforts.[69] On February 1, 1942, the sixty-six members of the Gustavus Choir and accompanying orchestra set out for Mitchell, South Dakota. Over the next two weeks the groups performed in parts of Iowa, Nebraska, Wisconsin, and Illinois, before presenting its final concert in Minneapolis.[70]

Fig. 2-8 Percy Grainger Greets People at Gustavus
Photo courtesy Gustavus Adolphus College Archives, GACA Collection 162, P-4521.

---

[68] "Manager Charts Six-State Tour," *The Gustavian Weekly*, 2 December 1941, 3.
[69] "Dynamic Pianist Performs and Directs Choir," *The Gustavian Weekly*, 2 December 1941, 4.
[70] "Minneapolis Concert Ends '42 Choir Tour," *The Gustavian Weekly*, 10 December 1942, 3.

The following fall, the choir began a typical year with auditions that included a large turnout by the freshman class. Nelson planned the repertoire, which again included the use of a small orchestra on some selections.[71] But the increasing tensions around the world associated with World War II made this year different than any other. The choir would not tour during 1943 and the performance schedule was dramatically decreased. They joined with the Choral Club to present J. S. Bach's *Christmas Oratorio* in December and a group was formed to present parts of this piece and others for the Lutheran League Conference in Minneapolis.[72] The call of the armed services and other war related activities was too great, and the numbers began to dwindle. The final performance of the choir was April 8, 1943 as part of a program to benefit the Red Cross.[73]

As the 1943-1944 school year began, many changes occurred on the campus of Gustavus Adolphus College. The school was selected as part of the V-12 program to train naval officers for the government, which brought 400 additional male students to campus. The decision to become part of this program probably saved the college from the financial strains of the war.[74] While the campus was re-establishing itself, the same could not be said for the Gustavus Choir. In July of 1943, Adolph Nelson announced that the choir would be temporarily divided into two performance organizations, a male chorus and the Schumann Chorus. He would also work to assemble small ensembles to appear at chapel and on the college radio broadcasts. This decision was made due to the lack of female singers on campus.[75] With the men of the country off to war, many of the women were forced to forgo college plans in order to work. The V-12 program brought many male voices to campus with the male chorus

---

[71] "Large Frosh Turnout for Choir Announced," *The Gustavian Weekly*, 23 September 1942, 1.
[72] "Choir Sings Oratorio Sunday, December 13," *The Gustavian Weekly*, 25 November 1942, 1 and "Choir Appears at L.L. Conference," *The Gustavian Weekly*, 17 December 1943, 1.
[73] "Nelson Announces Choir in Concert Thursday Evening," *The Gustavus Weekly*, 7 April 1943, 1.
[74] Richard Elvee, interview by author, 6 June 2006, St. Peter, MN. Tape Recording. Gustavus Adolphus College, St. Peter, MN and Michael Haeuser, interview by author, 12 June 2006, St. Peter, MN. Tape Recording. Gustavus Adolphus College, St. Peter, MN and Aldrich Bloomquist, "Gustavus at War," *Greater Gustavus Association Quarterly* (31 October 1944), 11.
[75] "Choir Divides in Two Units," *The Gustavian Weekly*, 21 July 1943, 1.

consisting of 90% service men.[76] A mixed chorus continued to survive, performing with the band on three concerts during the year, but the Gustavus Choir as it had been known ceased to exist.

Nelson remained a faculty member and continued to head the Gustavus Department of Music, but he no longer served as director of the choirs once they were split in two. Over the next two years, the choral conducting duties for the Male Chorus were left to band director Frederic Hilary and new faculty member, June Stromgren, led the Schumann Ladies Chorus. In August of 1945, Gustav Adolph Nelson resigned his position as head of the music department at Gustavus Adolphus College in a letter to President Edgar Carlson from the Interlochen National Music Camp, in his native Michigan, where he had spent the summer teaching.[77] While he left the college in a time of choral despair, the legacy he created was one of great success for the choir department. He elevated the choral program from one of mediocrity to a level of excellence on par with the other great a cappella choirs of the time period. He introduced the concept of touring with the mixed choir to Gustavus and through these concerts brought the a cappella style of singing from the college to the Eastern United States. G. Adolph Nelson, through his dedication to choral singing and to Gustavus Adolphus College, his innate musicality, and his pioneering spirit, gave birth to the ensemble now known as the Gustavus Choir.

---

[76] "Schumann – Male Choruses," in *The Gustavian* (St. Peter, MN: Gustavus Adolphus College, 1944), 50.
[77] "Nelson Resigns as College Music Head," Gustavus Adolphus College Archives; Faculty Staff Clippings: Neson, G. Adolph.

CHAPTER THREE

THE REBIRTH OF THE GUSTAVUS CHOIR
FROM 1945-1954:
THE WILBUR SWANSON
AND EUGENE CASSELMAN YEARS

The fall of 1945 brought an influx of new students to Gustavus Adolphus College, especially in the freshman class, which was the largest to date. Due to the increased number of students on campus, newly hired head of the Department of Music, Wilbur Swanson, decided to re-establish the a cappella choir, which had been dormant over the previous two years due to World War II. It was his intention to bring back a mixed choir to Gustavus in the tradition of previous editions. Swanson listened to auditions over a three-day period in his campus studio. Despite some difficulty attracting enough male vocalists, forcing Swanson to put out a campus wide call for singers, the initial response to the reorganization of a mixed chorus at Gustavus was one of excitement. More than 125 students attended tryouts.[1] After the additional week of auditions he added to attract sufficient men to fill out the ensemble, Swanson announced that a fifty-one member choir had been assembled, consisting of thirty-one women and twenty men. Rehearsals commenced on Friday, September 21, 1945, and thus, the Gustavus Choir was reborn.[2]

### Wilbur Swanson

Wilbur Swanson gained his formal music education at St. Olaf College where he earned a Bachelor of Music degree with a major in organ

---

[1] "Swanson to Conduct A Capella Tryouts," *The Gustavian Weekly*, 12 September 1945, 1 and "More Men Needed for A Capella Choir," *The Gustavian Weekly*, 19 September 1945, 1.
[2] "Swanson Announces Choir Personnel," *The Gustavian Weekly*, 26 September 1945, 1.

performance. While at St. Olaf, Swanson had the opportunity to study choral music under the tutelage of F. Melius Christiansen, whom he patterned much of his conducting after. Following his time in Northfield, Swanson moved to New York to continue his schooling at the Eastman School of Music. While at Eastman, he earned a Master's degree while focusing his studies on musicology, with a minor in organ. Swanson then began doctoral studies at the University of Iowa in musicology, but he did not complete the degree.

An accomplished organist, Swanson held numerous church positions prior to arriving at Gustavus. His keyboard skills, which were often described as sensitive and musical, served him well and enhanced his career as a musician. He was an associate in the American Guild of Organists, and served as dean of the Tri-City chapter of this organization, in Illinois, for six years.

Fig. 3-1 Wilbur Swanson
Photo courtesy Gustavus Adolphus College Archives, GACA Collection 162, P-1433.

His work in academia included a stop at Wheaton College in Illinois where he gained choral conducting experience as the director of the Messiah Chorus. In the years that followed, Swanson served on the faculty of Augustana College in Rock Island, Illinois, where he was dean of the School of Music and head of the departments of organ and theory, and conducted the Seminary Chorus. In August of 1945, Wilbur Swanson was appointed the head of the Department of Music at Gustavus Adolphus College. In addition to his administrative duties, Swanson taught organ and theory, and chaired the choral department.[3] His decision to re-establish the Gustavus Choir and his commitment to its excellence ensured that the choral legacy established by G. Adolph Nelson would continue.

## The Gustavus Choir is Reborn

The end of World War II marked the beginning of a renaissance on college campuses throughout the United States. Many young men returned from the war and went to school to complete college degrees thanks the government sponsored GI Bill. Gustavus Adolphus College was no different. As the men returned, so did the opportunities for the Gustavus Choir. With the auditions complete, the ensemble set to work, rehearsing Tuesday through Friday afternoons. It was determined, in order to enhance the viability of the a cappella choir, that the Schumann Chorus would no longer be a separate organization. It would again be made up of the women in the mixed chorus. Former Schumann director and current Gustavus voice faculty member, June Stromgren, would remain an important individual in the choir program. She would begin serving as assistant director for the a cappella group.[4]

It wasn't long before the Gustavus Choir appeared at campus chapel services and presented music on the local radio station.[5] Rehearsals intensified as the first full concert performance approached. The fourth annual campus Christmas program marked the choir's return to the concert stage. In past years, the Schumann and Male Choruses, in addition to their own contributions to the program, had been combined to provide mixed choral music at this event, since the college's mixed choir ceased to exist.

On the evening of December 16, 1945, before a capacity audience, the choir returned to an enthusiastic response. In addition to the choir's first

---

[3] "Eight New Instructors are Added to the Gustavus Adolphus Faculty," *The Gustavian Weekly*, 12 September 1945, 1.
[4] "Swanson Announces Choir Personnel," *The Gustavian Weekly*, 26 September 1945, 1.
[5] "Choir Practicing for Concert Tour," *The Gustavian Weekly*, 5 December 1945, 1.

concert appearance after a three-year hiatus, the program showcased performances by the college band, vocal soloists, and organ works performed by Swanson. The pieces for this concert were selected to include a wide variety of Christmas music. The choir again performed standards of the a cappella repertoire, including compositions by Gretchaninoff and F. Melius Christiansen. The evening concluded with all participants joining together in the hymn, "O Come All Ye Faithful," a song that, years later would be arranged for the annual finale of the Christmas in Christ Chapel program. In all, the concert was considered a tremendous success.[6]

The spring term of 1946 brought with it the return of the Gustavus Choir's annual concert tour. The two-week tour would take the choir on a 2000-mile adventure with performances presented in churches throughout the Minnesota Conference. Swanson programmed the music of Bach, Gretchaninoff, Christiansen, and others rooted in the Lutheran Choral School tradition, and he also featured the Schumann Ladies Chorus performing a set of pieces sung with piano accompaniment.

The ensemble presented its first formal concert prior to the tour on April 14 at First Lutheran Church in St. Paul. While choir members were determined to improve following this performance, they believed that they would be prepared musically for the tour. After two more weeks of intensive rehearsal, on April 26, members of the Gustavus Choir began their tour with a performance at Augustana Lutheran Church in Minneapolis.[7] Over the next few weeks, the choir presented concerts throughout the state of Minnesota to very receptive audiences. Choir members and administrators deemed the tour a success. Critics agreed that this edition of the ensemble lived up to the legacy previously established. Margaret Morris, music critic for the Duluth Herald wrote,

> Lifting their voices in hymns of praise, they (the Gustavus Choir) sang with a true joy of singing that boasts breadth and strength, a restrained but effective emotional appeal, unity and balance, jewel-like tone and dynamic shading.[8]

Upon its return, the choir presented the Home Concert on May 22 in the college auditorium. This performance not only provided the opportunity

---

[6] "A Capella Choir, Symphonic Band, Music Faculty Give Annual Concert," *The Gustavian Weekly*, 19 December 1945, 1.
[7] "Choir Ready for Tour April 26," *The Gustavian Weekly*, 17 April 1946, 1.
[8] "Swanson Directs Choir in Benefit Concert Tonight," *The Gustavian Weekly*, 22 May 1946, 1.

for the Gustavus and surrounding communities to hear the latest edition of the a cappella choir, but it served as a benefit for Bud Lindberg. While on tour, Lindberg, a choir member, had become very ill and was confined to a hospital in Willmar for nearly three weeks. He was released from the hospital days after the benefit, but did not accompany the choir on its weekend tour to Sioux Falls, South Dakota and Worthington, Minnesota which brought the school year to a close.[9]

Due to the success and popularity of the reorganized Gustavus Choir, the fall of 1946 brought with it the formation of a second major choir on campus. The faculty held auditions as usual over an eight-day period in September. When notice of the fifty-six member college choir was finally released, it was also announced that the personnel of the newly formed Chapel Choir would be released later the same week.[10] Swanson formed the Chapel Choir to train students to sing the standards of choral literature which would prepare them for future membership in the Gustavus Choir. He also used this ensemble, which met twice a week, as a lab choir for the training of prospective school music teachers enrolled at Gustavus.[11]

The 1946-47 school year also brought significant recognition to the music department at Gustavus Adolphus College when administrators announced that the department would be accepted as an associate member in the National Association of Schools of Music. They would earn full membership ten years later. Wilbur Swanson, who was instrumental in bringing this honor to Augustana College in Rock Island, headed the institution's efforts for membership. Professor Edwin Kappelmann, from the University of Wisconsin Conservatory of Music in Milwaukee, examined the music department in February and recommended Gustavus. Acceptance into this organization testified to the quality of work being done by the Department of Music and ensured its status among other institutions of higher learning.[12]

The Gustavus Choir began its year with a performance of three selections at the Saturday morning chapel service as part of homecoming weekend.[13] Throughout the year they maintained a hectic schedule singing at chapel services, at various local gatherings and at the Christmas

---

[9] Ibid.
[10] "Prof. Swanson Picks Choir," *The Gustavian Weekly*, 2 October 1946, 1.
[11] *Bulletin of Gustavus Adolphus College Cataloge, 1945-1946*, (St. Peter, MN: Gustavus Adolphus College, 1946), 18 and *Bulletin of Gustavus Adolphus College Cataloge, 1947-1948*, (St. Peter, MN: Gustavus Adolphus College, 1948), 22.
[12] "Nat'l Music Group Accepts G. A.," *The Gustavian Weekly*, 25 March 1947, 1.
[13] "Choir to Sing for Alumni Service Sat.," *The Gustavian Weekly*, 23 October 1946, 1.

Concert. In 1947 Swanson planned a nine-day concert tour that took the choir to northern Minnesota over a nine-day period beginning with a March 22 concert in Chisago City. In addition, he scheduled other off campus concerts later in the year, including a performance in Minneapolis in late April.[14]

The choir performed the home concert in conjunction with the May Music Festival on May 4, 1947, which was attended by 800 members of churches from throughout the Minnesota Conference. As part of the weekend of music and education, all singers joined together to form a mass choir, under the direction of Swanson, to perform six selections as part of concert in the college gymnasium on Sunday afternoon.[15]

As the semester came to a close, the Gustavus Choir spent eight hours in a recording session for the production of the ensemble's first full-length record. Norman Nelson, of the Norman Nelson Recording Company in Emmons, Minnesota, brought his studio equipment to the college auditorium for the session. The two record set, processed by RCA Victor, showcased a third of the 1947 concert program for the choir. Included in the seven selections on the recording were the "Alma Mater" for the college, "Hail, Gladdening Light," and the Scandinavian favorite, "Tryggare Kan Ingen Vara." The record also featured a performance of the F. Melius Christiansen arrangement of "Wake, Awake for Night is Flying," a piece that choir members deemed very meaningful to the ensemble and became a sort of signature selection for the choir during Wilbur Swanson's tenure. The recording was released the following November and sold in the campus bookstore where they experienced an enthusiastic reaction to its availability.[16]

For the 1947-1948 school year, new robes were purchased for the ensemble from the Collegiate Cap and Gown Company for $1247. The new robes were maroon, trimmed with gold, however, they were not made of velvet as the uniform would be known beginning in the 1980s. One audience member remarked at the choir's first appearance, "I wonder if that choir is as angelic as it looks."[17]

From 1947 to 1950, the reputation of the choir continued to grow. Members busied themselves each year preparing programs for homecoming,

---

[14] "60 Voice Gustavus Choir Prepares for NW Journey," *The Gustavian Weekly*, 11 March 1947.

[15] "800 Guest Singers Coming to Gustavus May Festival," *The Gustavian Weekly*, 23 April 1947, 1.

[16] Howard Holcomb, "2 Choir Recordings Made Last Spring Now on Sale at Bookstore," *The Gustavian Weekly*, 18 November 1947, 1.

[17] June Erickson, "The Music Box," *The Gustavian Weekly*, 21 October 1947, 2.

Christmas, and other campus and community activities, as well as for its annual tours. In 1948, Philip Knautz (Gustavus Choir director 1954-1980) sang as a member of the ensemble and served as the group's assistant conductor. The choir travelled over 3000 miles on a twelve-day concert tour to the east coast in March. Presenting concerts in seven states, choir members traveled as far east as Pennsylvania and Washington, D.C. [18] While in Washington, Congressman Joseph O'Hara welcomed the choir to town with a motorcycle escort, even ensuring that the policemen were of Swedish decent. The congressmen adopted the choir during its stay by hosting a reception for the group and making all arrangements for touring the nation's capitol. The following year, choir officials made O'Hara an honorary member of the Gustavus Choir at a reception in his honor on campus.[19] The ensemble's 1948 Home Concert was presented on Palm Sunday in the Myrum Memorial Fieldhouse on campus, an event that became a tradition for the next three years.[20] The year concluded with an historic service at the 90th annual convention of the Minnesota Conference of the Augustana Synod. The choir sang seven selections at the service and Gustavus president, Edgar Carlson, presented a message. Wilbur Swanson, also contributed at the organ for the event.[21]

The concert tour for 1949 was primarily throughout the state of Minnesota. The tour, which was split into two parts with the Home Concert falling in the middle, briefly, took the choir into Iowa, and for one performance into Illinois, at Rockefeller Chapel on the campus of the University of Chicago.[22]

The fall of 1949 brought about major changes in the music department at Gustavus Adolphus College. Wilbur Swanson, who was an outstanding public speaker, gave up his administrative responsibilities at the college to focus more time to his lecture work. Audiences responded enthusiastically to his speech on the history of music, which was sponsored by the University of Minnesota Artists and Lecture Bureau, and he was invited to appear throughout the region at least twice a week. In June of 1949 he was invited to speak at the International Speakers Platform convention at

---

[18] "The College Choir," in *The Gustavian* (St. Peter, MN: Gustavus Adolphus College, 1948), 138.
[19] "O'Hara 'Joins' Choir Greets Choirsters with Swede Escort," *The Gustavian Weekly*, 7 December 1948, 1.
[20] "Unrestrained Recognition Meets Choir," *The Gustavian Weekly*, 23 March 1948, 1.
[21] "Dr. Carlson, Choir at 90th Synod Meet," *The Gustavian Weekly*, 4 May 1948, 1.
[22] "College Choir," in *The Gustavian* (St. Peter, MN: Gustavus Adolphus College, 1948), 133.

the University of North Carolina in Chapel Hill. At Gustavus, Swanson focused his efforts on teaching organ and as directing the choir. College officials appointed Dr. Daryl Gibson as head of the music department in September of 1949.[23]

Later that fall, the choir joined with the college orchestra to perform J. S. Bach's *Cantata No. 5*. This performance, which occurred during the homecoming festivities, marked the first time since the orchestra's founding as a separate organization in 1948 that these two ensembles appeared together. The performance took place in the college field house and featured a sermon by Dr. George Hall between the movements. Daryl Gibson, conductor of the orchestra and new head of the music department, directed the opening half of the cantata. Following the sermon, Wilbur Swanson conducted the second half.[24]

The choir toured to the northern portions of Minnesota as well as a stop in Ironwood, Michigan as part of its 1950 January itinerary. This was the first time the choir traveled in January, during the break between the first and second semesters, as opposed to its customary spring tour. The tour also marked the final appearances for director, Wilbur Swanson, who decided to step aside to focus full time on his lecture schedule. Paul Karvonen, conductor of the Gustavus Male Chorus, temporarily assumed the directorship of the Gustavus Choir for the remainder of the school year.[25]

During his five years on the music faculty at Gustavus Adolphus College, Wilbur Swanson reorganized the a cappella choir, which had fallen dormant during World War II, brought back the choir's annual concert tour, and began the annual Christmas Concert tradition. Students and faculty recognized his musicianship and artistry, and appreciated the expressiveness and warmth he brought to the group. Perhaps his most significant contributions to Gustavus were his efforts to re-establish the Gustavus Choir as an outstanding a cappella choir within the Lutheran choral tradition.

---

[23] "Music Faculty Revamped; Swanson on U Tour Slate," *The Gustavian Weekly*, 15 March 1949, 1.
[24] "Services Feature Hall Sermon, Bach Cantata," *The Gustavian Weekly*, 15 October 1949, 1-2.
[25] "Choir Plans Pre-Tour Bernadotte Concert," *The Gustavian Weekly*, 13 January 1950, 1.

## The Eugene Casselman Years

Eugene Casselman succeeded Wilbur Swanson as director of the Gustavus Choir in the fall of 1950, becoming the third director in the ensemble's history. Casselman earned a Bachelor of Music degree from Heidelberg College in Tiffin, Ohio and master's degree in music from Westminster Choir College, where he sang as a member of the Westminster Choir. He also received formal musical training at the American Conservatory of Music in Chicago, and the Detroit Institute of Musical Art. Casselman was an accomplished singer, performing both as a soloist in various oratorios and as a concert performer. His scholarly work in the pedagogy of singing led to the publication of several articles on the topic. Prior to his arrival at Gustavus, Casselman was on the music faculty of Colorado College in Colorado Springs.[26]

Fig. 3-2 Eugene Casselman with the Choir
Photo courtesy Gustavus Adolphus College Archives, GACA Collection 162, P-2717.

Casselman maintained a busy schedule with the choir, and in January of his first year, he took the ensemble throughout the northern part of Minnesota. An instrumental group joined the choir on tour for the first time since Adolph Nelson was director. The group consisted of a violin, flute, and piano, which accompanied the ensemble on three numbers. Upon his return from the Gustavus Choir tour, Casselman immediately embarked on a four state tour with the Gustavian Male Chorus, fulfilling department head, Daryl Gibson's, plan to increase the visibility of the

---

[26] Gustavus Adolphus College, *Gustavus Adolphus Choir Season of 1951-52*, Concert Program Notes, 1952.

men's choir. Both groups presented Home Concerts in mid-February to conclude a successful tour season.[27]

For the concert tour of 1952, Casselman planned for the Gustavus Choir and the Gustavian Male Chorus to tour together and organized a female ensemble, later renamed the Schumann Chorus, to tour as well. These ensembles, made up entirely of Gustavus Choir members, traveled through the states of Minnesota, Iowa, Nebraska, and Illinois during a twelve-day period in early February.[28] Casselman also planned a series of five concerts to be presented throughout southern Minnesota in March of 1952. Unfortunately, an early spring blizzard caused Casselman to cancel concerts in Red Wing and Cannon Falls. The bus transporting the ensemble stalled in Minneapolis forcing the members to seek shelter in family homes and crowded hotels. The next day the bus finally returned to St. Peter, only to head back out the following day to take the weary choir members to a performance in Taylor Falls. The choirs performed their annual Home Concert the following weekend in conjunction with the Palm Sunday festivities on campus.[29]

Despite these challenges, and an exhausting schedule, the tour proved to be successful. Singing to near capacity audiences throughout their travels, The Gustavus Choir demonstrated technique and musicality that was lauded by critics. Clifford Bloom, of the Des Moines Register, wrote, "Their work was most effective and always in the best of musical taste. It was evident that these singers were not merely fine vocalists, but trained to all musical values."[30] Eugene Casselman agreed that the tour was a positive endeavor for all involved, complementing the choir members for the experience, "The choir exhibited a wonderfully fine spirit; every member cooperated to make the trip a success."[31]

The 1951-1952 school year ended in similar fashion to the previous years, with two final performances. The first was at an evening session of the Minnesota Conference of the Augustana Lutheran Church convention, where the choir presented selections for convention delegates. The ensemble's last performance came in conjunction with the annual May

---

[27] "Choruses to Give Concert Here," *The Gustavian Weekly*, 2 February 1951, 1 and "Post-Tour Choir Concert Tuesday," *The Gustavian Weekly*, 16 February 1951, 1.
[28] "Choir Tour of Four states Slated to Begin January 31," *The Gustavian Weekly*, 18 January 1952, 1.
[29] "Stormy Weather Halts College Choir," *The Gustavian Weekly*, 28 March 1952, 2.
[30] "Gustavus Choir Tour Ends; Omaha Critic Lauds Director," *The Gustavian Weekly*, 15 February 1952, 1.
[31] Ibid.

Festival on campus. The choir sang individual selections, and joined with choruses from area churches in a concert to conclude the festival weekend's activities.[32]

The next two years brought a change to the annual Christmas traditions for the choir. Instead of the combined band and choir holiday program, Eugene Casselman, drawing on his experience as an oratorio performer, instituted the performance of *Messiah*, by G. F. Handel. By combining the Gustavus Choir with the Chapel Choir, more than 100 singers participated in the event, which was accompanied by chapel organist, and faculty member, Paul Allwardt. The performers performed only the first and second parts of the oratorio and the concert ended with the well-known "Hallelujah Chorus."[33]

The Gustavus Choir did continue to present a concert each year in combination with the band, but the performance took place in the spring following each ensemble's concert tours. The concert was staged in Myrum Memorial Fieldhouse and featured shortened versions of each group's tour program. The choir portion of this concert included performances by the male and female choruses as well as numbers that showcased the full choir.[34]

The choir's travel schedule for the 1953 and 1954 seasons progressed in much the same manner. The program, which consisted of five parts, continued to be shared with the Gustavian Male Chorus and Schumann Women's Chorus, with each group responsible for one complete set. The centerpiece of the choral performance was the Brahms *Motet, Opus 74*. This had been a multiyear process to prepare the work for concert, but once installed, became the highlight of each tour performance.

In 1953, the choir participated in two concert tours: the first in January immediately following the completion of semester exams. The choir traveled to five states, Minnesota, South Dakota, Nebraska, Kansas, and Missouri over a twelve-day period.[35] The second tour occurred two weeks after the choir presented its annual Palm Sunday performance on campus. This ten-day tour marked the first time the Gustavus Choir traveled

---

[32] "Choir to Present Afternoon Concert," *The Gustavian Weekly*, 4 April 1952, 1.

[33] Gustavus Adolphus College, *The Messiah*, Concert Program, 7 December 1952 and Gustavus Adolphus College, *The Messiah*, Concert Program, 6 December1953.

[34] Gustavus Adolphus College, *The Gustavus Symphony Band and The Gustavus Choir*, Concert Program, 24 May 1953 and "Band-Choir Concert to be given Sunday," *The Gustavian Weekly*, 9 April 1954, 1.

[35] Carol Christensen, "Choir Home from Travels," *The Gustavian Weekly*, 13 February 1953, 2.

outside the United States as they ventured in Canada for concerts in Winnipeg and Kenora. The choir also performed at churches throughout northern Minnesota.[36] Concerts on both tours were well received by audiences and they provided the choir the opportunity to be heard in new locations. The 1954 season featured only one tour, which occurred after January exams. Over the two weeks, the choir performed in six Midwestern states: Minnesota, Iowa, Illinois, Indiana, Michigan, and Ohio.[37]

As the choir continued to travel, it received accolades from numerous critics around the country. Vernon Hoyt, of the *Morning World-Herald* in Omaha, Nebraska, wrote, "When you say 'Gustavus Adolphus Choir' you have almost said enough. Those who have heard the choir in the past know what you mean. For those who have not heard it, it is a nearly hopeless task to explain."[38] As its director, Eugene Casselman's reputation as a conductor continued to rise with each concert the choir presented. He received critical acclaim for his leadership of the ensemble and became a rising star in the choral field. Hoyt continued, "He must have great talent, patience, insight, and love of choral music to blend 58 individual voices into the perfect whole as Mr. Casselman has done with the Gustavus Adolphus College Choir."[39]

At the end of the school year in 1954, Eugene Casselman resigned his position as Gustavus Choir director in order to take a new position at Milwaukee-Downer College. In his four short years at Gustavus, Casselman and the choir gained wide recognition in music circles.[40] He left an indelible mark on the choir and instilled in the students a passion they kept in their memories. His relatively quick departure, combined with Swanson's short tenure, left choir members wondering if Gustavus Adolphus College would ever be seen as a premiere musical institution. In a baseball analogy comparing Gustavus to the minor leagues, student Denny Bergman wrote, "We have lost two valuable players from our music 'diamond' in the last four years. When will Gustavus become more

---

[36] "College Choir to Go on Tour to Canada," *The Gustavian Weekly*, 10 April 1953, 3.
[37] Mary Lou Pittack, "Gustavus Choir to Leave on Two Weeks Tour," *The Gustavian Weekly*, 8 January 1954, 1.
[38] Richard De Remee, "Ambassadors of Song: Gustavus Choir Goes on Winter Tour," *The Lutheran Companion*, 4 February 1953, 8.
[39] Ibid.
[40] "Gustavus Choir Director Eugene Casselman Resigns," *Greater Gustavus Quarterly 10*, no. 2 (1954): 4.

than a 'feeding ground' for the 'big leagues' in this extensive, field of music?"[41]

Despite the loss of Casselman, the Gustavus Choir had built a reputation as a top quality choral ensemble. It was during his brief time as director that the choir's reputation soared. His traditions were not as rooted in the Lutheran A Cappella Choral School as the college's other directors. Casselman brought variety in his selection of concert literature. He was the only Gustavus Choir director not to program any music by F. Melius Christiansen, and also the only director with a relative balance in style and time period. He made the Schumann Women's Chorus and Gustavian Male Chorus into integral parts of the Gustavus Choir's concert tours. Despite his differences in ideology, Eugene Casselman led the Gustavus Choir through an era of rebirth and transition.

---

[41] Denny Bergman, "'Prof' Casselman Build GA Choir in Short Stay," *The Gustavian Weekly*, 14 May 1954, 4.

# Chapter Four

## The Gustavus Choir from 1954 to 1980: The Philip Knautz Years

Upon the resignation of Eugene Casselman, Gustavus Adolphus College appointed one of its own graduates, Philip Knautz, as the director of the Gustavus Choir: a position he would hold for the next twenty-six years. He first came to Gustavus as a student in 1946, following his membership in the armed services during World War II. After six successful years on the faculty at Texas Lutheran College, he was offered the opportunity to return to his alma mater. In the quarter century Knautz served as director, he conducted the Gustavus Choir in more than 500 performances and traveled over 75,000 miles on their annual concert tours.

Philip Frederick Knautz was born on July 12, 1923, in Finshafen, New Guinea. When Knautz was very young, he and his family moved to the United States, settling in Fargo, North Dakota, where he eventually earned his diploma at Central High School. His musical involvement began at an early age and was influenced greatly by his parents. As a child, Knautz would hear music in the family home and at church. His father loved to sing, and his mother, in addition to singing, would play the piano and organ. Young Philip simply followed their lead becoming involved in his parents' musical life and continuing to sing throughout junior high and high school.[1]

Upon finishing high school, Knautz enrolled at nearby Concordia College, in Moorhead, Minnesota, where he immediately joined the college choir. The year and a half he spent as a member of this ensemble, under the direction of Paul J. Christiansen, was the most influential in his musical development, and it was during this time that many of his ideas for music selection, rehearsal techniques, and choral tone and blend were developed. Knautz believed that singing with Christiansen shaped him as

---

[1] Philip Knautz, interview by author, 9 June 2006, St. Peter, MN, Tape Recording, Gustavus Adolphus College, St. Peter, MN.

a conductor, and he in turn adapted many of these techniques and philosophies into his own teaching style.[2]

Fig. 4-1 Philip Knautz at Piano
Photo courtesy Gustavus Adolphus College Archives, GACA Collection 162, P-2645.

Before he finished his studies at Concordia, Knautz was called to serve in Europe during World War II. After two and half years in the military, during which he received numerous commendations, including the Purple Heart and Bronze Star, he returned to the United States seeking to complete his college degree. Instead of returning to Concordia, he followed his future wife, Ruth Clauson, to Gustavus Adolphus College where he continued his musical studies. During his time as a student at Gustavus, Phil Knautz sang as a member of the tenor section in the first a cappella choir after its brief hiatus during World War II. He also held the position of student director for the Gustavus Choir, under conductor Wilbur Swanson. This allowed him to continue to hone his skills as a

---

[2] Ibid.

conductor and provided the opportunity for him to work with a college ensemble. In 1948, Knautz graduated from Gustavus Adolphus College earning a Bachelor of Arts in Music.[3]

Upon the completion of his degree, Knautz accepted a position on the faculty at Texas Lutheran College in Seguin, Texas. Here he served as the director of the Texas Lutheran Choir and the college band, and taught classes in theory, music education, conducting, and voice. He spent six years at the college building the reputation of the choir. Through his leadership, the choir produced their first recording and toured throughout the United States, including a stop at Gustavus in April of 1953. Showing his choral heritage, Knautz programmed many selections for this concert that were rooted in the Christiansen traditions, as well as those he performed as a member of the choir at Gustavus.[4]

While teaching at Texas Lutheran, Knautz continued his musical training, spending two summers studying at the University of Colorado in Boulder. Ultimately, he decided, in 1950, to stay closer to home at the University of Texas at Austin, where, over the next several years, he steadily worked on his education, earning a Master of Music degree in 1954.

Once he and his family settled in Texas, Knautz fell in love with the state, its people, and the lifestyle. He had built a good life for himself and believed that he had found a permanent home is Seguin. So when Gustavus Adolphus College called in the spring of 1954 to offer him the opportunity to return to his alma mater as its choir director, the decision was not easily made. He spent two days mulling over the offer and talking with his wife before eventually accepting the position. In the fall of 1954, Phil Knautz became the fourth director of the Gustavus Choir, and began a twenty-six year tenure as the leader of this organization.[5]

## Philip Knautz's Choral Approach

Philip Knautz approached choral performance and rehearsal in a manner that was greatly influenced by his mentor Paul J. Christiansen. He believed that the Christiansen legacy was already firmly ensconced at Gustavus prior to his arrival and that it was his responsibility to continue that tradition. His choice of music for the Gustavus Choir was deeply

---

[3] Ibid.
[4] "Lutheran Choir from Texas to Appear at GA Tuesday," *The Gustavian Weekly*, 10 April 1953, 3.
[5] Knautz, interview.

rooted in the Lutheran Choral Heritage. Knautz would first draw upon the music he performed as a student at Concordia, then focus on those pieces he sang as a member of the Gustavus Choir before reading through new music. The literature chosen was primarily a cappella, as that was easiest to perform during the concert tours. Occasionally he would choose music with keyboard accompaniment, having someone travel with the choir or, at times, having someone from each individual town accompany the choir in performance. He generally shied away from accompanied music, because the performance venues often did not have a piano. Even if a piano was available, the quality of the instrument was often not consistent with the performance standards of the ensemble.

Text and poetry were also taken into account when selecting repertoire. Knautz believed that the traditions of the college should be reflected in the choir's performance. Therefore, sacred literature, especially pieces composed by those associated with the Lutheran tradition, like Bach and Christiansen, were regularly programmed during his tenure. Arrangements of music from the Scandinavian countries were also performed, placing a specific emphasis on Swedish folk songs, as they tied directly to the Gustavus heritage.[6]

Phil Knautz believed the key to success for the Gustavus Choir was the rehearsal, and he was known as a very demanding conductor who commanded the room and required great focus and attention from his singers. He had a clear idea of how things should run, and it was his way or no way.[7] On the first day of rehearsal Knautz would say to the newly assembled choir, "Work hard. It will be tough, and that's just the way it is." In rehearsal, he let the music dictate the pace. His concern was that the students make the music better using any means necessary. It was his goal to create a sound that matched the choral tone he learned while studying under Paul Christiansen. Despite his militaristic style, Knautz also had fun with the group and knew when to let them relax. He believed that hard work mixed with fun was the best way to build camaraderie, and a close bond, which benefited the choir in performance.[8]

Each year Philip Knautz focused much of his effort on the annual concert tour in the spring. He auditioned students for the following year's choir upon completion of the tour each spring. It was the responsibility of the outgoing seniors to help the new members learn the tour program for

---

[6] Ibid.
[7] Al Behrends, interview by author, 15 June 2006, St. Peter, MN, Tape Recording, Gustavus Adolphus College, St. Peter, MN.
[8] Knautz, interview.

the following year during the late part of the spring semester.[9] Knautz believed that the tour was first and foremost to provide performance opportunities for the choir away from the Gustavus campus, but also as a tool to raise awareness for the college and the choir. The administration, specifically President Edgar Carlson, was extremely supportive of these ventures. The first decision Knautz made each year was, "which direction should we go?" From there, the tour was planned primarily using churches as venues. He also strongly encouraged student home stays while traveling to form relationships that showcased the best Gustavus had to offer.

The choir adhered to a strict schedule and Knautz clearly articulated his expectations of the students while on tour. He believed that a successful tour involved a great deal of discipline. The choir spent time each morning on the bus working on schoolwork for classes being missed. In the afternoon Knautz allowed the students to be more relaxed and play cards. Once the group arrived at the concert venue, they rehearsed, ate dinner (usually potluck was served), and then they would perform the concert. Following the performance, students would meet the local families who would house them and the next morning the process would begin again.[10]

Philip Knautz demanded a great deal of discipline in all aspects of the life of the choir. He approached the choir in such a way that students would build both a musical ensemble and a community of members. He believed that performance brought the choir members together and created an atmosphere of pride: "If they do well singing, they know it, and then they can be proud."[11] It is through this philosophy that Philip Knautz led the Gustavus Choir from 1954 to 1980.

## The Philip Knautz Era

In the fall of 1954, Philip Knautz assumed the directorship and began assembling a choir of fifty-six singers, which then started rehearsals for his first concert season. As the year began, Knautz made one addition to the choral music offerings at the college by adding a new ensemble: The Gustavus Singers, which was a select chamber choir made up of members of the Gustavus Choir. The Singers appeared at campus events throughout

---

[9] Fienen, interview.
[10] Knautz, interview.
[11] Ibid.

the year, and performed an optional set of pieces as an encore for the 1955 tour program.[12]

Another change instituted upon Knautz arrival was the choir's participation in the Christmas program at Gustavus Adolphus College. The previous few years the college choir had combined with the Chapel Choir to present the oratorio *Messiah*. On December 14, 1954, these groups, and the newly formed Gustavus Singers, combined with small ensembles from the symphony band to put on a "Festival of Nine Lessons and Carols" style service in the college chapel. The program featured the reading of nine scripture lessons, each followed by appropriate Christmas music. The carol service was based on the traditional English orders of service with plainsong inflections added. The evening ended with the audience members joining the choruses and the brass choir in the singing of "O Come All Ye Faithful."[13]

The first concert tour of Knautz's tenure began on February 9, 1955. Members of the choir presented eleven concerts in twelve days and they traveled through Minnesota and Wisconsin. Audiences ranged from around 400 to well over 1000 people at joint concert with the Gustavus Band in Duluth, Minnesota on February 13. The program featured the Gustavus Choir singing primarily sacred music in English, Latin and Swedish. The Gustavian Male Chorus performed one set of pieces, and the Gustavus Singers concluded the evening with a section of lighter music as an encore.[14] The choir presented its "Home Concert" following the tour on March 6 in the college auditorium. This marked the only full concert performance by the ensemble on the Gustavus campus for the 1954-1955 school year. A free will offering was collected at the event to raise funds for the purchase of new choir robes, which the ensemble wore the following year. After the concert on campus, the choir's only other full concert performances for the year were in the Twin Cities in late April.[15]

Attired in brand new choir robes of black with golden trim, the Gustavus Choir continued to excel during the 1956 concert season,

---

[12] Bulletin of Gustavus Adolphus College 1958-1960 Catalog, (St. Peter, MN: Gustavus Adolphus College, 1946), 41 and Gustavus Adolphus College, *The Gustavus Choir*, Concert Program, 1955.
[13] "Christmas Music Keynotes Yule Spirit," *The Gustavus Weekly*, 10 December 1954, 2.
[14] "Band and Chorus Return in Midst of Snowstorm," *The Gustavian Weekly*, 25 February 1955, 1.
[15] "Choir Presents Homecoming Concert Sunday Night," *The Gustavus Weekly*, 4 March 1955, 1.

performing over a two-week period and traveling over 3000 miles through eight Midwest and Rocky Mountain states during early February.[16] The ensemble performed a varied program that featured soloists and included individual selections by both the male and female members of the group.[17]

Fig. 4-2 Gustavus Choir in Robes with Conductor Philip Knautz
Photo courtesy Gustavus Adolphus College Archives, GACA Collection 162, P-2500.

In the spring of 1956 Knautz organized a new venture for the entire choral program. In April, the Gustavus Choir joined forces with the Chapel Choir and combined with the Gustavus Band to present one of the largest productions in school history. The choirs rehearsed together to prepare two Romantic masterworks. The first was Felix Mendelssohn's motet, "Hear My Prayer" which was accompanied at the organ by chapel organist and head of the music department, Paul Allwardt. The concert concluded with the two choirs uniting with the band on three movements of Anton

---

[16] "'56 Choir Purchases New Robes," in *The Gustavian* (St. Peter, MN: Gustavus Adolphus College, 1956), 75.
[17] "GA College Choir Presents Concerts in Eight States During Two Week Tour," *The Gustavian Weekly*, 20 January 1956, 1.

Bruckner's *Mass in E Minor*, a piece for choir and sixteen brass and woodwind instruments.[18]

As the concert tours became an established activity for the choir, Knautz was able to plan longer trips. He used shorter weekend excursions before and after the tour to build the choir's reputation in the regional area. These concerts were largely presented in communities around Minnesota with at least a couple of performances each year in the Minneapolis-St. Paul area. In 1957, Knautz planned a two-week tour, during which they performed fourteen times. The choir left St. Peter on February 1, and traveled eastward though eleven states, going as far as New York City and Washington D.C.[19] As part of the ensemble's itinerary while in Washington, Representative Joseph O'Hara again welcomed the choir with open arms. In addition to hosting the group and providing sightseeing opportunities, he also arranged an audience with then Vice President Richard Nixon during their stay.[20] With so many of the tour's performances outside of the Gustavus Adolphus College home territory, eleven additional tour concerts were scheduled for the weekends both before and after the east coast trip. All but one of these concerts was presented within the state of Minnesota.[21]

Beginning with the tour of 1958 and continuing for the next fifteen years, the Gustavus Choir used a three-year rotation system for planning its concert tours. The first year of the rotation would include traveling throughout the Upper Midwestern United States and, sometimes, into Canada. Knautz believed that the Gustavus Choir was the first of the Lutheran Colleges to make regular concert tours into Canada. These Upper Midwestern tours incorporated numerous performances in Minnesota and the surrounding states of Wisconsin, Iowa, and North and South Dakota. Knautz used these performances to recruit perspective students and to keep in contact with a large population of alumni. The second and third year of this rotation would take the choir from St. Peter to points in one geographical direction. Once Knautz determined the direction of the tour, he would contact individuals in several locations to schedule performances. These tours provided students an opportunity to

---

[18] "Falck-Knautz to Direct GA Band-Choir Production," *The Gustavian Weekly*, 6 April 1956, 1.
[19] "Gustavus Choir to Go East for Annual Tour," *The Gustavian Weekly*, 18 January 1957, 1.
[20] "Gustavus Choir Plans Concert on Sunday," *Mankato Free Press*, 16 February 1957, 6.
[21] Philip Knautz, "Choir Concert Season Record," Personal File.

explore the United States and to sing in varying locations and venues away from the Gustavus campus.[22]

Fig. 4-3 Congressman O'Hara with the Choir in 1957
Photo courtesy Gustavus Adolphus College Archives, GACA Collection 162, P-2724.

Following the concert tour in 1958, two significant events for the Gustavus Choir unfolded. The first came in the early part of March, when the ensemble gathered for a recording session in order to produce the first record of the Knautz Era. The session, which lasted eight hours, took place at Trinity Lutheran Church in St. Peter. The final product was thirty-eight minutes of music produced on an RCA Victor custom labeled album that went on sale to the public in early April.[23]

In May of 1958, the Gustavus Choir began a tradition of presenting a concert in conjunction with the Parents' Day activities each year. The

---

[22] Ibid. and Knautz, interview.
[23] "No Coughing Please!" *St. Peter Herald*, 6 March 1958, 8.

1958 performance provided Gustavus Adolphus College one of its largest choral presentations to date. The Gustavus Choir combined with the Chapel Choir and congregational choirs from First Lutheran and Trinity Lutheran Church in St. Peter to present J. S. Bach's *Passion of St. John*. The concert, featuring Paul Allwardt accompanying at the organ, blended more than 200 singers and concluded the day's events in the college chapel. The Gustavus Choir and Chapel Choir were used as the crowd in the Passion story. The Trinity and First Lutheran Choirs joined the Chapel Choir in presenting the chorales throughout the work.[24]

As the years progressed, the choir continued to make regular campus appearances at Homecoming, Christmas, and Graduation, as well as the Home Concert that followed tours each year. The Parents' Day Concert took a departmental approach after the success of the *St. John Passion*. The choirs were joined by the band in presenting a joint concert each May, which featured individual sets by these ensembles. It was, however, their concert tours and other off campus events that were the focal point for the choir each year.

During the 1958-1959 school year, the choir presented performances at two significant conferences. The first came in September. With classes barely underway, the choir presented several selections for the more than 3000 people who attended the closing convocation of the Women's Missionary Society at Central Lutheran Church in Minneapolis.[25] Just two months later, the ensemble performed at the International Junior Chamber of Commerce Convention by presenting two selections at the opening convocation. This event, which took place in the Minneapolis Auditorium, brought together people from around the world and featured an address by President Dwight D. Eisenhower.[26] The annual concert tour, which for the first time under Knautz, did not include performances by the men and women of the choir individually, took the choir more than 3500 miles to six states reaching as far south as Texas. Included among the fifteen performances was a concert in Seguin, Texas, at Texas Lutheran College, where Philip Knautz taught for six years prior to his coming to Gustavus.[27]

---

[24] "Worship Service, Oratorio, Dorm Open House Highlight Program for Parent's Day," *The Gustavian Weekly*, 2 May 1958, 1.
[25] "Gustie Choristers Lay Season Plans," *The Gustavian Weekly*, 26 September 1958, 4.
[26] "Choir, Eisenhower Highlight JC Meet," *The Gustavian Weekly*, 14 November 1958, 1.
[27] "Choir to Embark Feb. 6 on Six-State Venture," *The Gustavian Weekly*, 23 January 1959, 1.

Over the next several years, the choir maintained an active schedule, performing both on and off campus. In addition to the regularly presented concerts, the ensemble also produced its third recording in 1960. The record, sponsored by the Faculty Women's Club, consisted of twenty-four hymns from the new Lutheran Service Book and Hymnal.[28] The concert tour for 1960 was "a pioneering trip" that took the Gustavus Choir to the Pacific Coast for the first time. The eighteen-day tour, which looped through nine states and encompassed 4500 miles, began on February 3. The choir presented concerts as far west as Oregon and Washington.[29] Throughout the tour the group performed for large and enthusiastic audiences, including a performance in Seattle that drew more than 1200 people. Knautz described the ensemble's concerts as "consistent" during what was the most extensive tour in the history of the Gustavus Choir to date.[30]

Later that spring, the choir and band were selected to participate in one of a series of broadcasts for the Armed Forces Radio Network. The choir and band each performed several selections on a thirty-minute show that was broadcast throughout the world on Armed Forces Radio. The program included information about the college as a part of the broadcast.[31]

With classes barely underway in the fall of 1960, the Gustavus Choir prepared holiday music at the request of the Columbia Company. The recording corporation approached the choir to produce a record that was distributed during the Christmas season as a gift for customers. This was the first time that the choir was recorded by the prestigious Columbia Recording Company, which produced around 10,000 records. In a recording session that lasted more than eight hours, the choir recorded several popular carols and hymns for the forty-five minute album. Phil Knautz said of the opportunity, "it is a definite privilege and honor to be even requested by Columbia to make such a record."[32]

The 1961 concert tour saw the choir travel extensively through Canada for the first time. During the trip, the ensemble presented concerts in four Canadian provinces in addition to the states of Minnesota and North Dakota. This was the first extended tour outside of the United States for

---

[28] "Superb Gustavus Choir Brings Wide Acclaim," in *The Gustavian* (St. Peter, MN: Gustavus Adolphus College, 1960), 72.
[29] "Gustavus Musicians Slate Tours," *The Gustavian Weekly*, 22 January 1960, 1.
[30] "Sunday Finishes Big Tour," *The Gustavian Weekly*, 19 February 1960, 5.
[31] "Musicians Serenade World," *The Gustavian Weekly*, 11 March 1960, 1.
[32] "Choir Records New Songs at Request of Columbia Co.," *The Gustavian Weekly*, 30 September 1960, 4.

the Gustavus Choir.[33] Concerts throughout the tour were well received. Critics heralded the choir's performance at numerous stops. In Calgary, reviewer Lawrence Cluderay, of the Calgary Hearld, wrote of the choir's concert in the newly constructed Jubilee Auditorium:

> The Jubilee Auditorium, balconies and all, should have been fully occupied with every choir director and choralist from miles around, for both the program and its performance was an object lesson from which there was much to be learned.
>
> Not for a long time have I enjoyed every minute of a choral evening so much. Not for a long time have I heard a choir with such purity of tone, expressive range, extending from the utmost delicacy to glowing brilliance, plus magnificent flexibility which enabled the group to cope successfully with music of widely differing periods.
>
> The Gustavus choir's singing here was nicely balanced and scrupulous in its intonation. I was particularly impressed with their tonal contracts and praising, especially to the imitative fugal sections.[34]

During the concert tour of 1962, the choir traveled eastward for two weeks through Chicago, New York and Washington D.C. among other locations. The trip included a performance at Orchestra Hall in Chicago and in the Senate Rotunda during a visit to the Capitol.[35] Perhaps the most significant event for the choir came upon its return to campus. The Home Concert took place on February 18, and was their first such concert presented in the newly constructed and dedicated Christ Chapel.[36] The completion of the chapel provided a space for worship on campus and an excellent venue in which to house concerts for the Gustavus Choir. This structure dramatically changed the landscape of Gustavus Adolphus College both in a literal and figurative way.

---

[33] "Choir and Band Prepare for Tours," *The Gustavian Weekly*, 20 January 1961, 1.
[34] "Calgary and Regina Critics Laud Choir's Performance," *The Gustavian Weekly*, 17 February 1961, 2.
[35] "Memorable Experiences Fill Minds of Gustavus Songsters," *The Gustavian Weekly*, 16 Febaruty 1962, 6.
[36] "Gustavus Choir Gives Concert February 18," *The Gustavian Weekly*, 16 February 1962, 6.

## Christ Chapel

On Sunday, January 7, 1962, to open the celebration for the centennial year of Gustavus Adolphus College, the newly constructed Christ Chapel was dedicated at a service in the building. The structure, in the center of the campus, would become the heart of the college, both geographically and as the ritual centerpiece for everything that would happen at the college. Long-time Gustavus Chaplain, Richard Elvee, described the opening of Christ Chapel as, "re-emphasizing the importance of the church as the center of the Lutheran liberal arts education."[37] Dr. Leonard Kendall, president of the Lutheran Minnesota Conference presided over the dedication ceremony, which was attended by 2000 people, including more than 60 pastors. Dr. Malvin Lundeen, president of the Augustana Lutheran Church, delivered the keynote address, entitled, "Christ and the Campus."[38] In an editorial for *The Gustavian Weekly*, college president, Edgar Carlson, wrote of the dedication service,

> Once in a while something happens about which you have the feeling that it was just as it should be. Nothing could have been added, or omitted, or changed, without detracting from it…
>
> This was my feeling about the dedication service for Christ Chapel last Sunday. The sermon was excellent, the music was superb, the liturgy was expertly and reverently done, the dedication rite was dignified and impressive, everything proceeded on schedule (including the final Amen), and the total impact was overwhelming. I can recall very few worship experiences that have been as inspiring and edifying. What a marvelous beginning for a Centennial year!

Carlson went on to call the completion of Christ Chapel the "realization of a dream" and declared of the structure, "Now it belongs to all of us."[39]

The idea for Christ Chapel began in the 1950s as the Board of Trustees began to consider the need for a worshipful place for the Gustavus students on campus. Before the erection of Christ Chapel, worship services took place in a room in Old Main, the chapel in the Auditorium, or in the Little Theater at one time or another.[40] In 1958, the project was

---

[37] Elvee, interview
[38] "Chapel Dedication Begins '62 Centennial," *The Gustavian Weekly*, 12 January 1962, 1.
[39] Edgar M. Carlson, "The Chapel – Now it is Finished and Dedicated," *The Gustavian Weekly*, 12 January 1962, 2.
[40] Lund, 176.

nearly scrapped as bids for construction totaled nearly $900,000, far beyond the $600,000 budgeted. The design by the architects had captivated the board and they were reluctant to scrap the ideas, believing there was no assurance a redesigned, more conventional building, would cost any less. When a contractor volunteered to erect the building within the budget if he could work with all parties in finding possible economies, the project began.[41] Through $504,600 in contributions from churches in the Minnesota Conference, individual gifts and memorials given to the college totaling $135,157, and other funding, enough money was raised to cover the total construction cost of nearly $750,000.

Fig. 4-4 Christ Chaple Dedication
Photo courtesy Gustavus Adolphus College Archives, GACA Collection 162, P-2364-02.

The architecture of Christ Chapel suggests the ancient symbol of the cross and crown. The structural unit is the folded elongated triangle. Alternate units point up and down, with the upward unit reaching higher to

---

[41] Carlson, 2.

form the crown at the top and to let light in below.[42] Atop the structure is a 187-foot spire, which is visible for miles around the campus, with a cross reaching to its peak.[43] Inside, the chapel is acoustically alive, with hard surfaces throughout to allow for maximum reverberation, which particularly enhances the music of the chapel's organ.

Fig. 4-5 Christ Chapel Construction
Photo courtesy Gustavus Adolphus College Archives, GACA Collection 162, P-2362-02 & P-2362-06.

To coincide with the opening of the chapel, President Carlson, hired Richard Elvee to assume the duties of Chaplain for the college. He was called to guide the religious direction of Gustavus Adolphus College. He teamed with music head and organist, Paul Allwardt, who was greatly involved in the design of the building pushing for the more Anglican tradition of King's College, to form the Chapel team. The structure hosted daily services for the students, which were optional, musical concerts, and most significant events on the campus.[44]

The Gustavus Adolphus College community has perceived the chapel as much more than a building for worship. The students see the structure as a focal point representing both the religious ideals of the college and its social center. This was most apparent following the tornado of 1998 that devastated much of the campus. The storm knocked the spire from the

---

[42] "Chapel Dedication Begins '62 Centennial," *The Gustavian Weekly*, 12 January 1962, 1.
[43] Lund, 176.
[44] Elvee, interview.

chapel, broke many of the windows, and caused significant water damage inside the building. What students remember most, however, is that through the devastation, the eternal flame within Christ Chapel was never extinguished. This light at the center of the campus gave the Gustavus community the strength to rebuild. To this day, Christ Chapel symbolizes the "heart" of Gustavus Adolphus College.[45]

Fig. 4-6 Christ Chapel Inside
Photo courtesy Gustavus Adolphus College Archives, GACA Collection 162, P-2403.

## The Continued Contributions of Philip Knautz

The enthusiasm generated by the opening of Christ Chapel and the success of the Gustavus Choir continued into the 1962-1963 school year. Knautz began the year by assembling a new seventy-voice ensemble with fifteen freshmen, making this the "youngest" group he could recall. The choir participated in the traditional campus performances, including Homecoming, Parent's Day, and various chapel services. In December, the choir traveled to Minneapolis for the purpose of taping a television

---

[45] Ibid.

show that would be shown on WCCO-TV on Christmas Day. The program, which was sponsored by First Federal Savings of Minneapolis, showed the robed choir performing holiday selections with an announcer's commentary. The television station videotaped the program in segments and the show took approximately three-and-a-half hours to produce. [46] The event proved to be successful and was repeated over the next several years, which continued to increase the visibility and reputation of the ensemble.

Fig. 4-7 Knautz Rehearsing in Chapel
Photo courtesy Gustavus Adolphus College Archives, GACA Collection 162, P-2709.

Christ Chapel provided a more appropriate home for the choir's annual performance of the Service of Carols and Lessons for Christmas, which continued to be a prominent feature in the Gustavus holiday festivities. Paul Allwardt organized the service and invited members of the college

---

[46] Bea Tourtelot, "GA Choir Presents TV Show," *The Gustavian Weekly*, 14 December 1962, 3.

community at large to read scriptures from the New and Old Testament between the selections performed by the Gustavus Choir, the Chapel Choir, and various other campus musical ensembles. The music faculty chose music for this concert that emphasized the elements of worship rather than the pageantry surrounding the holiday.[47]

Concert tours over the next five years alternated between the West Coast, the Upper Midwest and Canada, and the East Coast. Each tour saw at least ten performances over a ten-day to two-week period. In addition to these concentrated trips away from campus, the choir presented many weekend concerts, both before and after tour, throughout Minnesota. In 1965, one of these off-campus stops included the sharing of a concert with the St. Paul Chamber Orchestra at the Guthrie Theater in the Twin Cities. The concert, which was repeated on campus, featured the choir joining forces with the orchestra to in the presentation of Franz Schubert's *Mass in G*. This marked the first performance by the Gustavus Choir at the Guthrie Theater.[48]

In addition to the annual mid-winter concert tour through the upper Midwest, 1967 was the year of another first for the Gustavus Choir: a summer tour through Scandinavia, billed the Jussi Bjorling Memorial Concert Tour in honor of the Swedish born Metropolitan Opera star and father of Gustavus assistant business manager Anders Bjorling. The choir left Minneapolis on June 4, arriving eight hours later in Stockholm, Sweden, where members of the Swedish press and the widow of Jussi Bjorling met them. A highlight for the members of the choir occurred on June 6, when they were presented the flag of Sweden from Crown Prince Carl Gustav as the official representative of the United States at the annual Flag Day Ceremony.[49]

Just two days later, the choir performed a concert for King Gustav Adolph VI of Sweden. Students remember this performance because they had an opportunity to shake hands with the king, and because of the actions of Eisei, the king's small Pekingese. As the choir began to sing, the dog ran down the steps of the platform barking until the king himself was forced to come forward, pick up the dog, and have it removed from the room. The remainder of the concert went on without a hitch, but the

---

[47] "Chapel Carol services to Open Holiday Festivities at Gustavus," *The Gustavian Weekly*, 6 December 1963, 1.
[48] Janey Davis, "Choir to Repeat Guthrie Program," *The Gustavian Weekly*, 3 December 1965, 4 and "Gustavus Choir: Chamber Singers Add to Sacred Music," in *The 1966 Gustavian* (St. Peter, MN: Gustavus Adolphus College, 1966), 74.
[49] Charles Neuleib, "Students Sing for King of Sweden During Concert Tour of Europe," *The Gustavian Weekly*, 15 September 1967, 1.

Swedish newspapers greatly publicized this event with headlines reading "New Member for Choir" and "King's Dog is Music Critic."[50]

Fig. 4-8 King Gustav Adolph VI with Choir 1967
Photo courtesy Gustavus Adolphus College Archives, GACA Collection 162, P-2505.

Perhaps the most moving moment of the tour came as the choir participated in a wreath-laying ceremony at the grave of Jussi Bjorling. As part of the ceremony, director Philip Knautz placed a wreath on the grave and the choir sang a song of homage. The choir then presented a concert to an overflow audience in the Stora Tuna church. Bjorling's name would later be attached to the recital hall in the music building of the Fine Arts complex that opened in the early 1970s.[51]

In all, the European tour consisted of eighteen concerts in eighteen days throughout Scandinavia. The Scandinavian people responded to the choir enthusiastically and treated individuals within the choir with great hospitality. Following the performance portion of the tour, students were

---

[50] Ibid.
[51] "Gustavus Choir Returns from Scandinavian Tour," *St. Peter Herald*, 13 July 1967, 4.

allotted two more weeks to explore England and continental Europe before leaving Copenhagen on July 6 for the return to the United States.[52]

The Scandinavian tour marked the only non-Canadian international travel for the Gustavus Choir during Philip Knautz's tenure at the college. In 1968, the choir resumed its usual rotation by following the previous year's mid-winter concert tour to the upper Midwest with a trip to the Southern United States. This choir traveled into Texas for the first time in ten years.[53] The rotation continued over the next three years with an East Coast trip and a tour of the Western United States book ending a journey through the upper Midwest and Canada.[54]

In the spring of 1971 a new fine arts center was completed on the campus of Gustavus Adolphus College. On April 5, the music department moved into the facilities, which were described as a "mansion" compared to the cramped quarters of previous arts building. By April 13 the students, who were returning from break, were taking classes in the newly constructed building, which included instrumental storage rooms with lockers, an electric piano lab, lecture spaces, a shared rehearsal room for the band and orchestra, numerous practice rooms and faculty studios, a music library complete with listening stations, and the Jussi Bjorling Concert Hall, a smaller performance venue generally used for recitals. While the majority of the choir's on campus concerts continued to be in Christ Chapel, Bjorling Hall served as a rehearsal venue for the Gustavus Choir.[55]

In 1972, the Gustavus Choir and Gustavus Band toured together for the first and only time in the history of college. Three directors and 137 students toured for two weeks to California and Hawaii. Traveling over 8000 miles, the largest group of Gustavus musicians ever to tour together presented a varied program of music at military bases and churches. In addition to the band and choir performances, the concert program also featured the Gustavus Stage Band and the Chamber Singers, as well as two selections pairing the Gustavus Choir with a brass ensemble.[56] Every concert, with the exception of one, included all four of the performance

---

[52] Neuleib, 1.
[53] "Gustavus Band, Choir Schedule Annual Winter Concert Tours," *The Gustavian Weekly*, 19 January 1968, 6.
[54] Philip Knautz, "Choir Concert Season Record," Personal File.
[55] "Music Department Moves Into New Fine Arts Center," *Greater Gustavus Quarterly*, May 1971, 12-13.
[56] "Choir, Bands Travel 8,000 Miles on 1972 Winter Tour to Hawaii," *Greater Gustavus Quarterly*, February 1972, 12.

organizations.[57] Audiences throughout the tour responded enthusiastically and the tour increased recognition of Gustavus Adolphus College, making the joint tour a success.

Fig. 4-9  Fine Arts Building Completed in 1971
Photo courtesy Gustavus Adolphus College Archives, GACA Collection 162, P-2476-03.

The following year, Knautz planned a more traditional tour throughout Minnesota, Wisconsin, Michigan and Ontario, Canada. He programmed an increasing variety of music for the tour concert, utilizing the Chamber Singers and Male Chorus to introduce more popular music to the repertoire. The majority of the Gustavus Choir's literature, however, continued to be drawn from the a cappella choral standards of composers like Bach, Gretchaninoff, and Christiansen.[58]

In December of 1973, Richard Elvee and other key members of the Music Department devised a unique program that would change the Christmas traditions at Gustavus Adolphus College forever. The program used the music of the campus ensembles interspersed with the liturgy of the birth of Christ, all set in the spiritual center of the college. When these aspects came together, Christmas in Christ Chapel was born.

---

[57] "Choir and Band Begin Hawaii Tour," *Junction*, 28 January 1972, 1.
[58] Gustavus Adolphus College, *The Gustavus Choir*, Concert Program 1973.

## Christmas in Christ Chapel

Christmas in Christ Chapel began its development in the fall of 1973. When Paul Allwardt, who had been head of the music department, Chapel Choir director, and chapel organist for years, retired, the faculty decided it was a good time to explore changing the annual Christmas program. Allwardt, who had been very protective of the chapel and the events within, preferred the Kings College model of Lessons and Carols, which was performed on campus until 1973. Over the years, this event became a Chapel Choir only service and Philip Knautz and the Gustavus Choir were no longer involved. Allwardt had believed that the Chapel Choir was the singing organization for the chapel and that the college choir was for the road. The carol service, which was presented twice each year, did not draw a large audience, and with Allwardt's retirement, Knautz believed it was time to bring additional ensembles from within the music department back to the chapel. Chaplain Richard Elvee agreed, opening the chapel services throughout the school year to performances by various musical organizations.[59]

Fig. 4-10 Paul Allwardt at Christ Chapel Organ
Photo courtesy Gustavus Adolphus College Archives, GACA Collection 162, P-0029.

---

[59] Elvee, interview and Fienen, interview.

At the urging of Richard Elvee, the college hired David Fienen to replace Paul Allwardt as organist and director of the Chapel Choir. He split his time between the music department and the Christ Chapel staff. Fienen's appointment brought what Elvee called a "Lutheran's Lutheran" to the chapel. This was seen as a way to transition back to the Lutheran heritage of the college and away from the Anglican traditions that had been established by Paul Allwardt.[60]

With the pieces in place, Knautz, Elvee, Fienen, and members of the music and public relations departments met in the college canteen on the campus of Gustavus Adolphus College in the fall of 1973 to begin to plan the Christmas program. Throughout the planning, it was clear that this committee wanted a broader, more inclusive event that would be "uniquely Gustavus." A decision was made early on that this event would take place in Christ Chapel. In order to capitalize on the spiritual nature of this venue, the program would not be a pre-planned concert where music is simply inserted each year. Instead, the event would be an annually changing worship service centered on the story of the birth of Jesus Christ.[61] The emphasis on the worship aspect of this event was to make the service unique when compared to the Christmas concerts of surrounding Lutheran institutions. The program would blend scripture, congregational hymns, pastoral reflections, and musical performance in a themed telling of the Christmas story.[62] At the conclusion of the performance weekend, the slate is wiped completely clean and a new service is planned for the following year from scratch.[63]

The planning of the event usually begins with the establishment of a theme around which the entire program will be based. In the years Richard Elvee was chaplain, this task usually fell upon him. Elvee, who would serve in the capacity of "artistic director" said, "the theme would be revealed to him." Other members of the creative team would present ideas, but until Elvee had his epiphany the theme was never set. In later years, current chaplain, Brian Johnson, made the final decision on each year's theme. The selection of a theme shaped the liturgical direction of the service and provided the foundation for all other aspects of the production.[64]

---

[60] Elvee, interview.
[61] Fienen, interview.
[62] Dean Wahlund, interview by author, 12 June 2006, St. Peter, MN, Tape Recording, Gustavus Adolphus College, St. Peter, MN.
[63] Fienen, interview.
[64] Elvee, interview, Fienen, interview, and Gregory Aune, phone interview by author, 5 October 2006, Tape Recording.

With the theme in place, the individual directors of the Gustavus Choir, Chapel Choir, Lucia Singers, Gustavus Orchestra, Brass Choir and Chapel Handbell Choir typically selected the literature. The conductor of the Gustavus Choir serves as the music director for the event and works in tandem with the chaplain to plan the order of worship. Music is chosen to fit with both the Christmas story and the annual theme of the service. For example, if the theme was a German Christmas, repertoire would include Mendelssohn and Bach, German folk music, and traditional holiday hymns.[65] The performances would be interspersed with scripture readings or other, more grandiose, events, such as puppetry or interpretive dance, to enhance the theme while telling the biblical story. Each year the chapel was decorated, at times very elaborately, to create the mood of the service.[66]

Fig. 4-11 Christmas in Christ Chapel from the 1980s
Photo courtesy Gustavus Adolphus College Archives, GACA Collection 162, P-2692.

The capstone for the service occurred in 1976 when Chaplain Elvee approached Winston Cassler, a music professor at St. Olaf College, about composing an arrangement of "O Come All Ye Faithful" which would conclude the subsequent services. In the previous years, the choir and

---

[65] Erickson, interview.
[66] Elvee, interview.

congregation had sung this hymn from the hymnal. What Elvee wanted was something inspiring to bring this celebration to a close and this arrangement has come to signify Christmas in Christ Chapel.[67] The work opens with herald trumpets declaring the hymn melody before giving way to the organ and brass choir. The introduction swells to the initial entrance of the choirs and the seated congregation. As the work progresses it builds in intensity and excitement until the organ and brass choir introduce the final verse, supported by a soprano descant, for which the congregation stands. Chaplain Elvee believed the uplifting sentiment this song projects provided a fitting conclusion to the service.

Fig. 4-12 O Come All Ye Faithful with Herald Trumpets at Christmas in Christ Chapel in 2005
Photo courtesy Gustavus Adolphus College Public Relations Office.

The first Christmas in Christ Chapel, which was themed as a Christmas Choral Vespers, took place on December 3, 1973 at 3:30 and 7:30 p.m. Neither performance was sold out, but audiences responded to both enthusiastically. Performances were added each of the next two years bringing the total number of services each year to four over a three-day period. Ten years later, in 1986, an additional service was added to Saturday afternoon to accommodate the high demand for tickets. The five performances bring more than 6,000 people to Christ Chapel each year.

---

[67] Ibid.

When all the musical, liturgical, and dramatic aspects are drawn together, the service creates in the words of Richard Elvee, "a music drama."[68] This successful formula made the Christmas celebration uniquely Gustavus, but more than that, Christmas in Christ Chapel became the cultural event on the campus of Gustavus Adolphus College.

## The Final Years of the Phil Knautz Tenure

With Christmas in Christ Chapel now established as a holiday tradition on campus, the Gustavus Choir fell into a yearly routine of performances. The year began with chapel services and the Parent's Day Concert, with Christmas in Christ Chapel capping the fall schedule. However, from the very start of the year, Knautz planned rehearsals that prepared the choir for the annual tour. The choir continued to travel during the break between terms at the end of January or beginning of February, and traveled in all directions from St. Peter, with the upper Midwest being a standard tour every two or three years.

In 1975, the Gustavus Choir made its first trip to Florida, performing nine times on the ten-day tour. The choir and band both traveled throughout the state, leaving by chartered plane from the Twin Cities on January 30, in below zero weather. Upon their arrival in the eighty-degree warmth of Miami, the two ensembles went their separate ways. The choir toured primarily the Gulf Coast area, while the band's performances centered along the Atlantic seaboard. Throughout the tour, the choir was met by large audiences and received enthusiastic receptions. A comment that was representative of those received on tour came from Robert Keys, a church pastor in Fort Meyers, "I want to tell you how tremendously pleased we were in Fort Meyers with your appearance February 1st. From the time your choir arrived until the time they left, they were a real blessing to our church."[69]

In May, the Music Department presented a concert in honor of Gustavus president, Dr. Frank Barth. It was their intention to show appreciation for the support and encouragement Dr. Barth had extended to the department throughout his tenure. The program featured performances by numerous college ensembles.[70] For this event, the Gustavus Choir combined forces with the newly formed College Chorus, which was

---

[68] Ibid.
[69] "Gustavus Band, Choir Return from Successful Tours," *Greater Gustavus Quarterly 36*, no. 4 (1975): 15.
[70] Gustavus Adolphus College, *President's Day Concert*, Concert Program, 4 May 1975.

formed to provide another auditioned ensemble for the study of sacred and secular choral literature on the campus.[71] The concert was highlighted by the performance of F. Melius Christiansen's "Praise to the Lord," as conducted by the composer's son, Olaf.[72] The appearance of the former St. Olaf Choir director reinforced the Gustavus Choir's status among the Lutheran Choral tradition.

Over the next three years, the choir's travels kept them a bit closer to home. The Midwestern tour of 1976 saw the choir travel through five regional states presenting eight concerts. In addition to the standard a cappella repertoire the choir was known for, the program also featured music chosen to honor America's Bicentennial, showcasing composers and poets from the United States.[73]

In 1977, the ensemble traveled eastward, as far as western Pennsylvania. The trip included performances in the states of Wisconsin, Illinois, Michigan, and Ohio. For this tour, Knautz programmed Krysztof Penderecki's "Stabat Mater."[74] This piece, which was a departure from the choir's traditional repertoire, proved to be a challenge for the group. The dissonant harmonies and disjunctive nature of the vocal lines made the choir members work to grasp the selection. As a result of diligent rehearsals, Knautz believed the choir soon mastered the complexities of the work. The performance of the *Stabat Mater* had a profound influence on the members of the Gustavus Choir and the piece became a symbol to the ensemble of their status in the choral world.[75] The choir returned to Canada in 1978. In addition to its own concert performances, the choir presented three joint Minnesota performances with the band, including a concert at Orchestra Hall in Minneapolis to culminate the tour.[76]

As the spring term of 1978 came to a close, Philip Knautz recognized that his years of service to the Gustavus Choir were beginning to wear on him both physically and mentally. In order to reassess his priorities and determine his future, Knautz decided to take a leave of absence from the college for the entire 1978-1979 school year.[77] Despite the director's

---

[71] Bulletin of Gustavus Adolphus College Catalog Issue 1974-75. St. Peter, MN: Gustavus Adolphus College, [1974], 82.
[72] *President's Day Concert.*
[73] "GAC Band and Choir Tours Cover Midwest," *The Gustavian Weekly*, 23 January 1976, 6.
[74] "Band and Choir Return for Concerts," *The Gustavian Weekly*, 11 February 1977, 3.
[75] Behrends, interview.
[76] "Choir and Band Tours," *Greater Gustavus Quarterly 41*, no. 1 (1977): 13.
[77] Knautz, interview.

sabbatical, the choir continued with its typical busy concert schedule. David Engen assumed the choir's conducting responsibilities and programmed a tour concert entirely of sacred music. While the singing of sacred literature was not a unique experience for the Gustavus Choir, Engen's choice of repertoire did push the envelope. His program included works by composers for which the choir was known, but he also incorporated a great number of contemporary works that stretched the ears of the listeners. In addition to the standard a cappella music of Bach and Christiansen, Engen programmed Ligeti, Duruflé, and Pinkham. He further diverged from the standard Gustavus Choir program with the performance of Daniel Pinkham's "Alleluia." This piece was written for the singers to be accompanied by a pre-recorded electronic tape.[78]

With this unique and challenging program learned, the choir set out on its annual concert tour in February of 1979. The tour, which again mirrored that of the Gustavus Band, took the choir back to the state of Texas, passing through Iowa, Nebraska, Kansas, and Oklahoma along the way. While the band did not travel with the choir, the two organizations met twice for joint concerts, once at Midland College in Fremont, Nebraska, and again in Plano, Texas.[79]

In the spring of 1979, a significant choral event took place on the campus of Gustavus Adolphus College. The Music Department, in the most ambitious concert attempted to date, presented the *Mass in B Minor* by J. S. Bach on May 4 in Christ Chapel. The event involved virtually the entire music faculty, the combined the Gustavus and Chapel Choirs, the Gustavus Orchestra, and community members from St. Peter and Mankato.[80] This concert marked the first such performance of an extended masterwork since the college presented *Messiah* in 1971.

The following year, Philip Knautz returned from leave for what would be his final season as director of the Gustavus Choir. The year progressed as many others had before it. The choir busied itself with its annual fall performances before embarking on a concert tour through California. The choir and band departed the Minneapolis airport on February 2, 1980, for Los Angeles. Upon their arrival, the groups parted ways with the choir touring the suburbs and communities north of Los Angeles while band took the southern route. The tour was the shortest of Knautz's tenure with

---

[78] Gustavus Adolphus College, *The Gustavus Choir Winter Concerts – 1979*, Concert Program, 1979.
[79] "Texas Sun Awaits GAC Band & Choir," *The Gustavian Weekly*, 31 January 1979, 2.
[80] "Mass in B Minor on May 4," *Greater Gustavus Quarterly 43*, no. 1 (1979): 5.

only six performances during the trip.[81] At the Home Concert, which followed the tour, Knautz was honored with a reception, at which nearly 200 alumni and friends of the Gustavus Choir expressed their appreciation for his twenty-six years of service.[82] The year concluded with the choir again combining with the Chapel Choir for the presentation of two large-scale masterworks. The performance of J.S. Bach's *Cantata 131* and Anton Bruckner's *Mass in E Minor* on May 18, 1980, brought the tenure of Philip Knautz to a close.

Philip Knautz resigned his position as director of the Gustavus Choir to assume the responsibilities of as Director of Fine Arts Programs at the college, a position he would hold until his retirement in June of 1986. His resignation was met with a combination of sadness and happiness. While he would no longer lead the choral program that he had built so admirably during his years as conductor, his expertise and commitment to the fine arts would benefit the entire Gustavus community.[83] The contributions made by Philip Knautz during his time at Gustavus were numerous. In twenty-six years as director of the Gustavus Choir, Philip Knautz conducted the ensemble in more than 500 concerts. Under his leadership, the choir traveled to forty of the fifty U.S. states, several Canadian provinces, and took its first overseas international tour. He witnessed the construction of Christ Chapel and the new fine arts facilities on campus and worked to utilize them to their fullest. He was part of the team that gave birth to Christmas in Christ Chapel and became part of the legacy of this traditional holiday event. Through his commitment to musical excellence, the Gustavus Choir developed a reputation as a world-class performing ensemble that was rooted in the traditions of the Lutheran Choral School. Knautz remained a visible figure in the Gustavus and St. Peter community following his retirement. He was routinely seen on campus conducting reunion choirs and chatting with students and faculty. Knautz died on April 26, 2010 in Colby, Wisconsin at the age of 86. In his forty years of affiliation with Gustavus Adolphus College, as a student and faculty member, Philip Knautz came to embody the spirit of this institution.

---

[81] "Band and Choir to Tour in California," *Great Gustavus Quarterly 44*, no. 1 (1979): 13.
[82] "Philip Knautz to Direct G.A. Fine Arts Programs," *Greater Gustavus Quarterly 44*, no. 2 (1980): 8.
[83] Ibid.

Fig. 4-13 Philip Knautz Conducts the Gustavus Choir
Photo courtesy Gustavus Adolphus College Archives, GACA Collection 162, P-2649.

# CHAPTER FIVE

# THE GUSTAVUS CHOIR FROM 1980 TO 1994: THE KARLE ERICKSON YEARS

Soon after Philip Knautz decided to accept the position as Director of Fine Arts at Gustavus Adolphus College, administrators immediately began its search for a new director of the Gustavus Choir. Within months, they decided to appoint Dr. Karle Erickson, a Minnesota native, to the position. Erickson had a distinguished reputation in music circles serving as the conductor of various All-State Choirs throughout the country, including the Minnesota All-State in 1976-1977.[1] From the day he arrived, Karle Erickson pushed the choir to reach new levels of excellence. Administrators believed that Erickson's tenacity and dedication was exactly what the ensemble needed to advance.[2] During his years of service as conductor, the Gustavus Choir began regular international concert tours, worked with some of the finest choral musicians throughout the world, and further established its legacy as a program built on the traditions embodied by the Lutheran Choral School.

Karle Joseph Erickson was born and raised in Rush City, Minnesota. From an early age he showed an interest and proficiency in music and enjoyed the discipline needed to master a musical craft. His mother encouraged him to take private lessons, which he did in both clarinet and piano. Erickson's piano teachers always included the study of music theory as a vital part of his private instruction. The study of the inner workings of music allowed the young Erickson to develop an appreciation and deeper understanding of musical structure that went far beyond the technical requirements of playing a piece. This quest for knowledge and understanding developed into a passion for the art of music.[3]

---

[1] "Karle Erickson Named Director of Concert Choir," *Greater Gustavus Quarterly* **44**, no. 3 (1980): 11.
[2] Wahlund, interview.
[3] Erickson, interview.

Fig. 5-1 Karle Erickson
Photo courtesy Karle Erickson

In the small community of Rush City, Minnesota, Erickson involved himself with numerous musical activities. He played clarinet in the band, sang in a church choir, and participated in the High School Concert Choir, which he was allowed to join as a sixth grade alto. The idea of becoming a conductor was firmly established in Erickson early in his life, and as a high school student, he was often called upon to step in and lead rehearsals of the school's musical groups in the event of the music teacher's absence. Prior to his graduation, he also served as director of a local church choir.

Upon earning his diploma, Karle Erickson attended St. Olaf College because of its stellar reputation as a music school. He entered St. Olaf as a music education major with visions of becoming a band director before recognizing that his calling was in the choral realm. His focus changed because he believed that choir provided a more personal expression of musical ideas. The text and how composers set music to enhance its message became an important factor in his study. St. Olaf Choir director Olaf Christiansen, whom Erickson describes as his main choral influence, helped him develop these ideas. Christiansen also taught Erickson the importance of discipline and commitment. Throughout his work at St. Olaf, Erickson worked to hone his ear to hear the subtle nuances of choral tuning, and Christiansen taught him the importance of working to attain the ring of the overtones. Above all, Erickson believed that his undergraduate education instilled in him the ethic to work endlessly to achieve excellence in the art of choral music.[4]

---

[4] Ibid.

In 1960, Karle Erickson graduated from St. Olaf College with a Bachelor of Arts degree in Choral and Instrumental Music. He began his teaching career in St. James, Minnesota, where he taught all aspects of junior and senior high school music. After two years, he moved to Sterling, Illinois, and assumed the duties of choir director at Sterling High School. During summer breaks from the high school, Erickson pursued graduate studies in music at the University of Illinois in Champaign.

Upon the completion of his master's degree, he resigned his position at Sterling High School and enrolled at the university full time in pursuit of his doctorate. As a student at Illinois, Erickson studied with Harold Decker who taught him the solfege sight-reading system and the significance of its use in the choral rehearsal. This approach for the teaching of music literacy skills would become a cornerstone in Erickson's methodology. He completed his coursework in 1967 and three years later finished the dissertation that earned him the degree of Doctor of Education.[5]

Karle Erickson's first collegiate teaching position was at Lawrence University in Appleton, Wisconsin. He began his work in the Conservatory at Lawrence in 1967, eventually rising to the rank of associate professor. He conducted several choral ensembles, taught classes in conducting and music education, and recruited prospective students. In addition to his efforts at the university, Erickson founded a choir of select high school students in Wisconsin that toured Europe annually and he taught at the International Music Camp at International Peace Gardens in Bottineau, North Dakota. After thirteen years on the music faculty at Lawrence University, he seized the opportunity to return to his roots in the Lutheran colleges of Minnesota. In the fall of 1980, Karle Erickson became the fifth director in the history of the Gustavus Choir.[6]

## Karle Erickson's Choral Approach

Upon his arrival at Gustavus Adolphus College, Karle Erickson's aim was to build a legacy of quality similar to that which he experienced as an undergraduate at St. Olaf College. In an attempt to achieve this goal, Erickson drew on the ideals of F. Melius Christiansen and the Lutheran Choral School by identifying four concepts that he believed would advance the Gustavus Choir to the next level of excellence. These concepts included; the programming of quality concert literature, establishing energy and intensity in the rehearsal that would translate to artistic

---

[5] Ibid.
[6] Ibid.

performance, extensive touring throughout the United States and internationally, and building a sense of tradition within the choir.[7]

When selecting repertoire for the Gustavus Choir, Erickson's views did not deviate far from what Philip Knautz, and other directors, had already established as the norm. The music he selected tended to be a cappella and sacred, but Erickson favored more contemporary compositions than his predecessors.[8] Erickson programmed a wide array of literature to educate the singers, by making them aware of varied musical styles and time periods, but he did not pick a piece for educational purposes only. The music he selected was first and foremost music that he himself liked. To him, choral music was about the text and what message the composer was trying to express through its setting. Erickson would select literature in which the poetry and music supported each other.[9]

For Erickson, great performances were a result of quality rehearsals, and he provided the singers with an awareness of the music and of each individual's contribution to the overall sound or performance.[10] Through careful pre-analysis of the music and specific planning, Erickson structured fast paced rehearsals that would allow him to move beyond the technical difficulties to the expressive aspects of the music."[11]

To accomplish this, each member of the Gustavus Choir was asked to establish a high standard of personal discipline and commitment to the group. Singers were expected to learn to read music, both for what they did at Gustavus and for their musical lives after graduation. Erickson employed the solfege sight-reading method, both with the choir and music theory students at the college. Through this system he hoped to develop "independent musicians, not dumb singers." He believed that solfege was the key to accurately learning the score and a factor in improved tuning. Only after the pitches and rhythms were in place could the artistic beauty of the music be developed.[12] This approach permitted the Gustavus Choir to quickly learn new repertoire and allowed them to expand into more challenging literature. As their music reading skills improved, the choir

---

[7] Ibid.
[8] Behrends, interview.
[9] Erickson, interview.
[10] Karle Erickson, *The Gustavus Choir Handbook*, St. Peter, MN: Gustavus Adolphus College, Gustavus Adolphus College Archives, Box 16.1.2.2 "Gustavus Choir 1980-81 – 1986-87," Folder 2 "Gustavus Choir, 1981-82."
[11] Erickson, interview.
[12] Ibid.

developed a more unified, in tune sound, due to the increased rehearsal time available to polish, rather than learn notes.[13]

Choral tone and intonation were related entities in Karle Erickson's philosophy. He approached these concepts by attempting to achieve unity within each section while promoting the production of vocal freedom from each individual. He challenged the singers to unify vowel placement and tune chords by listening for the overtones to lock into place.

He devised a careful "placement method" for the choir to effectively utilize the varying timbre of the individual voices. If the concert order would allow, the seating would change according to the style of music being performed. In his standard formation, Erickson would place those singers with a brighter tone in the center of the choir and as he moved away from the center the singer's tone would be darker. This process would be reversed in order to achieve a more Romantic quality. Above all, Erickson strived for the choir to produce performances with impeccable intonation. As he rehearsed the ensemble, he would often proclaim, "if it's not in tune…" to which the choir would respond in unison, "it's ugly."[14]

Erickson believed that the choral program he inherited at Gustavus included a long history of performance excellence, but lacked a heritage of tradition passed from one class to the next. In 1981, he first programmed "Praise to the Lord" by F. Melius Christiansen for the annual concert tour and it has remained the signature selection for the choir ever since. Erickson wanted a piece that would signify the ensemble much in the same way "Beautiful Savior" had represented St. Olaf. He decided on "Praise to the Lord" because of its ties to Christiansen and the Lutheran Choral School, but also because of its uplifting message and lively compositional style. He believed that this piece of music would profoundly influence the singers in the ensemble and reach out to them many ways.[15] Over the years, this selection has become one that the alumni expect to hear and one that the choristers expect to learn when they become members of the choir. The singing of "Praise to the Lord" has become a defining moment in every Gustavus Choir concert.[16]

In order to further enhance the legacy of the Gustavus Choir as an ensemble of the Lutheran Choral Tradition, Erickson changed the group's appearance. In his second year, the choir purchased new robes. Drawing from the example of surrounding Lutheran colleges, the new robes were

---

[13] Fienen, interview.
[14] Erickson, interview.
[15] Ibid.
[16] Wahlund, interview.

velvet and crimson in color with cream-colored trim. He believed the change in uniform added an element of majesty and elegance to the choir's performance. This was Erickson's attempt to create an aura around each concert.

Fig. 5-2  Gustavus Choir in Velvet Robes
Photo courtesy Gustavus Adolphus College Archives, GACA Collection 162, P-4487.

Finally, he insisted that the members of the Gustavus Choir took ownership of the organization. He expanded the student board to include section leaders that would lead a sectional warm-up each day and would be responsible for their sections music and morale. Additionally, officers would take on more responsibility to lead and police the ensemble. Erickson established the tradition of singing the hymn "O God Our Help in Ages Past" as a post-concert bonding time for the ensemble. He would step out of this activity believing that this time belonged to the choir. Erickson used each new tradition to build a choir that would perform with excellence while also developing an emotional bond with each other and the college that would carry them far beyond their Gustavus Choir experience.[17]

Karle Erickson perhaps left his most indelible mark on the Gustavus program in the area of touring. He brought with him a philosophy of travel that he learned as a member of the St. Olaf Choir. He expanded the touring opportunities, both in duration and distance. He believed that tours needed to last for at least two weeks to provide singers the maximum experience. First and foremost, Erickson saw the concert tour as an educational experience that provided the opportunity to broaden the

---

[17] Erickson, interview.

students' exposure to different areas and cultures, as well as to grow with the art of choral music through repeated performance in varying venues.[18]

Upon his arrival, the choir's only extended travel occurred during the student break between January term and the spring semester. Shorter trips took place on the weekends before and after tour to reach communities within a short distance of St. Peter. Erickson worked with the college to extend the amount of time the students could be away from campus. He did this at first to allow for international travel for the choir. In 1987, he proposed the novel concept of creating a January Term class that combined extensive rehearsals with a course of study provided by a Gustavus faculty member from outside the music department. This allowed the students in the choir to register for a fully accredited course, learn about the history and culture of the tour location, and use the international travel as part of the class experience. Soon, this idea was expanded to include the extended tours within the United States as well.[19] For Erickson, this provided a way for the choir to take extended three-week concert tours, which immersed the choir members into the music and exposed them to a bigger world picture outside their Midwestern communities.[20]

The choir began to use a four-year travel rotation schedule. Within the four year period, the Gustavus Choir would twice tour in the upper Midwest during the break between terms, hitting the areas that tour manager, Dean Wahlund, called the "bread and butter." These tours provided a chance for local recruitment, fundraising, and to touch base with the largest number of Gustavus alumni, while providing performance opportunities for the choir members. The other two travel experiences, which alternated with the Midwestern tours, were more extensive and involved the outside faculty member and coursework throughout the January term. One of these excursions was an extended United States tour, in which a direction of travel from the college was determined and concerts were scheduled to put the choir in specific locations at certain times. [21] It was important to Erickson that, over the course of time, these tours encompassed the entire country. The fourth year of the travel rotation took the ensemble to an international site. Erickson's choice for international travel attempted to provide students with locations they would likely not experience without the Gustavus Choir.[22]

---

[18] Erickson, interview and Wahlund, interview.
[19] Wahlund, interview.
[20] Erickson, interview.
[21] Wahlund, interview.
[22] Erickson, interview.

During his tenure at Gustavus, Karle Erickson worked to build a lasting legacy of musical excellence with the Gustavus Choir. He implemented new methods and traditions aimed at building unity in the choir. Through his disciplined, energetic approach, Erickson played a significant role in the continued advancement of the Gustavus Choir, further enhancing its place among the elite college choirs of the Lutheran Choral Tradition.

## The Karle Erickson Era

In the fall of 1980, Dr. Karle Erickson assumed the duties as director of the Gustavus Choir. He immediately began the process of assembling his first choir. More than 150 students auditioned for membership. After trimming the roster to seventy singers, the Gustavus Choir began to prepare themselves for their annual schedule of fall events. The first performance for the Gustavus Choir under Erickson came on Sunday October 5, 1980, as part of the Parent's Weekend on campus. The choir, which performed four selections, shared the concert with the Gustavus Orchestra in Christ Chapel.[23] Just two days later, the choir presented the same selections at the Nobel Concert as part of the sixteenth annual Nobel Conference at Gustavus.[24] These performances provided the choir the opportunity to sing before large audiences with their new conductor, as preparations continued for Christmas in Christ Chapel and the first concert tour under Erickson.

In late January of 1981, the Gustavus Choir embarked on Midwestern tour that took the choir through Wisconsin, Illinois and upper Michigan. The travel took place during the interim period between January term and the spring semester, which has come to be known on campus as touring week. In order to keep a high profile in Minnesota with a new director, the choir traveled to locations within the state on the weekends prior to the extended tour.[25] Following this successful endeavor, the Gustavus Choir presented its annual home concert on February 14 in Christ Chapel. It was as part of this tour that the choir first performed F. Melius Christiansen's "Praise to the Lord" as the closing number for the concert.[26] This piece

---

[23] Gustavus Adolphus College, *Parent's Day Concert*, Concert Program, 5 October 1980.

[24] Mark Lammers, to Music Faculty, 11 September 1980, Memo: "Music for 1980 Nobel Conference," Archives, Folk Bernadotte Library, Gustavus Adolphus College, St. Peter, Minnesota.

[25] "Music Groups Prepare to Tour," *The Gustavian Weekly*, 23 January 1981, 2.

[26] Gustavus Adolphus College, *The Gustavus Choir*, Concert Program, 1981.

would continue to be programmed annually as the finale of the tour concert, and become the signature selection for the Gustavus Choir.

The concert year ended for the choir in the same manner as the previous several years, with the Gustavus Choir combining forces with the Chapel Choir in the performance of a major work. This year's edition featured the presentation of the *German Requiem* by Johannes Brahms. The "Gustavus Festival Orchestra," an ensemble formed for special events consisting of students, faculty members, and professionals from the area, provided the orchestral accompaniment for the work. The performance of the *Requiem*, which was conducted by Dr. Erickson, took place in Christ Chapel on Sunday May 17, 1981.[27]

The 1981-1982 school year commenced in the same manner as the previous year. As the choir busied itself with its fall activities and rehearsed for Christmas in Christ Chapel, they also prepared an event for the Minnesota chapter of the American Choral Directors Association. At the organization's state convention in November, which was on the Gustavus campus, the choir presented a program entitled, "We Sing the Year Round – A Celebration in Song." The concert, which took place in Christ Chapel, took the audience on a progression through the church calendar which included narration and the singing of a hymn appropriate to each of the church seasons. The performance also used the Chapel Brass and included congregational participation in the singing of the selected hymns.[28]

The 1982 concert tour, during which the Gustavus Choir wore for the first time the crimson and cream velvet robes for which they are known, again took the choir through the Midwestern United States. This time, the ensemble traveled west from St. Peter, through South Dakota and Nebraska, before spending the majority of the tour in Colorado.[29]

The school year concluded with two final performances. The Gustavus Choir again combined with the Chapel Choir and Festival Orchestra for a concert in Christ Chapel. This year's production included Igor Stravinsky's *Symphony of Psalms* and Antonio Vivaldi's *Gloria*.[30] In addition to the annual combined concert, the Gustavus Choir also had the opportunity to join the St. Paul Chamber Orchestra for a performance as part of the annual concert series. Following intermission the choir joined

---

[27] Gustavus Adolphus College, *Requiem*, Concert Program, 1981.
[28] American Choral Directors Association of Minnesota, *We Sing the Year Round – A Celebration in Song*, Concert Program, 21 November 1981.
[29] "Choir and Band to Tour in Colorado and Canada Respectively," *Greater Gustavus Quarterly 46*, no. 3 (1981): 7.
[30] "Choirs, Orchestra Go for Baroque," *The Gustavian Weekly*, 11 May 1982, 10.

the Chamber Orchestra for the presentation of *Mass No. 2 in G* by Franz Schubert.[31]

The following year provided many exciting opportunities for the Gustavus Choir. In addition to their regular busy schedule, the choir premiered a new piece of music at a performance for the 1982 Nobel Conference. The work, entitled *Dreamed in a Dark Millennium*, was commissioned of Minneapolis composer Ralph Johnson and featured the choir and orchestra with a baritone soloist. Its preparation was harried, as the completed work arrived only two weeks prior to its October 5 premiere performance.[32] Approximately one month later the choir provided special music for a convocation in Christ Chapel to greet the arrival of the King and Queen of Sweden. This event preceded the ensemble's first international tour since 1967, which would take the group to the Scandinavian country in January.[33]

Fig. 5-3 King and Queen of Sweden Greet Gustavus Choir Members
Photo courtesy Gustavus Adolphus College Archives, GACA Collection 162, P-2519.

The concert tour of 1983 marked the beginning of the four-year continuous travel rotation established, by Karle Erickson, to ensure the

---

[31] "Final SPCO Concert Slated for Tonight," *The Gustavian Weekly*, 20 April 1982, 11.
[32] "New Music Comes in Under Wire for Nobel," *The Gustavian Weekly*, 5 October 1982, 7.
[33] Carole Arwidson, "Swedish Majesties Pay Visit to Gustavus Campus," *The Gustavian Weekly*, 16 November 1982, 1-2.

Gustavus Choir would routinely participate in international touring. The three-week tour took the choir through five European countries, Norway, Sweden, Denmark, and East and West Germany. The choir presented nine formal concerts during their travels with all but one of these performances taking place in large European cathedrals. In East Germany, a communist state, the choir was closely monitored by police and was only allowed entrance as part of the 500$^{th}$ anniversary celebration of Martin Luther's birth.[34] The East German Government did manage to control the ensemble's concerts. They were originally allowed to perform three times at sites in the country, but the government altered the concert times so that they did not correspond to the strict transportation schedule. Since formal concerts were no longer possible, the choir improvised by "testing the acoustics" in the cathedral or singing an impromptu song after assembling for a picture. These informal performances, while important to the choir, were presented to an audience of passersby and, at times, no more than a janitor.[35]

The remainder of the tour was inspiring to the choir members. They had the opportunity to travel through the former Nazi Germany, sing for the King and Queen of Sweden, and tour the royal palace. While in Norway, the choir met with composer Knut Nystedt, whose piece "Sing and Rejoice" was commissioned for performance by the ensemble on this concert tour.[36] The choir's performances throughout the tour were met with wide acclaim. One performance at Karlstad's Cathedral in Sweden prompted critic Erland Rosell to write:

> From time to time it happens that a choir of American youths, usually prefaced by excerpts from glowing reviews, spills out of a bus and presents a choral greeting from "over there," with gospel music, Negro spirituals, and "Uti vår hage" (or something similar), perhaps for the chief reason of motivation and the financing of a trip to Europe.
>
> All such preconceived notions came to naught at the encounter with the Gustavus Choir in Karlstad's Cathedral. There were obviously many people who sensed this, because in spite of it being Friday evening, after a Christmas season of numerous choir concerts, and in addition being jammed between other musical events, there was nearly a full house. Even the 75 youthful choir members' perfect entrance in their tasteful burgundy choir gowns was a sight of beauty. When the vaults were suddenly filled

---

[34] Erickson, interview.
[35] Joel Stottrup, "European Choir Tour has Images of Horror, Beauty," *Princeton Union-Eagle*, 24 February 1983, 10.
[36] Ibid.

with their young voices' brilliance and splendor, the impression was – and there is no more appropriate description than this – stunning.[37]

Upon the choir's return from Europe, they immediately embarked on a ten-day tour of the state of Minnesota. This allowed the ensemble to continue to network within the state and touch base with its alumni. The choir, which presented the same program on both excursions, gave a total of eighteen performances. In all, the winter concert tour lasted an entire month beginning on January 10 in Oslo, Norway and concluding with the home concert in Christ Chapel on February 12.

The end of the tour season did not diminish the Gustavus Choir's hectic 1982-1983 schedule. The spring semester brought with it the annual choral concert with the Festival Orchestra, but for the first time, the choir stood alone in its presentation. While Erickson continued the tradition of doing a major work each spring by performing Handel's *Dettingen Te Deum*, the Chapel Choir did not join in this year's production, choosing instead to present its own major spring concert.[38] In addition to this performance, the Gustavus Choir also produced it first professional recording since the 1960s. At a grueling recording session on March 17, that lasted nearly nine hours, the choir performed thirteen familiar Christmas songs. The carols, such as "O Come All Ye Faithful" and "Joy to the World," were accompanied by organist David Fienen and the Gustavus Chapel Brass. The album, entitled simply, *Christmas*, was produced by Delta Records and went on sale in the late fall of 1983, in hopes of selling more than 5,000 copies.[39]

After the exhausting schedule of the 1982-1983 school year, the choir returned to the more standard calendar to which they were accustomed. Over the next three years, the ensemble, which grew to more than seventy-five singers, busied itself with annual fall and spring semester performances. They settled into a pattern of participation in four concerts each year. The fall produced a performance on Parent's Day of a short set of music that would be brought back as part of the concert tour. Christmas in Christ Chapel was the main emphasis during the early part of the school year. As the reputation of this event continued to grow, expectations of quality

---

[37] Erland Rosell, "Noteworthy Encounter with Swedish-America," translated from Swedish by Martha Lundholm Jansson, Karlstad Newpaper, photocopy located in Gustavus Adolphus College Archives, Box 16.1.2.2, "Gustavus Choir 1980-81 – 1986-87," Folder 4, "Gustavus Choir, Tour 1983."
[38] "Choir and Orchestra Perform in Harmony," *The Gustavian Weekly*, 10 May 1983, 5.
[39] "Gustavus Choir Records Album," *The Gustavus Weekly*, 12 April 1983, 7.

performance followed. The year concluded with the spring concert, which usually involved some sort of major work, often accompanied by orchestra. Erickson programmed a variety of repertoire for this concert through the years and it underwent several alterations, but it never became a hallmark performance of the choir. It was the annual January concert tour and the home concert, which opened the spring semester, on which the reputation of the Gustavus Choir was built.

The established travel rotation kept the choir in the United States for the next three years. Keeping with the design of the four-year plan, the ensemble toured closer to home in 1984 and 1985. They went eastward in 1984 making it all the way to Virginia for one performance. The bulk of the tour centered on the easternmost states in the Midwestern region. The choir presented ten concerts during the eight-day tour of Illinois, Indiana, Michigan, and Ohio.[40]

The following year, the group toured the area more central to the St. Peter campus from South Dakota to Indiana. In April of 1985, the Gustavus Choir was showcased at an event to celebrate the birthday of Carl XVI Gustaf, King of Sweden. The public celebration, which was a popular annual custom among Swedish Americans, took place at the newly opened Ordway Music Theatre in St. Paul. The choir was a natural choice for the celebration due to the college's Swedish heritage and the ensemble's recent performances for the king. Erickson felt fortunate that choir members would have the opportunity to sing in this exceptional new venue upon its January opening. The event, entitled "a musical toast," featured the choir's performance of John Rutter's *Gloria*, Beethoven's *Choral Fantasy*, and the music of Sweden.[41]

The 1985-1986 school year saw the production the Gustavus Choir's seventh album. This recording, again produced by Delta Records, consisted of simple versions of well-known Swedish hymns. Erickson believed that the recording provided good public relations for the college, but more importantly, increased the expectations of the choir members, cementing the idea that each individual is crucial to the ensemble.[42] In late January of 1986, the choir embarked on a seventeen-day concert tour during which they traveled to the Southeastern United States, with performances in

---

[40] "Gustavus Band and Choir Tours Scheduled West and East," *Greater Gustavus Quarterly 48*, no. 3 (1983): 9.
[41] "Choir to Sing King's Birthday Salute at Ordway Music Theatre," *Greater Gustavus Quarterly 49*, no. 4 (1985): 3.
[42] "Recording Artists Abound at Gustavus," *The Gustavian Weekly*, 1 October 1985, 9.

Florida, Georgia, and North Carolina, before concluding with several concerts in areas closer to home.[43]

The Gustavus Choir's 1987 concert tour of the Soviet Union, Poland, Czechoslovakia, and Sweden was an historic event for the ensemble and the college. The tour, which lasted from January 13 to February 6, took the choir behind the iron curtain and also kicked off the celebration of the 125th anniversary of Gustavus Adolphus College.[44] In addition to the historic locations and events included as part of this trip, the Gustavus Choir's tour for the first time included a course of study that allowed the students to receive a full January term credit for their participation. Members of the choir attended classes with Russian professor Vicki Frentz to learn about the culture and history of the area, while also rehearsing extensively in preparation for departure. It was Erickson's belief that the international tour should be much more than concertizing, but also a learning experience as part of the liberal arts tradition. He wanted to provide the students an important cultural experience that they were unlikely to encounter on their own. None of the members of the 1987 Gustavus Choir, nor Erickson himself, had ever been to Soviet Union.[45]

The choir presented fourteen concerts during the twenty-three days of the tour, which was completed without any major complications. They sang in the major cities of Moscow, Leningrad, Warsaw, Prague, and Stockholm and visited important historical landmarks such as the internment camp at Auschwitz, the Kremlin, and Lenin's tomb. Most importantly, the choir learned valuable cultural lessons and developed a greater appreciation for simple things in life they had taken for granted, prompting Heather Miller, a sophomore at the time, to say, "I have now come to appreciate corn flakes and milk."[46]

Perhaps the most important concert of this tour took place at the Royal Dramatic Theatre in Stockholm. When Karle Erickson stepped on the podium to open that evening's performance, he was also kicking off the 125th anniversary celebration of Gustavus Adolphus College. The concert, which featured Ann-Charlotte Bjorling as a soloist, was broadcast via

---

[43] "Touring Week Lasted 17 Days for Choir," *The Gustavian Weekly*, 20 February 1986, 7.
[44] "Choir's Soviet Union Tour Opens 125th Anniversary Year," *Greater Gustavus Quarterly 43*, no. 2 (1986): 1.
[45] Erickson, interview.
[46] Linda Herzog, "Band and Choir Tours End in Home Concerts," *The Gustavian Weekly*, 19 February 1987, 11.

satellite to an audience gathered for a gala dinner at the Minikahda Club in Minneapolis to salute the Gustavus anniversary.[47]

Fig. 5-4 The Gustavus Choir Performs in Poland
Photo courtesy Gustavus Adolphus College Archives, GACA Collection 162, P-2523-03.

While the tour was considered a monumental success, the choir did not come through it unscathed. Upon their return to campus, more than forty percent of the choir members developed severe gastro-intestinal symptoms. The students were soon diagnosed with Giardiasis, a disease contracted from water or food containing the parasite Giardia Lamblia. The students were likely exposed to this parasite while traveling in Europe. All choir members recovered quickly from the illness, and no long-term health concerns resulted from the outbreak.[48]

---

[47] "Choir's Soviet Union Tour Opens 125th Anniversary Year," *Greater Gustavus Quarterly 53*, no. 2 (1986): 1.
[48] Lori Day, "Choir Incur Lenin's Revenge," *The Gustavian Weekly*, 12 March 1987, 3.

Fig. 5-5 Erickson Rehearses the Choir for the 125th Anniversary Celebration
Photo courtesy Gustavus Adolphus College Archives, GACA Collection 162, P-2524-21.

With the Gustavus Choir coming off its extensive international tour the year prior, 1988 saw the ensemble remain closer to St. Peter. Erickson said this trip was made in an effort to "perform for the community close at hand," and "keep the public better informed about what we do at Gustavus Adolphus College."[49] The annual winter tour of Iowa, Kansas, and Nebraska was combined with several weekend trips to Minnesota locations. Three weeks after the tour concluded, the choir was honored by an invitation to sing at Orchestra Hall in Minneapolis as part of the American Choral Directors Association's North Central Division Convention. The Gustavus Choir was joined by two other colligate ensembles in the presentation of the convention's Finale Concert under the direction of Swedish conductor Eric Ericson.[50] In preparation for this event, Ericson spent several days on the Gustavus campus working extensively with the choir. The opportunity to work with one of the world's finest conductors gave the students the chance to explore a different approach to choral education. Choir members noted that Eric

---

[49] Wendy Levithan, "Choir Stays Close to Home," *The Gustavian Weekly*, 28 January 1988, 2.
[50] Ibid.

Ericson differed from their own director, Karle Erickson, in that he took a much more objective approach, placing a greater emphasis on the composer's original intentions. Despite the differences in technique, both men shared the same ultimate goal of striving for and achieving a high standard for choral performance.[51]

The 1988 school year ended with the American premiere performance of the Swedish opera *Saint Erik's Crown* in Christ Chapel. The piece, written by Eskil Hemberg, was an historical church opera about King Erik of Sweden. The five main characters were played by professional singers, while twenty members of the Gustavus Choir made up the "on stage chorus," with additional singers located in the balcony commenting on the action, similar to a Greek Chorus. The performance was conducted by Phillip Brunelle and staged by Steven Dietz who said of the performance level of the choir, "The Gustavus Choir is one of the reasons this opera is here."[52]

Fig. 5-6 Cast of St. Erik's Crown
Photo courtesy Gustavus Adolphus College Archives, GACA Collection 162, P-2535.

---

[51] Amanda Eggers, "Ericson Communicates with Unique Conducting Style," *The Gustavian Weekly*, 26 February 1988, 7.
[52] Doug Detisch, "Swedish Opera Premieres," *The Gustavian Weekly*, 28 April 1988, 8.

Each of the next two years continued the choir's established travel rotation. In 1989, the choir again took a more extended tour by traveling to the Western United States. This three-week tour marked the first time a domestic trip included educational instruction from an outside faculty member. The choir spent the first two weeks of the January term in seminars and rehearsals for the course entitled, "The Gustavus Choir in the American West." Gustavus geography professor, Robert Moline, instructed the choir members for two hours each day prior to their departure on the geographical influences in the different areas to be toured. He then joined the choir on the trip to provide a three-week field experience in geography, which was combined with concert performances. The ensemble traveled to eight U.S. states and Vancouver, Canada during the excursion, presenting eighteen concerts.[53] The following year, the choir returned to the upper Midwest traveling only on weekends and during the touring week through Minnesota, Iowa, Wisconsin and Illinois.

The 1990-1991 school year brought additional international recognition to the Gustavus Choir. In the fall, the King's Singers, from King's College in Cambridge, England, presented a concert in Christ Chapel. As part of their appearance on campus, the group utilized the Gustavus Choir in the recording of an educational video titled, *The Art of the King's Singers*. The video, which was recorded in Bjorling Concert Hall on November 5, 1990, featured the Gustavus Choir in a workshop setting that highlighted the instruction of the King's Singers. Two workshops were presented, both open to the public, from which excerpts could be used. Al Behrends, Fine Arts Coordinator for Gustavus, attributed the video opportunity to the growing reputation of the Gustavus Choir and its director, Karle Erickson. While acknowledging this endeavor would bring recognition to the choir, Erickson believed it more important to expose the students to a unique musical experience. Initially 100,000 videotapes were released and sold in stores and at King's Singers concerts worldwide.[54]

The spring semester brought about preparations for the choir's fourth international tour. The Gustavus Choir would be among the first United States collegiate organizations to present a concert tour in the People's Republic of China. In order to accommodate such a large undertaking, the choir deviated from its traditional January tour schedule in favor of a month long summer excursion.[55] The choir did participate in a January

---

[53] "1989 Gustavus Choir and Gustavus Band Tours are Westward Bound," *Greater Gustavus Quarterly 45*, no. 3 (1988): 12.
[54] Dana Wendorff, "Gustavus Choirs to Gain International Recognition," *The Gustavian Weekly*, 2 November 1990, 8.
[55] Erickson, interview.

term course, similar to past years, that both prepared the music for performance, and the students for emersion into a foreign culture. In preparation for the tour, the choir presented numerous concerts in Minnesota and Wisconsin in the weeks leading up to departure. Because the tour extended into the summer months, a traditional home concert at Christ Chapel was not feasible. Instead, the choir presented a performance at Orchestra Hall in Minneapolis, which also served as a major fundraiser for the Asian tour.[56] While tickets to the concert were sold for $25, they were also provided free of charge, along with transportation, to all Gustavus students. Erickson did this to create an atmosphere similar to that of a traditional home concert. The program for this concert was a preview of what the choir would be performing on tour. The repertoire consisted of an unusually wide variety of music, which encompassed classical choral works, American folk songs and spirituals, and music from Asian cultures, designed to complement their hosts. The Orchestra Hall performance would provide the choir a springboard into what would be a very successful tour.

The Asian tour was labeled as a concert/cultural event, because it was meant to be a learning experience as much a performance tour. The journey, which ran from May 28 to June 22, took the choir to four countries and ten cities in a culture halfway around the world. Joining the choir on this twenty-eight day expedition through the Far East was author, and Gustavus graduate, Bill Holm, who brought to the tour his own personal experiences as an exchange teacher in China, which he documented in a book called *Coming Home Crazy*. As someone who lived in the region, Holm added knowledge of the Chinese culture and political environment that helped the group avoid potentially difficult situations.[57]

The choir's travels through China corresponded with the tenth anniversary of the Tiananmen Square massacre, which heightened security and tensions throughout the tour. During a walking tour of the Forbidden City in Beijing, the choir assembled for a picture and an impromptu performance drawing a crowd of onlookers. As the choir sang, armed Chinese military police swarmed the area afraid these young foreigners were singing of freedom and revolution. As the ensemble finished singing, these men fell back into the crowd as the choir members collected

---

[56] Kathie Douma, interview by author, 2 November 2006, Phone interview.
[57] Douma, interview.

their belongings, shook hands with the Chinese citizens who had assembled, and left.[58]

Fig. 5-7 Choir Members Touring China
Photo courtesy Gustavus Adolphus College Archives, GACA Collection 162, P-2685-18.

Throughout the tour many different things touched the students, but the culture and lifestyle of the Chinese people opened many eyes. The choir traveled first-class on buses and trains while watching thousands of people commute on bicycles and dirty public transportation. Choir members were given special money called Foreign Exchange Currency as opposed to the "people's money." Several choir members were approached on the streets to exchange this currency, as it was extremely valuable on the black market.[59] Concerts also showed this divide as well as the Chinese Government's control of its people. At one performance, Erickson noticed an overflow crowd assembled in the balcony of the concert venue while the lower level was only sparsely filled. At that point he invited the standing room crowd to fill in the empty space on the lower level. This

---

[58] Bill Holm, "A Note to Parents and Sponsors: What Really Happened to Your Children in Asia?" *Greater Gustavus Quarterly 48*, no. 1 (1991): 11.
[59] Jane Simonsen, "Choir's Music Reaches Across the Globe," *The Gustavian Weekly*, 6 September 1991, 3.

was immediately stopped. Erickson would later learn this was an invasion of the established class system. These two groups were not allowed to intermingle on common footing.[60]

Perhaps the most moving event of the entire trip came as the ensemble toured Peace Park at ground zero in Hiroshima, Japan. As the group was visiting the monument, Erickson assembled them for the singing of the spiritual "Witness." As the choir performed, the students sensed the history and devastation of this place. A Japanese television station was so impressed by how moved the students appeared to be that they filmed the reaction and asked Erickson to have the choir sing the song again so they could capture it on video.[61]

Fig. 5-8  Film Crew Catches Choir Performance
Photo courtesy Gustavus Adolphus College Archives, GACA Collection 162, P-2685-12.

Karle Erickson described the Asian tour as his favorite travel experience while at Gustavus Adolphus College. The trip provided choir members the opportunity to perform in this foreign land, but also to experience a culture that they may never encounter again. The students walked along the Great Wall, experienced the destruction of Hiroshima and Pearl Harbor, and witnessed the workings of the Communist Party.

---

[60] Erickson, interview.
[61] Holm, 12, and Simonsen, 3.

Erickson believed that the Asian tour embodied everything that is important in the liberal arts education at Gustavus.[62]

During the final three years of Karle Erickson's tenure, the Gustavus Choir continued to build its reputation as a first rate collegiate ensemble. They busied themselves each year with the traditional school year performances, including the twentieth anniversary celebration of Christmas in Christ Chapel in December of 1992. The annual holiday service, in 1992 titled simply "Christmas in Christ Chapel," focused on the twenty-year history of the service itself instead of centering on a particular theme.[63] In addition to the annual campus performances, the choir also produced two new recordings; this time released on compact disc. The first of the two albums featured traditional concert literature while the second presented a selection of favorite Norwegian hymns in a collection that was similar to the Swedish recording the choir released a few years earlier.[64]

The organization's concert tours over this same period of years continued to follow the established travel rotation, with one slight deviation. Instead of the extended domestic tour falling between two shorter more regional tours, scheduling conflicts forced the three-week east coast trip to be delayed until January of 1994. In 1992, the Gustavus Choir traveled during touring week at the end of January term through the Midwest and south to Texas. This tour was highlighted by the world premiere of the piece, "The Modern Man I Sing." Composer Bob Chilcott wrote this selection at the request of Karle Erickson after the Gustavus Choir's work with the King's Singers on the documentary video the previous year. The song, based on poetry by Walt Whitman, deeply inspired the ensemble and was the centerpiece of the choir's tour program.[65] The following year, the group traveled through the upper Midwest reaching western portions of North and South Dakota and Montana for the first time in thirty years. This tour also featured the premiere performance of a challenging selection commissioned by Terry Burk called, "Psalm 66."[66] The extended east coast tour of 1994 again saw the partnership of the choir with a Gustavus faculty member to create a

---

[62] Erickson, interview.
[63] Deb Boelter, "Christmas in Christ Chapel Celebrates 20th Year of Worshipping Through Musical Talent," *The Gustavian Weekly*, 4 December 1992, 5.
[64] "The Gustavus Choir 1991-92," in *The 1991-92 Gustavian* (St. Peter, MN: Gustavus Adolphus College, 1992), 60.
[65] Ibid.
[66] Deb Boelter, "Musicians Travel Throughout the Country Performing Concerts During Touring Week," *The Gustavian Weekly*, 22 January 1993, 4.

January term course that was titled, "The Gustavus Choir in the American East." History professor, Kevin Byrne, accompanied the ensemble on its travels after spending the first two weeks of January lecturing daily on American history from the colonial times to eastern urbanization.[67] The tour, which took the choir to Boston, New York, and Washington D.C., including a performance at the National Cathedral, followed the eastward path of a cold front that brought record breaking cold temperatures at nearly every stop during the first week of travel. Despite the frigid weather, the group performed to the same large and enthusiastic audiences that had come to be expected at tour concerts for the Gustavus Choir.[68]

Shortly after the tour of 1994, Karle Erickson's duties as the director of the Gustavus Choir were suspended due to allegations of sexual harassment filed by student. On August 31, 1994, the Board of Trustees terminated Erickson's tenured position based on findings in conjunction with these charges. A month later, Erickson sued Gustavus Adolphus College for wrongful termination stemming from a violation of the sexual harassment grievance procedure outlined in the faculty guide.[69] In 1998, the two sides reached an out-of-court settlement for an undisclosed monetary award.[70] These events brought to an end an era of significant growth and development for the choir at Gustavus Adolphus College.

During his tenure, Karle Erickson brought a level of excellence to the Gustavus Choir that had a dynamic influence on the ensemble, the department of music, and the college. He was unable to accept the idea that Gustavus was any less than a first class citizen with respect to other Lutheran colleges. During his time as conductor, the choir began a travel rotation that included international touring once every four years, established interdisciplinary partnerships with Gustavus faculty members in order to create courses that corresponded with the choir's extended travel, and founded traditions within the organization that continue to be a part of the ensemble's legacy. He introduced F. Melius Christiansen's "Praise to the Lord" as the group's signature selection and purchased the velvet robes of crimson and cream for which the choir is known. Under the leadership of Karle Erickson, the Gustavus Choir furthered its

---

[67] Sara Tollefson, "Gustavus Choir Croons in the Big Apple," *The Gustavian Weekly*, 14 January 1994, 7.
[68] Wahlund, interview.
[69] Jeremy Jones, "Erickson Sues College, President," *The Gustavian Weekly*, 30 September 1994, 1.
[70] Elena Davis, "Lawsuit Against Gustavus Settled Out of Court," *The Gustavian Weekly*, 30 January 1998, 1.

international reputation as a quality collegiate ensemble, and reached new heights in its continued commitment to musical excellence.

Fig. 5-9  Karle Erickson Conducts the Gustavus Choir at Christmas in Christ Chapel
Photo courtesy Gustavus Adolphus College Archives, GACA Collection 162, P-5401.

CHAPTER SIX

THE GUSTAVUS CHOIR FROM 1995 TO 2007:
THE CONTRIBUTIONS OF GREGORY AUNE

Upon the departure of Karle Erickson, the Gustavus Choir entered into a period of transition. In order to allow an appropriate amount of time to conduct an exhaustive national search for the next director of the choir, the college appointed retired St. Olaf Choir director, Kenneth Jennings, as the interim conductor of the Gustavus Choir. He assumed leadership of the organization in September of 1994, and immediately began working with the group in preparation for its annual performance schedule.[1]

Events of the prior six months had caused the choir to lose some of its forward momentum. As rehearsals began in the fall, the ensemble had decreased in size to fifty-five members, as opposed to the more than seventy singers that had been customary in the past several years. Despite the smaller size, the choir and Jennings were determined not to experience any lessening in the quality of performance.[2] The ensemble engaged in the traditional fall concerts on Parent's Day and as part of the Christmas in Christ Chapel service, while also preparing for the January concert tour.

The 1995 concert tour continued the travel rotation established by Karle Erickson. Despite the period of transition, the Gustavus Choir embarked on January 18 for a seventeen-day international tour to Poland, Germany, Sweden, and Finland. As with past extended tours, the performance study was combined with the teachings of Dennis Johnson, vice president of church relations at Gustavus. The January term course, titled "The Legacy of the Christian Church from the Reformation to the Present," focused on the political, social, and cultural heritage of the Reformation in the northern part of Europe. Kenneth Jennings devised a concert program that would tie directly to the students' course of study by choosing literature that reflected either the composer or tour location's

---

[1] Fienen, interview.
[2] Behrends, interview.

102                           Chapter Six

Fig. 6-1 Kenneth and Carolyn Jennings with Gustavus President and First Lady on Tour - Photo provided by the author.

relationship to the Reformation.[3] During the trip, the choir toured or performed in several historic churches throughout northern Europe including Wittenberg, where Martin Luther nailed his treatise to the door that started the Reformation movement, and Leipzig, where J. S. Bach served as cantor and composer. The Scandinavian portion of the trip allowed the students to experience the culture and to better understand the evolutionary contributions made to Lutheran colleges across America. Jennings saw this tour as "an attempt to try to give something back to the culture which they are studying about."[4] The successful tour did not come off without its share of logistical issues, which made this tour among the most challenging for tour manager, Dean Wahlund. It began upon arrival in Poland, when the boxes carrying the choir's robes were not released from customs until hours before the first performance. It continued a few days later, when the hitch to the trailer carrying the choir's equipment broke while traveling between concert locations causing the bus to drive no faster than 25 miles per hour. The delay created by the slow speed, and the time needed for repairs caused the ensemble to miss a scheduled

---

[3] "Calendar Upcoming Events," *Greater Gustavus Quarterly 51*, no. 2 (1994): 83.
[4] Beth Russell, "G-Choir Celebrates Christianity in Europe," *The Gustavian Weekly*, 13 January 1995, 4.

performance. Despite these logistical problems, the Gustavus Choir presented eleven well-received concerts across four countries during the 1995 European tour.[5]

The end of tour did not bring a conclusion to the busy schedule for the 1994-1995 Gustavus Choir. In April of 1995, the choir in combination with the Chapel Choir and Gustavus Band presented the world premiere of David Holsinger's *Easter Symphony*. The commissioning of this work began in July of 1991 when Gustavus Band director, Douglas Nimmo, contacted Holsinger about obtaining additional movements of *The Easter Symphony*. The Gustavus Band had performed Holsinger's well-known piece "The Death Tree," which was intended to be the second movement of *The Easter Symphony*, during its 1990 concert tour. Nimmo discovered during his conversation with David Holsinger that due to financial problems, the remaining movements of the symphony, originally titled "Entry to Jerusalem" and The Resurrection," were never composed.[6] Financial hardship was not the only reason *The Easter Symphony* had never been completed. People who performed and listened to "The Death Tree" often told Holsinger that it stands alone and that he should not finish the work, but Douglas Nimmo disagreed.[7] After much prayer and soul searching, Nimmo decided to approach Holsinger about completing the symphony, because he believed that it would be much more powerful as a completed work. In January of 1992, Holsinger agreed to complete *The Easter Symphony*. As the final details of the commission were ironed out, it was decided that as part of the package, David Holsinger would spend time on the Gustavus campus leading to the premiere performance in April of 1995.[8]

As the first public performance approached, Holsinger's newly composed first and third movements, now entitled "Kings" and Symphonia Resurrectus," slowly got into the hands of the ensembles' directors.[9] Holsinger consulted with the directors, especially seeking the guidance of Kenneth Jennings in writing for voices, leading up to the premiere. He visited campus to meet with the conductors as he worked to complete and edit the final draft. Just four weeks prior to *The Easter Symphony's* debut, Doug Nimmo received the final 68 measures of the

---

[5] Wahlund, interview.
[6] Nimmo, interview.
[7] Debbie Boelter, "Gustavus Commissions Composer to Finish 'Easter Symphony,'" *The Gustavian Weekly*, 28 February 1992, 5.
[8] Nimmo, interview.
[9] Clinton Dietrich, "Musicians Anticipating *Easter* Premiere," *The Gustavian Weekly*, 24 March 1995, 1.

composition. He took the completed score and challenged himself and the ensembles to prepare and perform the piece "the best they could in the service of music."[10]

On April 28, 1995, the Gustavus Choir and Chapel Choir joined forces with the Gustavus Band in Christ Chapel to present the world premiere of David Holsinger's *The Easter Symphony* under the direction of Douglas Nimmo. The next evening an encore performance of the symphony was presented at Central Lutheran Church in Minneapolis. The second concert was intended as tribute to Bishop Herbert Chillstrom, who was retiring as Bishop of the Evangelical Lutheran Church of America. These performances brought the school year to a close, and with it, Kenneth Jennings' service to Gustavus Adolphus College.

## Gregory Aune Becomes Gustavus Choir Director

During the year Kenneth Jennings served as interim conductor of the choir, college administrators sought applications to fill the position on a permanent basis. During the winter of 1995, the search was completed when Dr. Gregory Aune was appointed as the sixth director of the Gustavus Choir. Under his leadership, the choir continued to thrive as an international touring ensemble, expanded it performance repertoire to include a wider variety of genres, and further enhanced its reputation as a member of the Lutheran Choral School.

Gregory John Aune was born and raised in Grand Rapids, Minnesota. As the son of a high school and church choir director and a piano teacher and organist, music was part of Aune's life from a very early age. He began piano studies as a child, taking lessons from his mother. These lessons proved somewhat unsuccessful, as the piano never became an instrument on which Aune acquired any significant skill. Throughout his childhood, Aune sang in church and school and developed an appreciation for the art of choral music, but it did not develop into a passion for him until later in his life.[11]

Upon graduation from high school, Aune was uncertain of his future. He enrolled in Itasca Community College in his hometown of Grand Rapids in an attempt to find a direction for his studies. It was during this year at Itasca that his outlook on life changed. The Concordia Choir from Concordia College in Moorhead, Minnesota, toured through Grand Rapids, as it had many times while Aune was growing up. This time, he

---

[10] Nimmo, interview.
[11] Aune, interview.

recognized that there was much more to the world than the small community in which he had grown up. It was time for him to spread his wings and branch out. The next year, Aune followed a high school friend to St. Cloud State University in St. Cloud, Minnesota. In his year at this university, Aune was still undecided in a major; however, music continued as a key interest in his life. At the end of the school year, he transferred again, this time to Concordia College where he began a track that would lead him to a profession in choral music. Gregory Aune spent three years at Concordia College studying with Paul J. Christiansen, the first significant influence in his choral development. In his first year on campus, he sang as a member of the Chapel Choir before spending his final two years in the Concordia Choir, the last of which, he served as an officer for the ensemble. As a member of the Concordia Choir, Aune learned the Christiansen philosophies and experienced firsthand the workings of a choral group rooted in the Lutheran traditions. He took with him Christiansen's ideas of tone production, programming, rehearsals, and touring, all of which he continued to develop and build upon as he progressed in his musical career.[12]

Fig. 6-2 Gregory Aune
Photo courtesy Gregory Aune.

---

[12] Ibid.

In 1976, Gregory Aune graduated from Concordia College with a Bachelor of Arts degree in Public School Music. He then moved to Sisseton, South Dakota, where his wife, whom he met while singing in the Concordia Choir, was already working as an elementary music teacher. Aune accepted a position as a music teacher in the small school district where he taught at both the junior and senior high school. His duties included directing two choirs at both schools as well as leading three bands at the junior high.[13]

During his third year in Sisseton, Aune decided it was time for him to seek additional education. During his time at Concordia, Aune realized that Paul Christiansen focused primarily on taking care of himself and his duties, so he was unable to seek advice on graduate programs. Instead, Aune contacted Lee Sataren, at Augsburg College in Minneapolis, with whom he had developed a collegial relationship. Sataren recommended Aune attend the University of Iowa for his graduate studies. In 1979, Gregory Aune enrolled in the master's program at Iowa, where he began his studies with the next significant influence in his choral development, Don Moses. Aune called Moses "a great teacher" who shaped his ideas on score study and rehearsal. As a Robert Shaw disciple, Moses guided Aune to understand the importance of rhythmic discipline, and gave him the opportunity to study great choral orchestral works, which honed his gesture in front of an instrumental ensemble. Upon entering the graduate program at the University of Iowa, Aune planned to pursue only his master's degree, but was convinced by Moses to stay on and complete his doctorate as well. He finished his course work in 1982 and five years later, Gregory Aune completed his dissertation and was awarded the degree of Doctor of Musical Arts in Choral Conducting.[14]

His first collegiate teaching job took Aune back to South Dakota where, in 1982, he assumed the position of Director of Choral Activities at Dakota Wesleyan University in Mitchell. In addition to his duties at the college, Aune also established a community choir called the "Dakota Chorale" which experienced a great deal of success during his tenure as director. In his third year with the ensemble, they were selected to perform at the American Choral Directors Association's North Central Division convention.[15]

After five years at Dakota Wesleyan, Aune resigned his position with the university to take a similar job at Bethany College in Lindsborg, Kansas. At Bethany, a Lutheran college, Aune was responsible for the

---

[13] Ibid.
[14] Ibid.
[15] Ibid.

choir, and in charge of the annual Messiah Festival. This festival, which dates back to the 19th century, featured multiple performances of major choral orchestral masterworks each year, most frequently G. F. Handel's *Messiah*. In his seven years as director of this festival, Aune had the opportunity to conduct *Messiah* fourteen times and did J. S. Bach's *St. Matthew Passion* another seven times. Part of his responsibilities at Bethany College included the leadership of the College Community Orchestra. As conductor of this ensemble, Aune further branched into the realm of instrumental music. He viewed the experience of conducting orchestral works, such as the Beethoven symphonies, as vital to his development as a musician. While at Bethany College, Aune had the opportunity to spend three January terms as a participant in the Robert Shaw Carnegie Hall symposiums. It was through these workshops that Aune learned directly from Robert Shaw, the third major influence on his choral study. His participation allowed him to enhance the philosophies he had learned at Iowa and helped to better shape his approach to the choral rehearsal.

When the choir job at Gustavus Adolphus College became available in 1994, Gregory Aune saw it as an opportunity to move up to an elite program. He wanted to teach in a private institution where he would have the chance to polish the music performed by the choir and saw this as that opportunity. He viewed the position as his "Utopia."[16] In the fall of 1995, after seven years at Bethany College, Gregory Aune became the sixth director in the history of the Gustavus Choir. His goal for the group was simply to "maintain the fine tradition of singing that has always been a part of Gustavus Adolphus College."[17]

## Gregory Aune's Choral Approach

Gregory Aune brought a very different approach to the teaching of choral music. His methods varied greatly from those of Erickson and Knautz. He conveyed a style of leadership that was more relaxed and less commanding. He worked to build a consensus among the choir and believed that respect goes both directions.[18] Though his methods were more thoughtful and subtle, the results produced more emotive singing from the choir. Through this softer tact, he was still able to produce an

---

[16] Ibid.
[17] Beth Russell, "Perserverance and Hard Work are Lessons New Choral Director Aune Hopes Students Will Learn," *The Gustavian Weekly*, 15 September 1995, 5.
[18] Berhends, interview, and Jorgensen, interview.

expressive ensemble that sang with technical accuracy and well blended intonation.[19] As the choir evolved each year, Aune attempted to create an atmosphere of a family, learning to work together on a musical project. Aune desires to establish an atmosphere where students work with him "not as the omnipotent maestro, but instead to make music as a collegial collaboration."[20]

Aune's approach to choral tone evolved greatly over the course of his career. It was influenced by each of his teachers over the years. In the beginning, he was influenced by Paul J. Christiansen as he worked to achieve a dark and covered sound that was focused on choral blend and removed the individual from the voice. While studying at Iowa, there was never talk of blend and the singers were allowed to sing and use the full color of their vibrato. After working with Robert Shaw he began to adapt the principles of his teachings that emphasized pitch and rhythm above all. He was also influenced by the choirs of Northern Europe, who used a strait tone, especially with the sopranos, to produce fine intonation. As Aune developed the sound of the Gustavus Choir, he combined these philosophies to produce a tone that was rich and full within the confines of each individual voice.[21] He employed more of a voice teaching approach to evolve a choral sound that is more free and musical, while promoting good vocal health.[22] Vibrato is used in a healthy manner, but is seen more as an expressive element that adds to the musical interpretation. Aune's approach to tone is not dictated by a set aural image of good choral sound, but instead, as a stylistic aspect that varies to accommodate the literature of different genres of music.[23]

Gregory Aune modeled his rehearsals with the Gustavus Choir after the philosophies of Robert Shaw. He used a layered approach in teaching the music to the students. He began by focusing the choir on learning pitches and rhythms. The learning of new music was Aune's least favorite part of the job, but also one he believed to be most important. The note-learning phase was often done in sectional rehearsal. Aune would set deadlines for which he expected pieces to be learned so that the group could come together in rehearsal. These deadlines, at times, were accompanied by mini exams in which the students would sing for Aune in quartets to test their knowledge of the score. Once the ensemble began to rehearse as a full choir, pitch issues were dealt with either by intervallic

---

[19] Fienen, interview.
[20] Aune, interview.
[21] Ibid.
[22] Jorgensen, interview.
[23] Aune, interview.

study or harmonically, based on Aune's interpretation of the problem. The solfege system, which under his leadership had moved to fixed do, was rarely used in this process.

Once the students became secure in their notes, Aune shifted the focus of the rehearsal to the text and how the music should be shaped to best interpret the poetry. From early in the learning process, Aune conducted the choir as he would in a final performance in hopes that the singers would observe some of his musical interpretation. As the rehearsal process continued, Aune worked with the students to develop the musical line beyond his conducting gesture. Through repeated performance, the interpretation would become somewhat instinctual. Finally, if the performance techniques did not prove successful in transferring the musical ideas, Aune would take time to have choir members mark every phrase detail into their scores. This ensured complete understanding of the musical ideas.[24]

The third layer of Aune's rehearsal plan allowed the choir the time it needed to sing the pieces in order to develop a comfort level. It is through this process that Aune believed the choir would ultimately make its connection with the music. As the choir sings, Aune continued to conduct the piece as if in performance, hoping the choir will continue to pick up on subtle nuances it was unable to distinguish in the reading stages. The final period of rehearsal also helped the choir to memorize its music in preparation for performance. Aune believed that music should be memorized to assure preparedness and to foster a connection between the choir and conductor in performance that would be blocked if they were holding scores. Throughout the rehearsal process, it was Aune's goal to create a choir that sings with impeccable accuracy while promoting an environment that allows musical expression and ultimately communicates meaning the with the audience.[25]

When selecting repertoire for the Gustavus Choir, Gregory Aune used the established conventions of the Lutheran Choral School and its directors as a starting point for the concert program. He believed this model to be evolving and expanding in scope to include literature that goes beyond the expectations of the traditional F. Melius Christiansen style choir. The majority of the music performed by the choir, especially on its concert tours, remained a cappella in nature. The a cappella heritage of the choir combined with the relative ease of extended touring without the added burden of instruments made programming this style of choral music

---

[24] Ibid.
[25] Ibid.

optimal. However, Aune suggested that the repertoire base is expanding among the Lutheran choirs. In his programming for the Gustavus Choir he worked to present choral literature representing a global perspective, as well as the time-honored sacred settings at the heart of the tradition, and noted that other directors also utilized this practice.[26]

Fig. 6-3  Aune Conducts the Gustavus Choir
Photo courtesy Gregory Aune

He also recognized what he called a "misconception" that these schools sing a more narrow range of literature, especially lacking in the performance of major works with an orchestra.[27] Aune brought to Gustavus Adolphus College his experience with choral orchestral compositions at Bethany. As the orchestra at the college reached higher levels of performance excellence, the two organizations combined more frequently in concert. Aune believed that the performance of masterworks was an important opportunity for the students to experience a new style of literature. Throughout his tenure at Gustavus, the spring concert evolved into an annual presentation of major choral orchestral works.[28]

When selecting repertoire for the Gustavus Choir, more than 75% of the music Aune programmed for the concert tours was from the 20th Century. He believed this style of music best fit the ensemble as it was, in his eyes, too large to sing early music. Aune stated that this period of choral music was his favorite, but he also believed it was important for

---

[26] Aune, 17.
[27] Ibid.
[28] Aune, interview.

him, as a college choir director, to champion the performance of new literature by contemporary composers. He further demonstrated this ideal through the commissioning of new works for the choir, believing this to be a great opportunity for the students and an important undertaking for the college. It was his goal that the Gustavus Choir would perform a newly composed work at least every other year.[29]

Gregory Aune ushered in a new era in the evolution of the Gustavus Choir; one that embraced its heritage of the Christiansen school of thought, while also expanding its perspective. He brought a more relaxed, collegial approach to the rehearsal, while maintaining high expectations for the students and their performance. Through his work with the choir, the group strived to develop a choral tone that was unique to each piece of music being performed. He pushed the choir to sing new and commissioned music and expanded its repertoire beyond the confines of the traditional Lutheran choir. Gregory Aune came to Gustavus Adolphus College to further the legacy of musical excellence established by the choir and its prior conductors. As its leader, Aune enhanced the reputation of the Gustavus Choir and secured its place among the elite college choirs.

## The Gregory Aune Era

In the fall of 1995, fifty-seven members of the Gustavus Choir were assembled and began rehearsals that marked the beginning of Gregory Aune's tenure at the college. The ensemble presented its traditional fall semester concert schedule, including a performance at Parent's Day and as part of Christmas in Christ Chapel, this year titled, "The Tree of Life." In January, the choir prepared, as usual, for its annual concert tour. The tour took the choir through the upper Midwestern states of Minnesota, Nebraska, Iowa, and Wisconsin. Throughout Aune's first tour the choir was well received. He programmed a varied concert of music ranging from Renaissance composers to a commissioned selection by Imant Raminsh. "Mighty River, Mighty Fire" was written specifically for the Gustavus Choir at the request of Karle Erickson a few years earlier.[30] The piece came to mean a lot to the choir and to Aune, who programmed the selection again the following year. As he rehearsed the piece in

---

[29] Ibid.
[30] Amber Rundle, "Nimmo, Aune Take Groups on the Road," *The Gustavian Weekly*, 19 January 1996, 5.

preparation for the tour, Aune identified with its meaning and felt he grew to understand the work better.[31]

In the spring, the Gustavus Choir continued its trend of singing larger scale accompanied works when it presented a concert with organist, and visiting Gustavus professor, Gregory Peterson. The performance, which took place in Christ Chapel, featured two Peterson organ solos, and the choir's renditions of Benjamin Britten's "Rejoice in the Lamb" and Jean Langlais' "Messe Solennelle." It was important to Aune to program accompanied literature to expose the choir and the audience to different textures and sounds after the a cappella concert tour.[32]

As the 1996-1997 school year began, the Gustavus Choir rehearsed diligently in preparation for the 125th anniversary celebration of the birth of F. Melius Christiansen. The ensemble participated in two performances at St. Olaf College as part of the celebration. The concerts, sponsored by the American Choral Director's Association, brought together five colleges that have come to represent the Christiansen Choral School and its philosophies. The choirs involved were from Gustavus, St. Olaf, Concordia College in Moorhead, Minnesota, Augsburg College in Minneapolis, and Luther College in Decorah, Iowa. Each ensemble presented a brief set of repertoire, with each group including a selection composed by Christiansen. The Gustavus Choir performed three pieces, including "Mighty River, Mighty Fire," and their signature selection, "Praise to the Lord" arranged by F. Melius Christiansen. In addition to individual performances by each ensemble, the choirs joined forces at the end to present four pieces that had been written by Christiansen. Conducting the combined choirs was the former interim director of the Gustavus Choir and longtime St. Olaf Choir director, Kenneth Jennings. It had been the organizers hope that F. Melius' son and former head of the Concordia Choir, Paul J. Christiansen, would be able to conduct the final two selections, but health concerns did not allow this. Aune saw this event as a unique opportunity for the five groups to perform together in a celebration of the Lutheran choral heritage they all share.[33]

The next two winter concert tours followed the travel rotation that had been established during Karle Erickson's tenure at the college. In 1997, the Gustavus Choir traveled to the Southeastern United States, but did not combine with a professor for an extended tour. During the ten-day trip,

---

[31] Aune, interview.
[32] Michelle Beissel, "Gustavus Choir to Perform Combination of Organ and Choral Music," *The Gustavian Weekly*, 26 April 1996, 7.
[33] Beth Russell, "125th Anniversary Celebration of F. Melius Christiansen Underway," *The Gustavian Weekly*, 15 November 1996, 8.

the ensemble presented concerts in five states traveling as far south as Sarasota, Florida.[34] The following year, the choir remained close to home traveling throughout the state of Minnesota during tour week. Aune saw the trip as an opportunity to "connect with roots in Minnesota." He viewed the 1998 tour as different than past trips in that the choir could reach more perspective students, alumni, and friends of the program. On the eleven-day tour, the ensemble presented seventeen concerts including several daytime performances at area high schools.[35]

In the spring of 1998, the landscape of Gustavus Adolphus College was changed forever. On March 29, at approximately 5:30 p.m. a tornado stretching more than a mile wide and packing wind gusts in excess of 200 miles per hour tore through the campus and St. Peter community. On the Gustavus campus every building sustained some damage. Approximately 80% of the campus' windows were broken, six student houses were destroyed, two resident halls sustained major damage, and the steeple was blown off of Christ Chapel. Fortunately, the vast majority of students were not on campus for the tornado as it occurred during spring break. The school remained closed an additional two weeks to allow for cleanup.[36]

Fig. 6-4 Christ Chapel is Damaged by the Tornado
Photo courtesy Gustavus Adolphus College

---

[34] Gustavus Adolphus College, *The Gustavus Choir*, Concert Program, 1997.
[35] Michelle Beissel, "Choir Ends Successful Tour," *The Gustavian Weekly*, 13 February 1998, 7.
[36] "Unseasonable Tornado Redefines Community, Brings Gusties Together Despite Tearing Apart the Campus," *The Gustavian Weekly*, 28 April 1998, 8.

When classes did resume on April 19, the academic schedule was dramatically altered. Five academic buildings remained temporarily closed, leaving only forty-five classrooms available to accommodate the entire course load. Students attended classes in buildings foreign to their subject matter and were required to move to a six-day week leaving only Sunday as a day of rest.[37]

The Fine Arts Building sustained significant damage to its roof and structure. Because of this, it was unable to open when students returned to campus. Therefore, the department was forced to schedule three hundred private lessons and twenty-five professors into three full and two partial classrooms and placed the entire performance component of the curriculum in jeopardy.[38] However, the students and faculty persevered. The Gustavus Choir not only presented its annual spring concert, a performance with the orchestra of Gabriel Fauré's *Requiem*, but also combined with the college's band and orchestra for a benefit concert in Minneapolis titled "Songs of Victory."[39]

As the 1998-1999 school year began, the Gustavus Adolphus College campus returned to some sort of normalcy despite reminders throughout of the devastation of the past March. The Gustavus Choir busied itself with its annual performances and prepared for an international concert tour. In January, the choir's seventy-three members embarked on an historic trip taking them to South Africa, the first visit by any Gustavus music ensemble to the African continent. The seed for the South African tour was planted in the summer of 1987 when then conductor, Karle Erickson, received an invitation for the Gustavus Choir to tour the area while he was attending the first World Symposium on Choral Music in Vienna. Unfortunately, the choir was unable to accept the invitation.[40] The college determined that while apartheid was in place in South Africa, no organization would tour the area. When apartheid fell and Nelson Mandela rose to power, the doors were opened and planning for the trip began.[41]

Preparations for the tour took in excess of two years. The itinerary included twelve concerts in eight South African cities, including three performances in both Port Elizabeth and Cape Town. In addition to the

---

[37] Sarah McCormick, "Faculty has Conquered a Whirlwind of Problems," *The Gustavian Weekly*, 28 April 1998, 1.
[38] Ibid.
[39] Gustavus Adolphus College, *Songs of Victory Spring Benefit Concert*, Concert Program, 17 May 1998.
[40] Levithan, 3.
[41] Wahlund, interview.

eight hours of daily rehearsals, the 1999 January term course, titled, "South Africa: The Heritage of Apartheid and the Hope of Freedom," required students to attend an hour and a half class each day, led by Dennis Johnson, to learn of the history, culture, and religions of the region. Each member of the choir was asked to read a book chronicling South African culture or history and report on its contents. While touring the area, the student's eyes were opened as they came in contact with third world poverty and experienced the difficult living conditions in the country.[42]

Fig. 6-5 Aune Talks Music with People in South Africa
Photo courtesy The Gustavus Quarterly, 55: 3 (Spring 1999).

The ensemble sang in Soweto, where the children's uprising began in 1976, and witnessed the conditions that gave rise to the music of liberation. Choir members toured Robben Island and lingered in the prison cell that held Nelson Mandela for so many years. They met with people who were directly involved in the South African freedom struggle, most notably Govan Mbeki, who was imprisoned on Robben Island with Mandela. They also had the opportunity to explore the Kruger National Park, the largest game reserve in the country, and take a boat cruise on Lake St. Lucia. Despite the scars left by apartheid, the choir witnessed signs of hope and harmony as they saw mixing of the races and in one case

---

[42] Michael R. Bukowski, "Choir Learns Music and More for South Africa Tour," *The Gustavian Weekly*, 27 January 1999, 5.

observed a black pastor baptize a white baby and then, with a white lay person, offer communion to all races.

Throughout the trip, it was the performance opportunities that meant the most to choir. Aune programmed a concert that included the choir's traditional literature as well as the folk music of the United States and South Africa. The repertoire was later recorded and released on a compact disc titled, "Sing South Africa." People throughout the country heaped praise upon the choir during the tour. The director of the Joy of Africa Choir remarked, "Your sound is different. It tears at the deepest recess of my soul and I feel as if I can touch God." The South Africa tour showed the members of the Gustavus Choir the power of choral music and allowed them to spread their goodwill to the African continent.[43]

Fig. 6-6 Gustavus Choir Performs with South African Dancers
Photo courtesy The Gustavus Quarterly, 55: 3 (Spring 1999).

Upon their return from this historic endeavor, the Gustavus Choir diligently worked in preparation for its second performance of David Holsinger's *Easter Symphony*. The choir again combined with the Gustavus Band for the presentation of the work. The piece was presented in remembrance of the one-year anniversary of the tornado that greatly damaged the community. The performance was free to all and did not require a ticket for admission. Band director, Doug Nimmo, wanted to

---

[43] Dennis Johnson, "The Gustavus Choir 'Sings South Africa,'" *Greater Gustavus Quarterly 55*, no. 3 (1999): 5-9.

create an atmosphere that would celebrate Easter's renewal of life through Christ and St. Peter's renewal as a community.[44]

The next year, the music department at Gustavus Adolphus College reached higher levels of status and performance quality. In April of 2000, the Gustavus Orchestra participated in a European tour during the college's spring break. This marked the first time that the ensemble had traveled internationally. The orchestra had been building toward a level of high caliber performance over an extended period of time. The overseas trip symbolized the group's arrival at that level. The success of the orchestra's excursion marked the addition of a third international touring ensemble at Gustavus. From this point forward, the music department began a rotation in which the three main performance groups on campus would each tour foreign lands within a four-year period.[45]

The Gustavus Choir continued its own travel rotation over the next three years. The concert tour of 2000 took the ensemble southward to Texas, with performances along the way in Minnesota, Iowa, Missouri, Kansas, and Oklahoma. As part of this touring week trip, current choir members had the opportunity to sing for former Gustavus Choir director, Phillip Knautz at a concert at Texas Lutheran University in Seguin, Texas.[46]

The following year, the group traveled extensively throughout the western United States. As part of this extended January term tour, the singers enrolled in a course titled "The Geography of the Pacific Northwest," taught by Gustavus professor, Robert Moline. The class emphasized the process by which people had affected the natural environment, by providing the students the opportunity to meet with city planners, and learn about the geographic features of the areas in which they traveled. During the three-week tour, the group presented twenty concerts in eight states before returning to Gustavus for the home concert.[47]

In the fall of 2001, the Gustavus Choir joined forces with the Chapel Choir, Lucia Singers, and Gustavus Orchestra, with help from the Mankato Children's Choir and the Metropolitan Boy Choir for the

---

[44] Jessica Risco, "'The Easter Symphony' in its Second Performance," *The Gustavian Weekly*, 30 April 1999, 5.
[45] Kathy Lenius, "GOY2UK International Tour a New Tradition for Orchestra," *The Gustavian Weekly*, 14 April 2000, 5.
[46] Katie Howe, "Tour 2000: Texas or Bust!" *Echoes & Overtones 1*, no. 1 (2000): 3.
[47] Angela Ziebarth, "Taking the West by Storm," *Echoes & Overtones 2*, no. 1 (2000): 1.

performance of the *Nobel Symphony* by Gustavus alumnus, Steve Heitzeg. The piece was commissioned by the college to celebrate the centennial of the first awarding of the Nobel Prize and presented in conjunction with the 37$^{th}$ Nobel Conference on campus.[48] The piece was set in six movements with each movement based on one of the various Nobel Prizes awarded in Chemistry, Physics, Economics, Physiology, Medicine, Literature, and Peace. Interspersed between the movements were a preamble, proclamations based on the Martin Luther King's essay "The Trumpet of Conscience," and a postlude for solo trumpet. The text of the symphony came from a group of Nobel laureates including; Desmond Tutu, Elie Wiesel, the Dalai Lama, Dag Hammerskjöld, Rigoberta Menchu, Nelson Mandela, Pablo Neruda, Samuell Beckett, Albert Camus, Alexander Solzhenitsyn, Mother Teresa, Amartya Sen, Perez Esquivel, and Toni Morrison. The thirty-minute work, which premiered on October 2, 2001, in Christ Chapel, was Heitzeg's attempt to address human rights and justice and to honor the vision and voices of the Nobel laureates.[49]

In late January of 2002, the Gustavus Choir embarked on a ten-day Upper Midwestern tour that took the group through Minnesota, Wisconsin, and Illinois. This tour again reached out to perspective students and alumni and featured performances in many area high schools. The most significant event of the school year came in March as the Gustavus Choir was selected to perform at the North Central American Choral Directors Association convention in Des Moines, Iowa. The performance, which was held in the Des Moines Civic Center on the morning of March 14, was the first time the choir had been selected to perform alone as part of this conference. Their only other performance came under Karle Erickson as part of a mass choir. The twenty-five minute presentation focused on the music of Scandinavian composers from the 19$^{th}$ and 20$^{th}$ Centuries.[50]

As the 2002-2003 school year began, the Gustavus Choir prepared for the traditional fall schedule. This year again included the group's performance as part of the Nobel Conference. The choir joined with the orchestra and Chapel Choir to present some of W. A. Mozart's most well-known works, including excerpts from the *Requiem*. Gustavus Orchestra director, Warren Friesen, designed the concert to tie into the conference's

---

[48] Dan Roeder and Paul Miller, "Nobel Symphony Generates Excitement," *Echoes & Overtones 3*, no. 1 (2001): 3.
[49] Gregory Aune, "Conductor's Column," *Echoes & Overtones 2*, no. 2 (2001): 2.
[50] Tobias Stalter, "Gustavus Choir Accepts Historic Invitation," *Echoes & Overtones 3*, no.1 (2001): 1.

theme "Nature of Nurture."[51] Later that semester, the choir participated in the thirtieth annual Christmas in Christ Chapel service. The event, themed "Julbön Christmas Prayer" centered on the texts of the Saints of the North and featured the music of Sweden. Gustavus chaplain, Brian Johnson, said, "To celebrate 30 years of Christmas in Christ Chapel, it seemed important to draw on the heritage of the college and its connection with Sweden." Each of the five Christmas services was again performed to a sold out audience.[52]

In January, the choir prepared for its annual concert tour, which in 2003 took the group on a seventeen-day excursion to Italy. As part of their preparations, the singers participated in classes, led by English professor, Joyce Sutphen, which introduced the culture and history of the country. As part of the trip, the choir had the opportunity to perform in four of Italy's grandest cathedrals: the Basilica of St. Peter in Rome, the Basilica Inferiore of Saint Francesco in Assisi, the Duomo in Florence, and the Basilica of Saint Mark in Venice. For the tour, Aune programmed varied literature that would be enhanced by the acoustics of the performance venues and would bring the musical tradition of Gustavus to the Italian people. In addition to performances, choir members explored the country's rich history, touring ancient Roman ruins and historic religious locations like the Vatican and St. Peter's Basilica. It was, however, the performances that defined the trip.[53] Throughout the tour, the choir was met with enthusiastic appreciation. At their very first concert in Rome, following the completion of the program, the audience's prolonged applause was followed by chants of "Bis! Bis," this means encore. The choir obliged this request three times before Aune was forced to thank the enthusiastic crowd and explain that they were finished. The appreciation overwhelmed and inspired the Gustavus Choir making the entire tour an exhilarating experience.[54]

Over the next several years, the Gustavus Choir continued its busy performance schedule with the annual concert tour highlighting each year. In 2004, the group traveled regionally through North Dakota, Colorado, Nebraska, and Minnesota. The trip began in St. Paul as a standard tour

---

[51] Kristin Kolich, "Nobel Concert: Mozart for the Masses," *The Gustavian Weekly*, 27 September 2002, 5.
[52] Megan Peterson, "Christmas is Christ Chapel Goes Swedish," *The Gustavian Weekly*, 13 December 2002, 1.
[53] Megan Peterson, "Gustavus Choir Departs on International Tour," *The Gustavian Weekly*, 17 January 2003, 3.
[54] Anna Felkey, "Concerto Inaugurale: Millennium in Musica," *Echoes & Overtones 4*, no. 2 (2003): 1.

week excursion. Within hours of the final notes being sung at Gloria Dei Lutheran Church, the ensemble's conductor, Gregory Aune was hospitalized with an appendicitis. The choir was not deterred. In a phone conversation the next morning from his hospital bed, Aune spoke with the ensemble's officers and it was determined that the tour must go on. Aune said, "The choir was confident they could do the tour. It felt good that the choir had the pride and confidence to continue." Rachael Seeley, who was a music major and a member of Aune's conducting class, assumed the directing responsibilities for three concerts before Aune returned to the podium in Colorado Springs. He led the remainder of the tour without incident.[55] The circumstances surrounding these events brought the choir closer together. Despite a trip that included the theft of nearly all their cash during a concert in Bismarck, North Dakota, and travel problems, including a car hitting the bus and later the bus breaking down, the Gustavus Choir persevered and presented quality performances that were well received by audiences.[56] Following the tour, the finishing touches were placed on a new compact disc entitled *How Can I Keep from Singing?*, which featured music recorded by the Gustavus Choir over the previous five years.[57]

Tours for the next two years followed the established travel rotation. The 2005 tour took the choir through nine eastern and southern states and Washington D. C., including a performance at the National Cathedral. Before a concert in Washington, the ensemble met Courtney Walker, a choir alumnus from 2002. Walker was battling cancer. Shortly after the performance, she took a turn for the worse forcing her to return home to South Dakota where she died in August. After the tour, officials at the Kennedy Center contacted Aune and offered to commission a piece in Walker's honor. Aune accepted the offer and recommended Stephen Paulus to complete the commission. Paulus set one of Walker's favorite biblical passages, Isaiah 43: 1-3. The following year, as part of the writing process, Paulus attended a Gustavus Choir rehearsal, which allowed the ensemble the opportunity to work with the famed composer. In the end, Paulus created a powerful piece titled "I Will Be With You," which served as the centerpiece for the 2006 concert tour through Minnesota and Wisconsin.[58]

---

[55] Aune, interview.
[56] Josh Williams, "Gusties Truly Shine," *The Gustavian Weekly*, 20 February 2004, 5.
[57] Gregory Aune, "Conductor's Column," *Echoes and Overtones* 5, no. 2 (2004): 2.
[58] Samuel Eckberg, "The New Commission," *Echoes & Overtones* 7, no. 1 (2006): 1-2.

The spring semesters of 2005 and 2006 brought the establishment of a new tradition to the Gustavus Adolphus College Music Department. On March 20, 2005, the three international touring organizations, the Gustavus Choir, the Gustavus Wind Orchestra, formerly the Gustavus Band, and the Gustavus Symphony Orchestra, presented a joint concert in Minneapolis entitled "Gustavus Music Showcase." The directors planned this event in the Twin Cities area to attract a large audience of alumni and other music enthusiasts to hear the quality work being done by the students at Gustavus.[59] The concert, which took place at St. Andrew Lutheran Church in Eden Prairie, featured individual performances by each ensemble before a combined finale brought the groups together in the performance of an adapted version of Ralph Vaughan Williams' "Sine Nomine."[60] The next year, the concert moved to its permanent location at Orchestra Hall in Minneapolis. Following the performance in this venue, the college and music department decided that the "Gustavus Music Showcase" would become an every other year event with the next rendition scheduled for 2008.[61]

The 2006-2007 school year marked the celebration of the 75th anniversary of the founding of the Gustavus Choir. In addition to the choir's traditional performances at Parent's Day and as part of Christmas in Christ Chapel, the group also sang as part of the F. Melius Christiansen festival, which celebrated the 135th anniversary of his birth. The concerts, which took place on November 19, mirrored the performances of ten years earlier. The festival performances took place at Orchestra Hall in Minneapolis this time, moving away from the St. Olaf campus. The F. Melius Christiansen Star of the North Festival Concert Series and the American Choral Directors Association of Minnesota sponsored the festival, with the concerts highlighting the organization's annual fall convention. The performances featured the same college choirs as the past celebration, with the exception of Luther College, which was replaced by Concordia University in St. Paul to keep all the institutions within the state of Minnesota. Each choir again performed individually led by its own conductor on the podium and then combined to form a mass choir, again, under the direction of Kenneth Jennings. Proceeds from the concert benefited the scholarship fund of the F. Melius Christiansen Endowment

---

[59] Wahlund, interview.
[60] Gustavus Adolphus College, *Gustavus Music Showcase*, Concert Program, March 20, 2005.
[61] Wahlund, interview.

Fund, which supports continuing education and graduate studies for young choral directors in Minnesota.[62]

In January, members of the ensemble enrolled in class entitled "The Gustavus Choir Tours Spain and Portugal." The class, which was co-taught by Spanish Professor Hayden Duncan and Gregory Aune, was designed to prepare the ensemble both culturally and musically for a three-week tour of the area. The group arrived in Lisbon on January 12, 2007, for a five day stay that included a concert and a performance at morning mass. Over the course of the tour, the Gustavus Choir performed ten times in locations around Spain and Portugal, including Madrid, Malaga, and Granada. This was the choir's eighth international tour and their first excursion into this region.[63]

Fig. 6-7 The Gustavus Choir Performs in Spain
Photo courtesy The Gustavus Quarterly, 63: 3 (Spring 2007).

In the spring of the year, the Gustavus Choir prepared itself for a gala celebration of the 75th anniversary of the ensemble's formation. At a

---

[62] "Choir to Appear at Christiansen Festival," *Echoes & Overtones* 7, no. 1 (2006): 6.
[63] Dean Wahlund, "The Gustavus Choir Will Reign in Spain (and Not Only on the Plane)," *Echoes and Overtones* 7, no. 1 (2006): 5.

concert on May 5, 2007, the choir officially marked the occasion with a performance and a festive reunion of past choir members, including the performance of an assembled alumni choir. The concert featured the current Gustavus Choir performing a variety of the ensemble's "greatest hits" and most performed selections of the past 75 years. The concert concluded with a group of alumni joining the choir to perform a few selections including the signature closing piece, "Praise to the Lord", by F. Melius Christiansen. The festivities recognized the enduring history of the Gustavus Choir and celebrated its legacy as an organization firmly rooted in the Swedish heritage of the college and the musical traditions of the Christiansen Choral School.

Fig. 6-8  75th Anniversary Reunion Choir
Photo courtesy The Gustavus Quarterly, 64: 1 (Winter 2007-2008).

During his time as director, Gregory Aune has continued to enhance the reputation and level of excellence of the Gustavus Choir. He brought a commitment to the students and the program that is obvious to those who hear their performances. Aune embraced the Lutheran heritage of the choir while he transformed the traditions to include new ideas and expanded repertoire. During his time as conductor, the Gustavus Choir continued to present first-rate concert tours, including groundbreaking international travel every four years. He introduced new styles of music by contemporary composers to the ensemble and commissioned pieces for the choir to debut. He brought an attitude of collegial collaboration to the musical learning and worked to provide his students with educational experiences that taught life lessons. Though the final chapter of his time at Gustavus Adolphus College has yet to be written, Gregory Aune has established his legacy at the college and has taken the Gustavus Choir to new levels of musical excellence.

# CHAPTER SEVEN

# CONCLUSION

From its inception, Gustavus Adolphus College has stressed the importance of singing and music instruction as a vital component to its liberal arts education. When the school opened its doors in Red Wing, Minnesota, in 1862, singing was listed as one of the core subjects taught by founder Erik Norelius. With the Gustavus Choir's formation in 1932, the ensemble became the flagship choral organization on campus. Throughout its history, the choir's performances have been steeped in the traditions established by F. Melius Christiansen. This Lutheran Choral School of singing involves the performance of primarily sacred, a cappella literature in a manner stressing the unity of the choir over the individual performer. The Gustavus Choir has demonstrated this philosophy throughout its history. Four of the choir's six conductors had the opportunity to study with a Christiansen and experience the a cappella choral tradition as an undergraduate. The Gustavus Choir has embraced this heritage and has come to be recognized as one of the major contributors to the Christiansen ideology through its performance, appearance, and touring philosophy.

The Gustavus Choir has built its reputation on a philosophy of performing excellence that is achieved through intensive rehearsal. Each conductor has brought his unique personality to the process, but in the end, the emphasis is placed on preparation for performance. The college strives to foster an environment that promotes intellectual growth and personal development as part of its mission. Throughout its existence, the choir has shared these ideals. Each conductor worked to create a learning environment that taught students the fundamentals of singing while seeking excellence in concert, but also provided them with opportunities to experience life beyond the rehearsal and concert venues.

As the top choral organization on the campus of Gustavus Adolphus College, the choir has developed an international reputation as a quality performance ensemble. The group represents the music department and the college at important functions both on and off campus, serving first as a performance ensemble, then as an outreach for the school. The Gustavus Choir is most noted for its performances at Christmas in Christ Chapel and for its annual concert tour. The Christmas in Christ Chapel service, through a successful blend of scripture, music, and venue all centered on an annually changing theme, has developed into a celebration that is unique to the college and has become the cultural event on the Gustavus campus.

The tradition of concert touring dates back to as early as 1878 for the music ensembles at Gustavus Adolphus College. From its inception, the Gustavus Choir has participated in an annual tour that has taken the ensemble throughout the United States and Canada, as well as on eight international excursions. The choir has performed in thirty-six U.S. states and sixteen foreign countries on four continents during its seventy-one concert tours. Touring provides the choir, first and foremost, the opportunity to perform its program on numerous occasions, fostering a deeper musical understanding of the literature, and developing the discipline and artistic integrity required to create musical excellence in varying acoustics and for diverse audiences. The tour also allows choir members the opportunity to experience a wide array of cultures and locations they may not encounter without the ensemble. The extended tours at Gustavus include an interdisciplinary course as part of their preparation, which promotes understanding of the culture and history of the areas to be toured. In addition, Gustavus Adolphus College benefits from the ensemble's travel, as the musicians provide an outreach to its constituents, including alumni, parents, perspective students, and possible donors. The school continues to support and promote touring as a vital part of the liberal arts education.

Gustavus Adolphus College is a church-related, residential liberal arts college firmly rooted in its Swedish and Lutheran heritage. For seventy-five years, The Gustavus Choir has shared this legacy. It has become a vital part of the educational environment of the college, providing the campus, and St. Peter community with an outstanding choral organization deeply rooted in the a cappella traditions of the Lutheran colleges. Throughout its history, the choir has gained an international reputation for high caliber choral performances. As its legacy continues to evolve, the Gustavus Choir will assuredly maintain its commitment to musical excellence.

# Appendix A

# Repertoire Performed by the Gustavus Choir on its Extended Concert Tours

| Title | Composer/ Arranger | Time Period | Accomp. | Text |
|---|---|---|---|---|
| **1933 Concert Tour Repertoire - G. Adolph Nelson, conductor** ||||||
| Blessing, Glory and Wisdom and Thanks | Wagner, Georg | Baroque | A cappella | sacred |
| Hear Us Lord | Soderman, August | 19$^{th}$ Century | A cappella | sacred |
| O God, Hear My Prayer | Gretchaninoff, Alexander | 20$^{th}$ Century | A cappella | sacred |
| Open Our Eyes | MacFarlane, Will | 20$^{th}$ Century | A cappella | sacred |
| Salvation is Created | Tchesnokoff, Paul | 20$^{th}$ Century | A cappella | sacred |
| The Three Kings | Romeu, Lluis | Folk | A cappella | sacred |
| Wake, Awake for Night is Flying | Christiansen, F. Melius | 20$^{th}$ Century | A cappella | sacred |

## 1934 Concert Tour Repertoire - G. Adolph Nelson, conductor

| | | | | |
|---|---|---|---|---|
| Agnus Dei | Kalinnikoff, Basil | 20th Century | A cappella | sacred |
| Benedictus Qui Venit | Soderman, August | 19th Century | A cappella | sacred |
| Go, Song of Mine | Elgar, Edward | 19th Century | A cappella | sacred |
| Lost in the Night | Christiansen, F. Melius | 20th Century | A cappella | sacred |
| O God, Hear My Prayer | Gretchaninoff, Alexander | 20th Century | A cappella | sacred |
| O Sacred Head | Hassler, Hans Leo | Renaissance | A cappella | sacred |
| O Watchers of the Stars | Cain, Noble | 20th Century | A cappella | sacred |
| The Spirit Also Helpeth Us | Bach, J.S. | Baroque | A cappella | sacred |
| Two Old Bohemian Carols | Riedel | Folk | A cappella | sacred |

## 1935 Concert Tour Repertoire - G. Adolph Nelson, conductor

| | | | | |
|---|---|---|---|---|
| Benedictus | Soderman, August | 19th Century | A cappella | sacred |
| Carol of the Birds | Cain, Noble | 20th Century | A cappella | sacred |
| Cherubim Song | Tcherepnin, Alexander | 20th Century | A cappella | sacred |
| Gloria in Excelsis | Lindegren, Johan | 19th Century | A cappella | sacred |
| Kyrie | Lindegren, Johan | 19th Century | A cappella | sacred |
| Now Sinks the Sun | Parker, Horatio | 20th Century | A cappella | sacred |
| Nunc Dimittis | Rachmaninoff, Sergei | 19th Century | A cappella | sacred |
| O God, Hear My Prayer | Gretchaninoff, Alexander | 20th Century | A cappella | sacred |
| O Watchers of the Stars | Cain, Noble | 20th Century | A cappella | sacred |
| Sing Ye to the Lord | Bach, J.S. | Baroque | A cappella | sacred |

## 1936 Concert Tour Repertoire - G. Adolph Nelson, conductor

| | | | | |
|---|---|---|---|---|
| A Passion Motet | Fryklof | 20th Century | A cappella | sacred |
| Benedictus | Soderman, August | 19th Century | A cappella | sacred |
| Domine | Soderman, August | 19th Century | A cappella | sacred |
| Gloria in Excelsis | Lindegren, Johan | 19th Century | A cappella | sacred |
| Hail, Gladdening Light | Wood, Charles | 20th Century | A cappella | sacred |
| Kyrie | Lindegren, Johan | 19th Century | A cappella | sacred |
| Noel of the Bressen Waits | Davis, Katherine | 20th Century | A cappella | sacred |
| O God, Hear My Prayer | Gretchaninoff, Alexander | 20th Century | A cappella | sacred |
| O Sacred Head, Now Wounded | Bergquist | 20th Century | A cappella | sacred |
| Offering of the Soul | Cain, Noble | 20th Century | A cappella | sacred |
| Sing Ye to the Lord | Bach, J.S. | Baroque | A cappella | sacred |

## 1937 Concert Tour Repertoire - G. Adolph Nelson, conductor

| | | | | |
|---|---|---|---|---|
| Come, Jesu, Come | Bach, J.S. | Baroque | A cappella | sacred |
| Gloria in Excelsis | Lindegren, Johan | 19th Century | A cappella | sacred |
| Glory be to God | Rachmaninoff, Sergei | 19th Century | A cappella | sacred |
| Good Friday Music in Catelonian Church | Nicolau, Antoni | 20th Century | A cappella | sacred |
| Kyrie | Soderman, August | 19th Century | A cappella | sacred |
| Noel of the Bressen Waits | Davis, Katherine | 20th Century | A cappella | sacred |
| O Brightness of the Immortal Father's Fate | Andrews | 20th Century | A cappella | sacred |
| O God, Hear My Prayer | Gretchaninoff, Alexander | 20th Century | A cappella | sacred |
| Offering of the Soul | Cain, Noble | 20th Century | A cappella | sacred |
| Souls of Righteous | Noble | 20th Century | A cappella | sacred |
| With Joyful Song | Schvedov, Constantine | 20th Century | A cappella | sacred |

## 1938 Concert Tour Repertoire - G. Adolph Nelson, conductor

| | | | | |
|---|---|---|---|---|
| Ara, vare Gud i Hojden | Lindegren, Johan | Folk | A cappella | secular |
| Benedictus | Soderman, August | 19th Century | A cappella | sacred |
| Born Today | Sweelinck, Jan | Renaissance | A cappella | sacred |
| Comfort My Soul with Thy Help, O Lord | Brahms, Johannes | 19th Century | A cappella | sacred |
| Herre, forbarma Dig | Lindegren, Johan | 19th Century | A cappella | sacred |
| Jesus, Du Hjertas Langtan | Wetterling | Folk | A cappella | sacred |
| Nunc Dimittis | Rachmaninoff, Sergei | 19th Century | A cappella | sacred |
| O God, Hear My Prayer | Gretchaninoff, Alexander | 20th Century | A cappella | sacred |
| Sleep Infant Divine | Biedermann | 20th Century | A cappella | sacred |
| Sverige | Stenhammer, Wilhelm | 20th Century | A cappella | secular |
| The Spirit Also Helpeth Us | Bach, J.S. | Baroque | A cappella | sacred |
| The Three Kings | Romeu, Lluis | Folk | A cappella | sacred |
| Wake, Awake for Night is Flying | Nelson, G. Adolph | 20th Century | A cappella | sacred |

## 1939 Concert Tour Repertoire - G. Adolph Nelson, conductor

| | | | | |
|---|---|---|---|---|
| Gladjens Blomster | Swedish Folk Song | Folk | A cappella | secular |
| Good Friday Music in Catelonian Church | Nicolau, Antoni | 20th Century | A cappella | sacred |
| It is a Good Thing to Give Thanks | Schvedoff | 20th Century | A cappella | sacred |
| Jesus, Du Hjertas Langtan | Wetterling | Folk | A cappella | sacred |
| Komm, heil'ger Geist | Schumann, Georg | 20th Century | A cappella | sacred |
| Make Me, O Lord God, Pure in Heart | Brahms, Johannes | 19th Century | A cappella | sacred |
| The Adoration of the Shepherds | Schindler, Kurt | 20th Century | A cappella | sacred |
| The Crimson Flood | Strom, Ralph Alvin | 20th Century | A cappella | sacred |
| The Earth is the Lord's | Nikolsky, Alexander | 20th Century | A cappella | sacred |
| Tonerna | Sjoberg, Birger | Folk | A cappella | secular |
| Wake, Awake for Night is Flying | Nelson, G. Adolph | 20th Century | A cappella | sacred |

| 1940 Concert Tour Repertoire - G. Adolph Nelson, conductor ||||||
|---|---|---|---|---|
| All Breathing Life, Sing, and Praise Ye the Lord | Bach, J.S. | Baroque | A cappella | sacred |
| Benedictus | Soderman, August | 19th Century | A cappella | sacred |
| Das ist ein Kostliches Ding | Schumann, Georg | 20th Century | A cappella | sacred |
| Hemlangtan | Soderman, August | 19th Century | A cappella | sacred |
| Hosanna | Christiansen, F. Melius | 20th Century | A cappella | sacred |
| Hosannah in the Highest | Soderman, August | 19th Century | A cappella | sacred |
| Lost in the Night | Christiansen, F. Melius | 20th Century | A cappella | sacred |
| My Soul Doth Magnify the Lord | Clokey, Joseph | 20th Century | A cappella | sacred |
| O Come, Let Us Worship | Rachmaninoff, Sergei | 19th Century | A cappella | sacred |
| O Lamb of God | Kalinnikoff, Vassily | 19th Century | A cappella | sacred |
| O Watchers of the Stars | Cain, Noble | 20th Century | A cappella | sacred |
| The Lord Said unto My Lord | Nikolsky, Alexander | 20th Century | A cappella | sacred |
| The Twenty-Third Psalm | Schreck, Gustav | 20th Century | A cappella | sacred |

| 1941 Concert Tour Repertoire - G. Adolph Nelson, conductor | | | | |
|---|---|---|---|---|
| Annunciation Carol | Old English | Folk | A cappella | sacred |
| Austrian Up-Country Song | Grainger, Percy | 20th Century | A cappella | secular |
| Brigg Fair | Grainger, Percy | 20th Century | A cappella | secular |
| Fierce was the Wild Billow | Noble | 20th Century | A cappella | sacred |
| Fireflies | Russian Folk Song | Folk | A cappella | secular |
| Grieve Not the Holy Spirit of God | Stainer, John | 19th Century | A cappella | sacred |
| Hospodi Pomilui, "Holy Lord Have Mercy" | Lvovsky | Folk | A cappella | sacred |
| Jesu, Priceless Treasure | Bach, J.S. | Baroque | Keyboard | sacred |
| O Be Joyful in the Lord | Gretchaninoff, Alexander | 20th Century | A cappella | sacred |
| O Holy Land | Dett, Nathaniel | 20th Century | A cappella | sacred |
| Pretty Swallow | Le Jeune | Renaissance | A cappella | secular |
| Psalm 46 God is Our Refuge and Strength | Strom, Ralph Alvin | 20th Century | A cappella | sacred |
| Swedish Liturgical Music | Lindegren, Johan | 19th Century | A cappella | sacred |
| The Three Kings | Romeu, Lluis | Folk | A cappella | sacred |
| Tryggare Kan Ingen Vara | Pearson | Folk | A cappella | sacred |

| 1942 Concert Tour Repertoire - G. Adolph Nelson, conductor | | | | |
|---|---|---|---|---|
| Alleluia, Let Us Sing | English 13th Century | Folk | A cappella | sacred |
| Because of Thy Sweet Son | English 13th Century | Folk | A cappella | sacred |
| Cantata 147 | Bach, J.S. | Baroque | Orchestra | sacred |
| Fireflies | Russian Folk Song | Folk | A cappella | secular |
| Flowers of the Field | Lineva | Folk | A cappella | secular |
| Kindlin' Wood | Lineva | Folk | A cappella | secular |
| Laud Ye the Name of the Lord | Rachmaninoff, Sergei | 19th Century | A cappella | sacred |
| Lullaby | Curtis-Burlin | Folk | A cappella | secular |
| O Saving Victim | Willaert, Adrian | Renaissance | A cappella | sacred |
| Song of Vermeland | Grainger, Percy | 20th Century | A cappella | secular |
| The Kipling Jungle Book Cycle | Grainger, Percy | 20th Century | Keyboard | secular |
| Three French Folk Songs | Fickensher | Folk | A cappella | secular |
| Tribute to Foster | Grainger, Percy | 20th Century | Keyboard | secular |
| | | | | |
| **1943 - 1945 No Concert Tour (Choir Dormant)** | | | | |

| 1946 Concert Tour Repertoire - Wilber Swanson, conductor | | | | |
|---|---|---|---|---|
| Air | Agnolucci, Mario | 20th Century | Cello & Violin | sacred |
| All Breathing Life, Sing, and Praise Ye the Lord | Bach, J.S. | Baroque | A cappella | sacred |
| And Now the Lord to Rest is Laid | Bach, J.S. | Baroque | Keyboard | sacred |
| Cherubim Song | Glinka, Michail | 19th Century | A cappella | sacred |
| Christus Factus Est | Anerio, Felice | Renaissance | A cappella | sacred |
| Fireflies | Russian Folk Song | Folk | A cappella | secular |
| Lullaby on Christmas Eve | Christiansen, F. Melius | 20th Century | A cappella | sacred |
| O Be Joyful, All Ye Lands | Gretchaninoff, Alexander | 20th Century | A cappella | sacred |
| Prayer for Marching Men | Winstead, Kenneth | 20th Century | A cappella | sacred |
| The Nicene Creed | Gretchaninoff, Alexander | 20th Century | A cappella | sacred |
| There is a Balm in Gilead | Dawson, William | 20th Century | A cappella | sacred |
| Tonerna | Sjoberg, Birger | Folk | A cappella | secular |
| Wake, Awake for Night is Flying | Christiansen, F. Melius | 20th Century | A cappella | sacred |

# Appendix A

| 1947 Concert Tour Repertoire - Wilber Swanson, conductor | | | | |
|---|---|---|---|---|
| Blessing, Glory and Wisdom and Thanks | Wagner, Georg | Baroque | A cappella | sacred |
| Christus Factus Est | Anerio, Felice | Renaissance | A cappella | sacred |
| Father Most Holy | Christiansen, F. Melius | 20th Century | A cappella | sacred |
| Hail, Gladdening Light | Wood, Charles | 20th Century | A cappella | sacred |
| Hauta Laulu | Kuula, Toivo | 20th Century | A cappella | secular |
| Hosanna | Christiansen, F. Melius | 20th Century | A cappella | sacred |
| How They So Softly Rest | Wilan, Healey | 20th Century | A cappella | secular |
| I Wonder as I Wander | Niles, John Jacob | 20th Century | A cappella | sacred |
| Now Shall The Grace | Bach, J.S. | Baroque | Keyboard | sacred |
| Nunc Dimittis | Gretchaninoff, Alexander | 20th Century | A cappella | sacred |
| Salvation is Created | Tchesnokoff, Paul | 20th Century | A cappella | sacred |
| Send Out Thy Spirit | Schuetky, Fr. Jos. | 19th Century | A cappella | sacred |
| The Day of Judgment | Archangelsky, Alexander | 20th Century | A cappella | sacred |
| The Nicene Creed | Gretchaninoff, Alexander | 20th Century | A cappella | sacred |
| Tryggare Kan Ingen Vara | Swanson, Wilber F. | Folk | A cappella | sacred |
| Wake, Awake for Night is Flying | Christiansen, F. Melius | 20th Century | A cappella | sacred |

| 1948 Concert Tour Repertoire - Wilber Swanson, conductor | | | | |
|---|---|---|---|---|
| A Mighty Fortress is Our God | Liemohm, Edwin | 20th Century | A cappella | sacred |
| Exaltation | Christiansen, F. Melius | 20th Century | A cappella | sacred |
| Hail, Gladdening Light | Wood, Charles | 20th Century | A cappella | sacred |
| Hvad est Du Dog Skjon | Grieg, Edvard | 19th Century | A cappella | secular |
| Ich Lasse Dich Nicht | Bach, J.C. | Classical | A cappella | secular |
| Listen to the Lambs | Dett, Nathaniel | 20th Century | A cappella | sacred |
| Now Shall the Grace | Bach, J.S. | Baroque | A cappella | sacred |
| O Domine Jesu Christe | Palestrina | Renaissance | A cappella | sacred |
| Out of the Silence | Jenkins, Cyril | 20th Century | A cappella | sacred |
| Praise to the Lord | Christiansen, F. Melius | 20th Century | A cappella | sacred |
| The Day of Judgment | Archangelsky, Alexander | 20th Century | A cappella | sacred |
| The Lord Bless You and Keep You | Lutkin, Peter | 20th Century | A cappella | sacred |
| To Thee We Sing | Tkach | 20th Century | A cappella | secular |
| Tryggare Kan Ingen Vara | Swanson, Wilber F. | 20th Century | A cappella | secular |

# Appendix A

| 1949 Concert Tour Repertoire - Wilber Swanson, conductor | | | | |
|---|---|---|---|---|
| Ain'a that Good News | Dawson, William | 20th Century | A cappella | sacred |
| All Breathing Life, Sing, and Praise Ye the Lord | Bach, J.S. | Baroque | A cappella | sacred |
| As a Flower of the Field | Christiansen, Paul J. | 20th Century | A cappella | secular |
| Cherubim Song | Glinka, Michail | 19th Century | A cappella | sacred |
| Lost in the Night | Christiansen, F. Melius | 20th Century | A cappella | sacred |
| Nunc Dimittis | Tschesnokoff | 20th Century | A cappella | sacred |
| O Be Joyful, All Ye Lands | Gretchaninoff, Alexander | 20th Century | A cappella | sacred |
| Surely, He Bore Our Sorrows | Victoria, Thomas Luis da | Renaissance | A cappella | sacred |
| The Earth is the Lord's | Nikolsky, Alexander | 20th Century | A cappella | sacred |
| The Lord Bless You and Keep You | Lutkin, Peter C. | 20th Century | A cappella | sacred |
| The Peaceable Kingdom (Selections from) | Thompson, Randall | 20th Century | A cappella | sacred |
| There is a Balm in Gilead | Dawson, William | 20th Century | A cappella | sacred |
| Tryggare Kan Ingen Vara | Swanson, Wilber F. | Folk | A cappella | sacred |
| Wake, Awake for Night is Flying | Christiansen, F. Melius | 20th Century | A cappella | sacred |

| 1950 Concert Tour Repertoire - Wilber Swanson, conductor ||||| 
|---|---|---|---|---|
| A Mighty Fortress is Our God | Liemohm, Edwin | 20th Century | A cappella | sacred |
| And Now the Lord to Rest is Laid | Bach, J.S. | Baroque | Keyboard | sacred |
| Christus Factus Est | Anerio, Felice | Renaissance | A cappella | sacred |
| God's Son Hath Set Me Free | Overby, Oscar | 19th Century | A cappella | sacred |
| Jesu, Priceless Treasure | Bach, J.S. | Baroque | Keyboard | sacred |
| Mary Had a Baby | Dawson, William | 20th Century | A cappella | sacred |
| Salvation is Created | Tchesnokoff, Paul | 20th Century | A cappella | sacred |
| Send Out Thy Spirit | Schuetky, Fr. Jos. | 19th Century | A cappella | sacred |
| The Lord Bless You and Keep You | Lutkin, Peter C. | 20th Century | A cappella | sacred |
| The Nicene Creed | Gretchaninoff, Alexander | 20th Century | A cappella | sacred |
| The Peaceable Kingdom (Selections from) | Thompson, Randall | 20th Century | A cappella | sacred |
| Tryggare Kan Ingen Vara | Swanson, Wilber F. | Folk | A cappella | sacred |

| 1951 Concert Tour Repertoire - Eugene Casselman, conductor ||||| |
|---|---|---|---|---|
| Be Glad Then, America | Billings, William | Classical | Keyboard | sacred |
| Be Unto Me a Tower of Strength | Byrd, William | Renaissance | A cappella | sacred |
| Exultate Deo | Scarlatti, Alessandro | Baroque | A cappella | sacred |
| Glory be to God | Rachmaninoff, Sergei | 19th Century | A cappella | sacred |
| I'm So Glad Trouble Don't Last Always | Niles, John Jacob | 20th Century | A cappella | sacred |
| Jesus, Jesus, Rest Your Head | Niles, John Jacob | 20th Century | A cappella | sacred |
| Let Us Lift Up Our Heart | Brahms, Johannes | 19th Century | A cappella | sacred |
| Look Down, O Lord | Byrd, William | Renaissance | A cappella | sacred |
| Lord Hosanna, The Son of David | Schreck, Gustav | 19th Century | A cappella | sacred |
| O My God, Forsake Thy People Nevermore | Bach, J.S. | Baroque | Keyboard, Violin | sacred |
| Resurrection | Koshetz, Alexander | Folk | A cappella | sacred |
| The Angels' Song | Tchesnokoff, Paul | 20th Century | A cappella | sacred |
| Tryggare Kan Ingen Vara | Swanson, Wilber F. | Folk | A cappella | sacred |
| Virga Jesse Floruit | Bruckner, Anton | 19th Century | A cappella | sacred |
| We Find Them Happy Which Endures in Patience | Brahms, Johannes | 19th Century | A cappella | sacred |
| Why Afflict Thyself, O My Spirit | Schutz, Heinrich | Baroque | Keyboard, Vln, Flt | sacred |

### 1952 Concert Tour Repertoire - Eugene Casselman, conductor

| | | | | |
|---|---|---|---|---|
| Ad Dominum cum tribularer | Hassler, Hans Leo | Renaissance | A cappella | sacred |
| Christus Factus Est | Pitoni, Giuseppe | Baroque | A cappella | sacred |
| Exultate Deo | Scarlatti, Alessandro | Baroque | A cappella | sacred |
| Hodie Christus Natus Est | Willan, Healey | 20th Century | A cappella | sacred |
| I See His Blood Upon the Rose | Benjamin | 20th Century | A cappella | sacred |
| I'm So Glad Trouble Don't Last Always | Niles, John Jacob | 20th Century | A cappella | sacred |
| Motet, Opus 74, No. 1 | Brahms, Johannes | 19th Century | A cappella | sacred |
| Of Household Rule | Hindemith, Paul | 20th Century | A cappella | sacred |
| Resurrection | Koshetz, Alexander | Folk | A cappella | sacred |

### 1953 Concert Tour Repertoire - Eugene Casselman, conductor

| | | | | |
|---|---|---|---|---|
| As by the Streams of Babylon | Dett, Nathaniel | 20th Century | A cappella | sacred |
| Cantate Domino | Byrd, William | Renaissance | A cappella | sacred |
| From Heights of Heavens | Schein, Hermann | Renaissance | A cappella | sacred |
| God is With Us | Kastalsky, Alexander | 19th Century | A cappella | sacred |
| Motet, Opus 74, No. 1 | Brahms, Johannes | 19th Century | A cappella | sacred |
| O Lord, Increase My Faith | Gibbons, Orlando | Renaissance | A cappella | sacred |
| Sicut Cervus | Palestrina | Renaissance | A cappella | sacred |
| The Three Kings | Schindler, Kurt | Folk | A cappella | sacred |
| Vinea mea Electa | Poulenc, Francis | 20th Century | A cappella | sacred |

## 1954 Concert Tour Repertoire - Eugene Casselman, conductor

| | | | | |
|---|---|---|---|---|
| Alleluia | Slovak Folk Song | Folk | A cappella | sacred |
| Blessing, Glory and Wisdom and Thanks | Wagner, Georg | Baroque | A cappella | sacred |
| Cantate Domino | Byrd, William | Renaissance | A cappella | sacred |
| Chorus of the Guilty | Milhaud, Darius | 20th Century | A cappella | sacred |
| Come Ye All to Bethlehem | Slovak Folk Song | Folk | A cappella | sacred |
| God's Own Hour | Milhaud, Darius | 20th Century | A cappella | sacred |
| Happy Bethlehem | Schindler, Kurt | Folk | A cappella | sacred |
| Motet, Opus 74, No. 1 | Brahms, Johannes | 19th Century | A cappella | sacred |
| On This Holy Christmas Morn | Kountz, Richard | Folk | A cappella | sacred |
| Psalm 96 | Sweelinck, Jan | Renaissance | A cappella | sacred |
| Surely, He Borne Our Griefs | Lotti, Antonio | Renaissance | A cappella | sacred |

| 1955 Concert Tour Repertoire - Philip Knautz, conductor | | | | |
|---|---|---|---|---|
| An Apostrophe to the Heavenly Hosts | Willan, Healey | 20th Century | A cappella | sacred |
| Bread of Tears | Christiansen, Paul J. | 20th Century | A cappella | sacred |
| Bring a Torch, Jeannette, Isabella | Dickinson, Clarence | 20th Century | A cappella | sacred |
| Come Rise Up Early | Kountz, Richard | 20th Century | A cappella | secular |
| Hallelujah, Amen | Handel, G.F. | Baroque | Keyboard | sacred |
| I Wonder as I Wander | Niles, John Jacob | 20th Century | A cappella | sacred |
| Jesu, Priceless Treasure | Bach, J.S. | Baroque | Keyboard | sacred |
| Lines | Bales, Richard | 20th Century | A cappella | sacred |
| Lost in the Night | Christiansen, F. Melius | 20th Century | A cappella | sacred |
| O Bone Jesu | Palestrina | Renaissance | A cappella | sacred |
| Prayer to Jesus | Oldroyd, George | 20th Century | A cappella | sacred |
| Set Down Servant | Shaw, Robert | 20th Century | Keyboard | sacred |
| The Three Kings | Romeu, Lluis | Folk | A cappella | sacred |
| Tonerna | Lundholm, Brynolf | Folk | A cappella | secular |

## 1956 Concert Tour Repertoire - Philip Knautz, conductor

| Title | Composer | Period | Style | Type |
|---|---|---|---|---|
| All Breathing Life, Sing, and Praise Ye the Lord | Bach, J.S. | Baroque | A cappella | sacred |
| Armenian Canticle of Thanksgiving | Gaul, Harvey | 20th Century | A cappella | sacred |
| Beautiful Savior | Christiansen, F. Melius | 20th Century | A cappella | sacred |
| Birthday Greeting | Kodaly, Zoltan | 20th Century | A cappella | sacred |
| Den Store Hvide Flok | Grieg, Edvard | 19th Century | A cappella | sacred |
| O Be Joyful, All Ye Lands | Gretchaninoff, Alexander | 20th Century | A cappella | sacred |
| Peace Comes to Me | Murray, Lynn | 20th Century | A cappella | sacred |
| Prayers of Steel | Christiansen, Paul J. | 20th Century | A cappella | sacred |
| Sing We Merrily Unto God Our Strength | Shaw, Martin | 20th Century | A cappella | sacred |
| Soon Ah Will Be Done | Dawson, William | 20th Century | A cappella | sacred |
| Tenebrae Factae Sunt | Ingegneri, Marc Antonio | Renaissance | A cappella | sacred |
| The Creation | Scott, Tom | 20th Century | A cappella | sacred |
| The Shepherd's Story | Dickinson, Clarence | 20th Century | A cappella | sacred |
| Tryggare Kan Ingen Vara | Swedish Folk Song | Folk | A cappella | sacred |

| 1957 Concert Tour Repertoire - Philip Knautz, conductor | | | | |
|---|---|---|---|---|
| Advent Motet | Schreck, Gustav | 20th Century | A cappella | sacred |
| Alleluia | Thompson, Randall | 20th Century | A cappella | sacred |
| An Apostrophe to the Heavenly Hosts | Willan, Healey | 20th Century | A cappella | sacred |
| As a Flower of the Field | Christiansen, Paul J. | 20th Century | A cappella | secular |
| Blessing, Glory and Wisdom and Thanks | Wagner, Georg | Baroque | A cappella | sacred |
| From Heaven Above | Christiansen, F. Melius | 20th Century | A cappella | sacred |
| Go Down, Death | Decker, Harold | 20th Century | A cappella | sacred |
| Go Tell It on the Mountain | Work, John | 20th Century | A cappella | sacred |
| God Is Gone Up With a Merry Noise | Hutchings, Arthur | 20th Century | A cappella | sacred |
| Hodie Christus Natus Est | Palestrina | Renaissance | A cappella | sacred |
| Let All Mortal Flesh Keep Silent | Bairstow, Edward C. | 20th Century | A cappella | sacred |
| Let All Things Now Living | Davis, Katherine | 20th Century | Keyboard | sacred |
| Peace Comes to Me | Murray, Lyn | 20th Century | A cappella | sacred |
| Surely, He Hath Borne Our Griefs | Lotti, Antonio | Baroque | A cappella | sacred |
| Tryggare Kan Ingen Vara | Swedish Folk Song | Folk | A cappella | sacred |
| Wade in de Water | Hall, Arthur | 20th Century | A cappella | sacred |

| 1958 Concert Tour Repertoire – Philip Knautz, conductor | | | | |
|---|---|---|---|---|
| Alleluia from *Brazilian Psalm* | Berger, Jean | 20th Century | A cappella | sacred |
| Cast Me Not Away from Thy Presence | Wesley, Samuel | 20th Century | A cappella | sacred |
| Celtic Hymn (The Outgoing of the Boats) | Roberton, Hugh | Folk | A cappella | sacred |
| Christus Factus Est | Anerio, Felice | Renaissance | A cappella | sacred |
| Four Chorales | Bach, J.S. | Baroque | A cappella | sacred |
| God Is Gone Up With a Merry Noise | Hutchings, Arthur | 20th Century | A cappella | sacred |
| Hail, Gladdening Light | Wood, Charles | 20th Century | A cappella | sacred |
| Lift Up Your Heads, Ye Mighty Gates | Leisring, Volkmar | Baroque | A cappella | sacred |
| Nar Juldagsmorgon Glimmar | German Melody | Folk | A cappella | sacred |
| O Clap Your Hands | Woodward, Henry | 20th Century | A cappella | sacred |
| Prayer of the Norwegian Child | Knautz, P. F. | 20th Century | A cappella | sacred |
| Psallite | Praetorius, Michael | Renaissance | A cappella | sacred |
| Round Me Falls the Night | Drese, Adam | 20th Century | A cappella | sacred |
| Sjungom Studenten | Swedish Folk Song | Folk | A cappella | secular |
| Spring | Christiansen Paul J. | 20th Century | A cappella | secular |
| Sverige | Stenhammer, Wilhelm | 20th Century | A cappella | secular |
| Te Deum | Holst, Gustav | 20th Century | Keyboard | sacred |

| 1959 Concert Tour Repertoire – Philip Knautz, conductor | | | | |
|---|---|---|---|---|
| Alleluia from *Brazilian Psalm* | Berger, Jean | 20th Century | A cappella | sacred |
| Carol of the Drum | Davis, Katherine | 20th Century | A cappella | sacred |
| Choral Scherzo | Kubik, Gail | 20th Century | A cappella | secular |
| Halsa dem Darhemma | Hansen, Curtis | Folk | A cappella | secular |
| Hosanna | Lockwood, Normand | 20th Century | A cappella | sacred |
| Jesu, Priceless Treasure | Bach, J.S. | Baroque | Keyboard | sacred |
| Lost in the Night | Christiansen, F. Melius | 20th Century | A cappella | sacred |
| Noah Found Grace in the Eyes of the Lord | Spiritual | Folk | A cappella | sacred |
| Prayer of the Norwegian Child | Knautz, P. F. | 20th Century | A cappella | sacred |
| Prayer to Jesus | Oldroyd, George | 20th Century | A cappella | sacred |
| Prelude for Voices | Schumann, William | 20th Century | A cappella | secular |
| Spring | Christiansen, Paul J. | 20th Century | A cappella | secular |
| The Paper Reeds by the Brooks from *Peaceable Kingdom* | Thompson, Randall | 20th Century | A cappella | sacred |
| The Three Kings | Romeu, Lluis | Folk | A cappella | sacred |
| The United Nations Charter | Simon, William | 20th Century | A cappella | secular |
| Vinea mea electra | Poulenc, Francis | 20th Century | A cappella | sacred |

## 1960 Concert Tour Repertoire - Philip Knautz, conductor

| Title | Composer | Period | Performance | Type |
|---|---|---|---|---|
| Ack, Varmeland | Swedish Folk Song | Folk | A cappella | secular |
| All Breathing Life, Sing, and Praise Ye the Lord | Bach, J.S. | Baroque | A cappella | sacred |
| Blessed is the Man | Rachmaninoff, Sergei | 19th Century | A cappella | sacred |
| Come to the Manger | Kountz, Richard | 20th Century | A cappella | sacred |
| Cry Out and Shout | Nystedt, Knut | 20th Century | A cappella | sacred |
| Ding Dong! Merrily on High | Wood, Charles | 20th Century | A cappella | sacred |
| God Be in My Head | Davies, Walford | 20th Century | A cappella | sacred |
| Hosanna | Christiansen, F. Melius | 20th Century | A cappella | sacred |
| I Sing of a Maiden | Shaw, Martin | 20th Century | A cappella | sacred |
| In Heaven Above | Christiansen, F. Melius | 20th Century | A cappella | sacred |
| Let All Mortal Flesh Keep Silent | Bairstow, Edward C. | 20th Century | A cappella | sacred |
| O Sons and Daughters | French Melody | Folk | A cappella | sacred |
| Prelude for Voices | Schumann, William | 20th Century | A cappella | secular |
| Sing We Merrily Unto God Our Strength | Shaw, Martin | 20th Century | A cappella | sacred |
| Tenebrae Factae Sunt | Ingegneri, Marc Antonio | Renaissance | A cappella | sacred |
| The Peaceable Kingdom (Selections from) | Thompson, Randall | 20th Century | A cappella | sacred |

| 1961 Concert Tour Repertoire - Philip Knautz, conductor | | | | |
|---|---|---|---|---|
| A La Nanita Nana | Luboff, Norman | 20th Century | A cappella | sacred |
| An Apostrophe to the Heavenly Hosts | Willan, Healey | 20th Century | A cappella | sacred |
| Blessing, Glory, and Wisdom, and Thanks | Wagner, Georg | Baroque | A cappella | sacred |
| Bread of Tears | Christiansen, Paul J. | 20th Century | A cappella | sacred |
| Children of the Heavenly Father | Swedish Folk Song | Folk | A cappella | sacred |
| Children's Blessing | Wasner, Franz | 20th Century | A cappella | sacred |
| For All the Saints | Vaughan Williams, Ralph | 20th Century | A cappella | sacred |
| Jesus and the Traders | Kodaly, Zoltan | 20th Century | A cappella | sacred |
| Let Down the Bars, O Death | Barber, Samuel | 20th Century | A cappella | sacred |
| O Bone Jesu | Palestrina | Renaissance | A cappella | sacred |
| O Bread of Life | Bach, J.S. | Baroque | A cappella | sacred |
| Patapan | Shaw, Martin | 20th Century | A cappella | secular |
| Peace Comes to Me | Murray, Lyn | 20th Century | A cappella | sacred |
| Set Me as a Seal | Walton, William | 20th Century | A cappella | sacred |
| The Creation | Scott, Tom | 20th Century | A cappella | sacred |
| The Peaceable Kingdom (Selections from) | Thompson, Randall | 20th Century | A cappella | sacred |
| Who is that Yonder | Spiritual | Folk | A cappella | sacred |

# Appendix A

| 1962 Concert Tour Repertoire - Philip Knautz, conductor | | | | |
|---|---|---|---|---|
| Alleluia from *Brazilian Psalm* | Berger, Jean | 20th Century | A cappella | sacred |
| Beati Quorum Via | Stanford, Charles | 19th Century | A cappella | sacred |
| Cantate Domino | Pitoni, Giuseppe | Baroque | A cappella | sacred |
| Cast Me Not Away from Thy Presence | Wesley, Samuel | 20th Century | A cappella | sacred |
| Choral Scherzo | Kubik, Gail | 20th Century | A cappella | secular |
| God Is Gone Up With a Merry Noise | Hutchings, Arthur | 20th Century | A cappella | sacred |
| Goin' Home | Lockwood, Normand | 20th Century | A cappella | sacred |
| How Blest are They | Tschaikovsky, Peter | 19th Century | A cappella | sacred |
| How Far is it to Bethlehem? | Parker, Alice & Shaw, Robert | 20th Century | A cappella | sacred |
| I Was Glad When They Said Unto Me | Parry, Hubert | 19th Century | Keyboard | sacred |
| O Day Full of Grace | Christiansen, F. Melius | 20th Century | A cappella | sacred |
| O Heiland Reiss Die Himmel Auf! | Brahms, Johannes | 19th Century | A cappella | sacred |
| Praise to The, Lord Jesus | Schutz, Heinrich | Baroque | A cappella | sacred |
| Spring | Christiansen, Paul J. | 20th Century | A cappella | secular |
| The Shepherd's Story | Dickinson, Clarence | 20th Century | A cappella | sacred |
| Three Far Eastern Carols | Sargent, Malcom | 20th Century | A cappella | secular |
| We Pause Beside this Door | Dickinson, Clarence | 20th Century | A cappella | sacred |

| 1963 Concert Tour Repertoire - Philip Knautz, conductor | | | | |
|---|---|---|---|---|
| Carol of the Drum | Davis, Katherine | 20th Century | A cappella | sacred |
| Choral Scherzo | Kubik, Gail | 20th Century | A cappella | secular |
| Devotional Songs | Berger, Jean | 20th Century | A cappella | sacred |
| I Sing of a Maiden | Shaw, Martin | 20th Century | A cappella | sacred |
| Jesu, Priceless Treasure | Bach, J.S. | Baroque | Keyboard | sacred |
| Noah Found Grace in the Eyes of the Lord | Spiritual | Folk | A cappella | sacred |
| O Be Joyful, All Ye Lands | Gretchaninoff, Alexander | 20th Century | A cappella | sacred |
| O Magnum Mysterium | Victoria, Thomas Luis da | Renaissance | A cappella | sacred |
| Patapan | Shaw, Martin | 20th Century | A cappella | secular |
| Prayer of the Norwegian Child | Knautz, P. F. | 20th Century | A cappella | sacred |
| Psalm 61 | King, Alvin | 20th Century | A cappella | sacred |
| Religious Folk Songs | Brahms, Johannes | 19th Century | A cappella | sacred |
| Spring | Christiansen, Paul J. | 20th Century | A cappella | secular |
| Sverige | Stenhammer, Wilhelm | 20th Century | A cappella | secular |
| Tryggare Kan Ingen Vara | Swedish Folk Song | Folk | A cappella | sacred |
| Two Motets | Stanford, Charles | 19th Century | A cappella | sacred |

| 1964 Concert Tour Repertoire - Philip Knautz, conductor ||||||
|---|---|---|---|---|
| A Spotless Rose | Howells, Herbert | 20th Century | A cappella | sacred |
| Benedictus | Christiansen, Olaf | 20th Century | A cappella | sacred |
| Canticle of Thanksgiving | Gaul, Harvey | 20th Century | A cappella | sacred |
| Fum, Fum, Fum | Parker, Alice & Shaw, Robert | 20th Century | A cappella | sacred |
| Hodie Christus Natus Est | Palestrina | Renaissance | A cappella | sacred |
| Jubilate Deo | Atcherson, Thomas | 20th Century | A cappella | sacred |
| Let All Mortal Flesh Keep Silent | Bairstow, Edward C. | 20th Century | A cappella | sacred |
| O Little One Sweet | Shaw, Martin | 20th Century | A cappella | sacred |
| On God, and Not on Human Trust | Pachelbel, Johann | Baroque | A cappella | sacred |
| Prelude for Voices | Schumann, William | 20th Century | A cappella | secular |
| Psalm 51 | Brahms, Johannes | 19th Century | A cappella | sacred |
| Shakespeare's Carol | Stevens, R.J.S. | Classical | A cappella | secular |
| Sing We Merrily Unto God Our Strength | Shaw, Martin | 20th Century | A cappella | sacred |
| Sing Ye to the Lord | Bach, J.S. | Baroque | A cappella | sacred |
| Tonerna | Sjoberg, Birger | Folk | A cappella | secular |
| Waters Ripple and Flow | Taylor, Deems | 20th Century | A cappella | secular |
| Yea, Though I Wander | Schumann, Georg | 20th Century | A cappella | sacred |

| 1965 Concert Tour Repertoire - Philip Knautz, conductor |||||
|---|---|---|---|---|
| Bleak Midwinter | Holst, Gustav | 20th Century | A cappella | sacred |
| Blessed is the Man | Rachmaninoff, Sergei | 19th Century | A cappella | sacred |
| Blessing, Glory, and Wisdom, and Thanks | Wagner, Georg | Baroque | A cappella | sacred |
| Down in Yon Forest | Vaughn Williams, Ralph | 20th Century | A cappella | sacred |
| Elf of Eve | Christiansen, Paul J. | 20th Century | A cappella | sacred |
| God Is Gone Up With a Merry Noise | Hutchings, Arthur | 20th Century | A cappella | sacred |
| Jubilate Deo Omnis Terra | Atcherson, Thomas | 20th Century | A cappella | sacred |
| Lift Up Your Heads, Ye Mighty Gates | Leisring, Volkmar | Baroque | A cappella | sacred |
| Nar Juldagsmorgon Glimmar | German Melody | Folk | A cappella | sacred |
| Peace I Leave With You | Nystedt, Knut | 20th Century | A cappella | sacred |
| Psalm 51 | Brahms, Johannes | 19th Century | A cappella | sacred |
| Tenebrae Factae Sunt | Ingegneri, Marc Antonio | Renaissance | A cappella | sacred |
| The Day of Judgment | Archangelsky, Alexander | 20th Century | A cappella | sacred |
| The Peaceable Kingdom (Selections from) | Thompson, Randall | 20th Century | A cappella | sacred |
| The Three Kings | Romeu, Lluis | Folk | A cappella | sacred |
| Tonerna | Sjoberg, Birger | Folk | A cappella | secular |
| Who is that Yonder | Spiritual | Folk | A cappella | sacred |

# Appendix A

| 1966 Concert Tour Repertoire - Philip Knautz, conductor | | | | |
|---|---|---|---|---|
| A Joyful Christmas Song | Gevaert, Francois | 20th Century | A cappella | sacred |
| Alleluia! We Sing with Joy | Handl, Jacob | Renaissance | A cappella | sacred |
| An Apostrophe to the Heavenly Hosts | Willan, Healey | 20th Century | A cappella | sacred |
| Come to the Manger | Kountz, Richard | 20th Century | A cappella | sacred |
| Crucifixus | Lotti, Antonio | Baroque | A cappella | sacred |
| Cry Out and Shout | Nystedt, Knut | 20th Century | A cappella | sacred |
| From Heaven Above | Christiansen, F. Melius | 20th Century | A cappella | sacred |
| Gloria from "Mass in G" | Schubert, Franz | 19th Century | Keyboard | sacred |
| Go Not Far from Me, O God | Zingarelli | Classical | A cappella | sacred |
| Nu Tandas Tusen Juleljus | Knautz, P. F. | 20th Century | A cappella | sacred |
| O Give Thanks Unto the Lord | Purcell, Henry | Baroque | A cappella | sacred |
| Peace Comes to Me | Murray, Lyn | 20th Century | A cappella | sacred |
| Peace I Leave With You | Nystedt, Knut | 20th Century | A cappella | sacred |
| Prayers of Steel | Christiansen, Paul J. | 20th Century | A cappella | sacred |
| Psalm 61 | King, Alvin | 20th Century | A cappella | sacred |
| Sing Ye Merrily | Sateren, Leland | 20th Century | A cappella | sacred |
| Surely He Hath Borne Our Griefs | Graun, Karl | Baroque | A cappella | sacred |
| The Creation | Scott, Tom | 20th Century | A cappella | sacred |

| 1967 Concert Tour Repertoire - Philip Knautz, conductor ||||| 
|---|---|---|---|---|
| Cantate Domino | Pitoni, Giuseppe | Baroque | A cappella | sacred |
| Choral Scherzo | Kubik, Gail | 20th Century | A cappella | secular |
| Christus Factus Est | Anerio, Felice | Renaissance | A cappella | sacred |
| Credo from *Mass in E minor* | Bruckner, Anton | 19th Century | Keyboard | sacred |
| Ding Dong Merrily on High | Wood, Charles | 20th Century | A cappella | sacred |
| Fum, Fum, Fum | Parker, Alice & Shaw, Robert | 20th Century | A cappella | sacred |
| I Wonder as I Wander | Niles, John Jacob | 20th Century | A cappella | sacred |
| Jesu, Priceless Treasure | Bach, J.S. | Baroque | Keyboard | sacred |
| Let Down the Bars, O Death | Barber, Samuel | 20th Century | A cappella | sacred |
| Noah Found Grace in the Eyes of the Lord | Spiritual | Folk | A cappella | sacred |
| O All Ye Works of the Lord | Fetler, Paul | 20th Century | A cappella | sacred |
| O Bread of Life from Heaven | Christiansen, F. Melius | 20th Century | A cappella | sacred |
| O Heiland Reiss Die Himmel Auf! | Brahms, Johannes | 19th Century | A cappella | sacred |
| Prayer of the Norwegian Child | Knautz, P. F. | 20th Century | A cappella | sacred |
| Prayer to Jesus | Oldroyd, George | 20th Century | A cappella | sacred |
| Sing Ye Merrily | Sateren, Leland | 20th Century | A cappella | sacred |
| Spring | Christiansen, Paul J. | 20th Century | A cappella | secular |
| Sverige | Stenhammer, Wilhelm | 20th Century | A cappella | secular |

## 1968 Concert Tour Repertoire - Philip Knautz, conductor

| | | | | |
|---|---|---|---|---|
| Alleluia | Kopyloff, Andre | 20th Century | A cappella | sacred |
| And with His Stripes We are Healed from *Messiah* | Handel, G.F. | Baroque | Keyboard | sacred |
| Be Not Afraid | Bach, J.S. | Baroque | A cappella | sacred |
| Benedictus | Christiansen, Olaf | 20th Century | A cappella | sacred |
| De Profundis | Nystedt, Knut | 20th Century | A cappella | sacred |
| Ehre Sei Dir, Christe | Schutz, Heinrich | Baroque | A cappella | sacred |
| God Keep You Merry, Gentlemen | Shaw, Martin | 20th Century | A cappella | sacred |
| Jesus, Think of Me | Back, Sven-Erik | 20th Century | A cappella | sacred |
| O Sing Unto the Lord | Purcell, Henry | Baroque | A cappella | sacred |
| Patapan | Shaw, Martin | 20th Century | A cappella | secular |
| Prelude for Voices | Schumann, William | 20th Century | A cappella | secular |
| The Cradle | Christiansen, Paul J. | 20th Century | A cappella | sacred |
| The Peaceable Kingdom (Selections from) | Thompson, Randall | 20th Century | A cappella | sacred |
| The Shepherd's Story | Dickinson, Clarence | 20th Century | A cappella | sacred |
| Tryggare Kan Ingen Vara | Swedish Folk Song | Folk | A cappella | sacred |
| Waters Ripple and Flow | Taylor, Deems | 20th Century | A cappella | secular |

| 1969 Concert Tour Repertoire - Philip Knautz, conductor ||||| 
|---|---|---|---|---|
| Adoramus Te | Gasparini, Quirino | Classical | A cappella | sacred |
| Angels We Have Heard on High | Barnes, Edward | 20th Century | A cappella | sacred |
| Benedictus | Gabrielli, Giovanni | Renaissance | A cappella | sacred |
| Bread of Tears | Christiansen, Paul J. | 20th Century | A cappella | sacred |
| Devotional Songs | Berger, Jean | 20th Century | A cappella | sacred |
| Finale – Sing Ye to the Lord | Bach, J.S. | Baroque | A cappella | sacred |
| Gloria from *Mass in G* | Schubert, Franz | 19th Century | Keyboard | sacred |
| I Sing of a Maiden | Shaw, Martin | 20th Century | A cappella | sacred |
| Look to this Day | Kittleson, Carl | 20th Century | A cappella | secular |
| Lord, Thou Hast Been Our Refuge | Vaughn Williams, Ralph | 20th Century | Keyboard | sacred |
| Lost in the Night | Christiansen, F. Melius | 20th Century | A cappella | sacred |
| O Day Full of Grace | Christiansen, F. Melius | 20th Century | A cappella | sacred |
| O Give Thanks Unto the Lord | Purcell, Henry | Baroque | A cappella | sacred |
| Presentation of Christ in the Temple | Eccard, Johannes | Renaissance | A cappella | sacred |
| Set Me as a Seal | Walton, William | 20th Century | A cappella | sacred |
| Song of the Hammer | Spiritual | Folk | A cappella | sacred |
| Spring | Christiansen, Paul J. | 20th Century | A cappella | secular |
| The Peaceable Kingdom (Selections from) | Thompson, Randall | 20th Century | A cappella | sacred |
| Vergorenheit | Wolf, Hugo | 20th Century | A cappella | secular |

## 1970 Concert Tour Repertoire - Philip Knautz, conductor

|  |  |  |  |  |
|---|---|---|---|---|
| A Shepherd's Carol | Britten, Benjamin | 20th Century | A cappella | sacred |
| Be Glad then America | Billings, William | Classical | Keyboard | sacred |
| Birthday Greeting | Koldaly, Zoltan | 20th Century | A cappella | sacred |
| Glory and Worship | Purcell, Henry | Baroque | A cappella | sacred |
| God Is Gone Up With a Merry Noise | Hutchings, Arthur | 20th Century | A cappella | sacred |
| Hvad est Du Dog Skjon | Grieg, Edvard | 19th Century | A cappella | sacred |
| I Was Glad When They Said Unto Me | Parry, Hubert | 19th Century | Keyboard | sacred |
| Let Us Break Bread Together | Lynn, George | 20th Century | A cappella | sacred |
| Look to this Day | Kittleson, Carl | 20th Century | A cappella | secular |
| Lord, Thou Hast Been Our Refuge | Vaughn Williams, Ralph | 20th Century | Keyboard | sacred |
| On God, and Not on Human Trust | Pachelbel, Johann | Baroque | A cappella | sacred |
| Peace Comes to Me | Murray, Lyn | 20th Century | A cappella | sacred |
| Peace I Leave With You | Nystedt, Knut | 20th Century | A cappella | sacred |
| Psallite | Praetorius, Michael | Renaissance | A cappella | sacred |
| Psalm 61 | King, Alvin | 20th Century | A cappella | sacred |
| Remember, O Thou Man | Oldham, Arthur | 20th Century | A cappella | sacred |
| Sing We Merrily Unto God Our Strength | Shaw, Martin | 20th Century | A cappella | sacred |
| Sleep, Thou, My Jewel | Bement, Gwynn | 20th Century | A cappella | sacred |
| Why Then has the Light Been Given | Brahms, Johannes | 19th Century | A cappella | sacred |

| 1971 Concert Tour Repertoire - Philip Knautz, conductor ||||| 
|---|---|---|---|---|
| Adoramus Te | Gasparini, Quirino | Classical | A cappella | sacred |
| Alleluia from *Brazilian Psalm* | Berger, Jean | 20th Century | A cappella | sacred |
| Alleluia, Come Good People | Davis, Katherine | 20th Century | A cappella | sacred |
| Be Not Afraid | Bach, J.S. | Baroque | A cappella | sacred |
| Cherubim Song | Glinka, Michail | 19th Century | A cappella | sacred |
| Come to the Manger | Kountz, Richard | 20th Century | A cappella | sacred |
| Hallelujah Chorus from *Mount of Olives* | Beethoven, Ludwig | 19th Century | Keyboard | sacred |
| He is Good and Handsome | Passereau, Pierre | Renaissance | A cappella | sacred |
| Jesus and the Traders | Kodaly, Zoltan | 20th Century | A cappella | sacred |
| Just a Closer Walk with Thee | Spiritual | Folk | A cappella | sacred |
| Let All Things Now Living | Davis, Katherine | 20th Century | Keyboard | sacred |
| O Be Joyful, All Ye Lands | Gretchaninoff, Alexander | 20th Century | A cappella | sacred |
| Prayer to Jesus | Stenhammer, Wilhelm | 20th Century | A cappella | sacred |
| Skip to My Lou | American Folk Song | Folk | A cappella | secular |
| Spring Returns | Marenzio, Luca | Renaissance | A cappella | secular |
| Studentsang | Satherberg, K.H. | Folk | A cappella | secular |
| The Path of the Just | Nystedt, Knut | 20th Century | A cappella | secular |
| Wade in the Water | Hall, Arthur | 20th Century | A cappella | sacred |
| Wake, Awake for Night is Flying | Christiansen, F. Melius | 20th Century | A cappella | sacred |

## 1972 Concert Tour Repertoire - Philip Knautz, conductor

|  |  |  |  |  |
|---|---|---|---|---|
| Alleluia | Kopyloff, Andre | 20th Century | A cappella | sacred |
| An American Hymn | Effinger, Cecil | 20th Century | Brass Ensemble | secular |
| An Apostrophe to the Heavenly Hosts | Willan, Healey | 20th Century | A cappella | sacred |
| Cry Out and Shout | Nystedt, Knut | 20th Century | A cappella | sacred |
| From Heaven Above | Christiansen, F. Melius | 20th Century | A cappella | sacred |
| Gloria in Excelsis Deo | Washburn, Robert | 20th Century | Brass Ensemble | sacred |
| Hail, Gladdening Light | Wood, Charles | 20th Century | A cappella | sacred |
| Jubilate Deo | Atcherson, Thomas | 20th Century | A cappella | sacred |
| Prayer of the Norwegian Child | Knautz, P. F. | 20th Century | A cappella | sacred |
| Psalm 23 | Berger, Jean | 20th Century | A cappella | sacred |
| Psalmkonzert | Zimmerman, Heinz Werner | 20th Century | A cappella | sacred |
| Rock-a My Soul | Kirk, Theron | 20th Century | A cappella | sacred |
| Surely He Hath Borne Our Griefs | Graun, Karl | Classical | A cappella | sacred |
| The 150th Psalm | Berger, Jean | 20th Century | A cappella | sacred |
| The Creation | Scott, Tom | 20th Century | A cappella | sacred |
| The Shepherd's Story | Dickinson, Clarence | 20th Century | A cappella | sacred |
| Tonerna | Sjoberg, Birger | Folk | A cappella | secular |

| 1973 Concert Tour Repertoire - Philip Knautz, conductor | | | | |
|---|---|---|---|---|
| A La Nanita Nana | Luboff, Norman | 20th Century | A cappella | sacred |
| Blessing, Glory, and Wisdom, and Thanks | Wagner, Georg | Baroque | A cappella | sacred |
| Carol of Service | Shaw, Martin | 20th Century | A cappella | sacred |
| De Profundis | Nystedt, Knut | 20th Century | A cappella | sacred |
| Deep River | Burleigh, H.T. | 20th Century | A cappella | sacred |
| Die mit Tranen Saen | Schein, Johann Hermann | Renaissance | A cappella | sacred |
| Hauta Lauta | Kuula, Tovio | 20th Century | A cappella | secular |
| I Will Lift Up Mine Eyes | Willan, Healey | 20th Century | A cappella | sacred |
| Nature Carol | Sargent, Malcom | 20th Century | A cappella | secular |
| O Bread of Life from Heaven | Christiansen, F. Melius | 20th Century | A cappella | sacred |
| O Day Full of Grace | Christiansen, F. Melius | 20th Century | A cappella | sacred |
| Pilgrim's Chorus | Wagner, Richard | 19th Century | Keyboard | sacred |
| Sing Ye Merrily | Sateren, Leland | 20th Century | A cappella | sacred |
| Tenebrae Factae Sunt | Ingegneri, Marc Antonio | Renaissance | A cappella | sacred |
| The Nicene Creed | Gretchaninoff, Alexander | 20th Century | A cappella | sacred |
| The Three Kings | Romeu, Lluis | Folk | A cappella | sacred |
| Welsh Carol | Jones, Griffith | 20th Century | A cappella | sacred |
| Worthy Art Thou, O Lord | Bruckner, Anton | 19th Century | A cappella | sacred |

| 1974 Concert Tour Repertoire - Philip Knautz, conductor | | | | |
|---|---|---|---|---|
| Angels We Have Heard on High | Barnes, Edward | 20th Century | A cappella | sacred |
| Benedictus | Christiansen, Olaf | 20th Century | A cappella | sacred |
| Disguised God | Larsson, Lars Eric | 20th Century | Keyboard | sacred |
| Have Ye Not Known from *Peaceable Kingdom* | Thompson, Randall | 20th Century | A cappella | sacred |
| Hodie Christus Natus Est | Palestrina | Renaissance | A cappella | sacred |
| I Was Glad When They Said Unto Me | Parry, Hubert | 19th Century | Keyboard | sacred |
| Jesu, Priceless Treasure | Bach, J.S. | Baroque | Keyboard | sacred |
| Prelude for Voices | Schumann, William | 20th Century | A cappella | secular |
| Psalm 61 | King, Alvin | 20th Century | A cappella | sacred |
| Set Down Servant | Shaw, Robert | 20th Century | A cappella | sacred |
| Soul of the World | Purcell, Henry | Baroque | A cappella | sacred |
| Vinea mea electra | Poulenc, Francis | 20th Century | A cappella | sacred |
| Ye Shall have a Song from *Peaceable Kingdom* | Thompson, Randall | 20th Century | A cappella | sacred |

## 1975 Concert Tour Repertoire - Philip Knautz, conductor

|  |  |  |  |  |
|---|---|---|---|---|
| A Joyful Christmas Song | Gevaert, Francois | 20th Century | A cappella | sacred |
| Be Glad then America | Billings, William | Classical | Keyboard | sacred |
| Finale - Sing Ye to the Lord | Bach, J.S. | Baroque | A cappella | sacred |
| Hallelujah Chorus from *Mount of Olives* | Beethoven, Ludwig | 19th Century | Keyboard | sacred |
| Let All Things Now Living | Davis, Katherine | 20th Century | Keyboard | sacred |
| Let Us Break Bread Together | Lynn, George | Folk | A cappella | sacred |
| Look to this Day | Kittleson, Carl | 20th Century | A cappella | secular |
| Midst the Deep Silence | Jennings, Carolyn | 20th Century | A cappella | sacred |
| Psalmkonzert | Zimmerman, Heinz Werner | 20th Century | A cappella | sacred |
| Set Me as a Seal | Walton, William | 20th Century | A cappella | sacred |
| Speak to One Another of Psalms | Berger, Jean | 20th Century | A cappella | sacred |
| Spring | Christiansen, Paul J. | 20th Century | A cappella | secular |
| Tonerna | Lundholm, Brynolf | Folk | A cappella | secular |
| Vergorenheit | Wolf, Hugo | 20th Century | A cappella | secular |

| 1976 Concert Tour Repertoire - Philip Knautz, conductor ||||||
|---|---|---|---|---|---|
| Alleluia from *Brazilian Psalm* | Berger, Jean | 20th Century | A cappella | sacred |
| Be Not Afraid | Bach, J.S. | Baroque | A cappella | sacred |
| Benedictus | Christiansen, Olaf | 20th Century | A cappella | sacred |
| Fum, Fum, Fum | Parker, Alice & Shaw, Robert | 20th Century | A cappella | sacred |
| Haec est Dies | Gallus, Jacobus | Renaissance | A cappella | sacred |
| Let All Mortal Flesh Keep Silent | Bairstow, Edward C. | 20th Century | A cappella | sacred |
| Let All the World Praise the Lord | Vivaldi, Antonio | Baroque | A cappella | sacred |
| Let Down the Bars, O Death | Barber, Samuel | 20th Century | A cappella | secular |
| Lost in the Stars | Weill, Kurt | 20th Century | A cappella | secular |
| National Hymn | Warren, George | 19th Century | A cappella | sacred |
| Prayers of Steel | Christiansen, Paul J. | 20th Century | A cappella | sacred |
| Stomp Your Foot | Copland, Aaron | 20th Century | Keyboard | secular |
| Suddenly There Came a Sound from Heaven | Aichinger, Gregor | Renaissance | A cappella | sacred |
| The Omnipotence | Schubert, Franz | 19th Century | Keyboard | sacred |
| The Shepherd's Story | Dickinson, Clarence | 20th Century | A cappella | sacred |
| Tonerna | Lundholm, Brynolf | Folk | A cappella | secular |
| Wake, Awake for Night is Flying | Christiansen, F. Melius | 20th Century | A cappella | sacred |
| Witness | Fissinger, Edwin | 20th Century | A cappella | sacred |

| 1977 Concert Tour Repertoire - Philip Knautz, conductor ||||| 
|---|---|---|---|---|
| A Babe is Born | Moe, Daniel | 20th Century | A cappella | sacred |
| Beati Quorum Via | Stanford, Charles | 19th Century | A cappella | sacred |
| Christus Factus Est | Anerio, Felice | Renaissance | A cappella | sacred |
| Ding Dong Merrily on High | Wood, Charles | 20th Century | A cappella | sacred |
| God Is Gone Up With a Merry Noise | Hutchings, Arthur | 20th Century | A cappella | sacred |
| Holy, Holy, Holy | Mendelssohn, Felix | 19th Century | A cappella | sacred |
| Hosanna | Lockwood, Normand | 20th Century | A cappella | sacred |
| I Will Lift Up Mine Eyes | Willan, Healey | 20th Century | A cappella | sacred |
| In Heaven Above | Christiansen, F. Melius | 20th Century | A cappella | sacred |
| Let Me Be Ready | Spiritual | Folk | A cappella | sacred |
| Lord, Thou Hast Been Our Refuge | Vaughn Williams, Ralph | 20th Century | Keyboard | sacred |
| O Day Full of Grace | Christiansen, F. Melius | 20th Century | A cappella | sacred |
| Praise to The, Lord Jesus | Schutz, Heinrich | Baroque | A cappella | sacred |
| Prayer to Jesus | Oldroyd, George | 20th Century | A cappella | sacred |
| Russian Picnic | Enders, Harvey | 20th Century | Keyboard | secular |
| Senses | Gold-Feldstein | 20th Century | Keyboard | secular |
| Stabat Mater | Penderecki, Krzysztof | 20th Century | A cappella | sacred |
| The Creation | Scott, Tom | 20th Century | A cappella | sacred |
| The Omnipotence | Schubert, Franz | 19th Century | Keyboard | sacred |
| Tryggare Kan Ingen Vara | Swedish Folk Song | Folk | A cappella | sacred |

| 1978 Concert Tour Repertoire - Philip Knautz, conductor | | | | |
|---|---|---|---|---|
| Advent Motet | Schreck, Gustav | Renaissance | A cappella | sacred |
| Alleluia | Thompson, Randall | 20th Century | A cappella | sacred |
| Benedictus | Christiansen, Olaf | 20th Century | A cappella | sacred |
| Carol of the Bells | Leontovich, M | 20th Century | A cappella | secular |
| Cry Out and Shout | Nystedt, Knut | 20th Century | A cappella | sacred |
| Great is the Lord | Berger, Jean | 20th Century | A cappella | sacred |
| Holy, Holy, Holy | Bach, J.S. | Baroque | Keyboard | sacred |
| I Sing of a Maiden | Shaw, Martin | 20th Century | A cappella | sacred |
| Jesus, Think of Me | Back, Sven-Erik | 20th Century | A cappella | sacred |
| Nature Carol | Sargent, Malcom | 20th Century | A cappella | secular |
| O Be Joyful, All Ye Lands | Gretchaninoff, Alexander | 20th Century | A cappella | sacred |
| Rock-a My Soul | Kirk, Theron | 20th Century | A cappella | sacred |
| Sing We Merrily Unto God Our Strength | Shaw, Martin | 20th Century | A cappella | sacred |
| Today There is Ringing | Christiansen, F. Melius | 20th Century | A cappella | sacred |
| Ye Shall have a Song from *Peaceable Kingdom* | Thompson, Randall | 20th Century | A cappella | sacred |

## 1979 Concert Tour Repertoire – David Engen, conductor

| | | | | |
|---|---|---|---|---|
| Alleluia | Pinkham, Daniel | 20th Century | Electronic Tape | sacred |
| Bred Dina Vida Vingar | Ohrwall, Anders | 20th Century | A cappella | sacred |
| Children of the Heavenly Father | Engen, David | 20th Century | A cappella | sacred |
| Come, Ye That Love the Lord | Parker, Alice | 20th Century | A cappella | sacred |
| Easter Carol | Pinkham, Daniel | 20th Century | A cappella | sacred |
| Fife and Drum | Bielawa, Herbert | 20th Century | A cappella | sacred |
| Laudi | Lidholm, Ingvar | 20th Century | A cappella | sacred |
| Magnificat | Berger, Jean | 20th Century | Flute, Tam, Triangle | sacred |
| Morning | Ligeti, Gyorgy | 20th Century | A cappella | sacred |
| Night | Ligeti, Gyorgy | 20th Century | A cappella | sacred |
| O Lord, Creator of All Things | Schutz, Heinrich | Baroque | A cappella | sacred |
| Psalm 50 | Christiansen, F. Melius | 20th Century | A cappella | sacred |
| Singet Dem Herren | Bach, J.S. | Baroque | A cappella | sacred |
| Surrexit Pastor Bonus | di Lasso, Orlando | Renaissance | A cappella | sacred |
| Tantum Ergo | Durufle, Maurice | 20th Century | A cappella | sacred |
| Ubi Caritas | Durufle, Maurice | 20th Century | A cappella | sacred |
| Varldens Fralsare Kom Nu Har | Ohrwall, Anders | 20th Century | Flute & Keyboard | sacred |

## 1980 Concert Tour Repertoire - Philip Knautz, conductor

|  |  |  |  |  |
|---|---|---|---|---|
| A Joyful Christmas Song | Gevaert, Francois | 20th Century | A cappella | sacred |
| A Rose Tree Blossoms | Hovhaness, Alan | 20th Century | A cappella | secular |
| An Apostrophe to the Heavenly Hosts | Willan, Healey | 20th Century | A cappella | sacred |
| Be Ye Joyful, Earth and Sky | Bender, Jan | 20th Century | A cappella | sacred |
| Carol of Service | Shaw, Martin | 20th Century | A cappella | sacred |
| Choral Scherzo | Kubik, Gail | 20th Century | A cappella | secular |
| Die mit Tranen Saen | Schein, Johann Hermann | Renaissance | A cappella | secular |
| Greater Love Hath No Man | Ireland, John | 20th Century | Keyboard | sacred |
| Hvad est Du Dog Skjon | Grieg, Edvard | 19th Century | A cappella | sacred |
| Just a Closer Walk with Thee | Spiritual | Folk | A cappella | sacred |
| Lost in the Night | Christiansen, F. Melius | 20th Century | A cappella | sacred |
| Midst the Deep Silence | Jennings, Carolyn | 20th Century | A cappella | sacred |
| O Give Thanks Unto the Lord | Purcell, Henry | Baroque | A cappella | sacred |
| Prelude for Voices | Schumann, William | 20th Century | A cappella | secular |
| Psalm 100 | Zimmerman, Heinz Werner | 20th Century | Bass & Keyboard | sacred |
| The Lord is Great | Manten, Eric | 20th Century | A cappella | sacred |
| Wake, Awake for Night is Flying | Christiansen, F. Melius | 20th Century | A cappella | sacred |

## 1981 Concert Tour Repertoire - Karle Erickson, conductor

| | | | | |
|---|---|---|---|---|
| Agnus Dei | Kalinnikoff, Basil | 20th Century | A cappella | sacred |
| Ain'a that Good News | Dawson, William | 20th Century | A cappella | sacred |
| Crown Him King of Glory | Christiansen, Olaf | 20th Century | A cappella | sacred |
| God is Our Refuge and Strength | Pachelbel, Johann | Baroque | A cappella | sacred |
| I Will Greatly Rejoice | Nystedt, Knut | 20th Century | A cappella | sacred |
| If You Receive My Words | Nystedt, Knut | 20th Century | A cappella | sacred |
| Jubilate Deo Omnis Terra | Peeters, Flor | 20th Century | Keyboard | sacred |
| Laudate Dominum | Mozart, W.A. | Classical | Keyboard | sacred |
| O Magnum Mysterium | Victoria, Thomas Luis da | Renaissance | A cappella | sacred |
| Only Begotten Son | Gretchaninoff, Alexander | 20th Century | A cappella | sacred |
| Praise to the Lord | Christiansen, F. Melius | 20th Century | A cappella | sacred |
| Psalm 100 | Schutz, Heinrich | Baroque | A cappella | sacred |
| The Son of God is Come to Earth | Brahms, Johannes | 19th Century | A cappella | sacred |
| Tota Pulchra Es | Durufle, Maurice | 20th Century | A cappella | sacred |
| Tryggare Kan Ingen Vara | Swanson, Wilber F. | Folk | A cappella | sacred |
| Ubi Caritas | Durufle, Maurice | 20th Century | A cappella | sacred |

## 1982 Concert Tour Repertoire - Karle Erickson, conductor

| | | | | |
|---|---|---|---|---|
| Bred Dina Vida Vingar | Ohrwall, Anders | 20th Century | A cappella | sacred |
| Cantate Domino | Sweelinck, Jan | Renaissance | A cappella | sacred |
| Heilig | Mendelssohn, Felix | 19th Century | A cappella | sacred |
| Hodie Christus Natus Est | Willan, Healey | 20th Century | A cappella | sacred |
| Jubilate Deo | Fetler, Paul | 20th Century | Keyboard | sacred |
| Mass in Honor of the Eucharist | Dello Joio, Norman | 20th Century | Keyboard | sacred |
| O Be Joyful, All Ye Lands | Gretchaninoff, Alexander | 20th Century | A cappella | sacred |
| O Come, O Come Emmanuel | French Processional | Folk | A cappella | sacred |
| O Gud, All Sannings Kalla | Ohrwall, Anders | 20th Century | Keyboard | sacred |
| Peace I Leave With You | Nystedt, Knut | 20th Century | A cappella | sacred |
| Praise to the Lord | Christiansen, F. Melius | 20th Century | A cappella | sacred |
| Praise to the Lord | Distler, Hugo | 20th Century | A cappella | sacred |
| The Eyes of All Wait Upon Thee | Berger, Jean | 20th Century | A cappella | sacred |
| Tota Pulchra Es | Durufle, Maurice | 20th Century | A cappella | sacred |
| Tu Es Petrus | Durufle, Maurice | 20th Century | A cappella | sacred |
| Ubi Caritas | Durufle, Maurice | 20th Century | A cappella | sacred |
| With a Voice of Singing | Jennings, Kenneth | 20th Century | A cappella | sacred |
| Ye Were Sometimes Darkness | Thompson, Randall | 20th Century | A cappella | sacred |

## 1983 Concert Tour Repertoire - Karle Erickson, conductor

| Title | Composer | Period | Performance | Type |
|---|---|---|---|---|
| Ave Verum | Liszt, Franz | 19th Century | A cappella | sacred |
| Bred Dina Vida Vingar | Ohrwall, Anders | 20th Century | A cappella | sacred |
| I Wonder as I Wander | Niles, John Jacob | 20th Century | A cappella | sacred |
| Jesus, As Thou Art Our Savior | Britten, Benjamin | 20th Century | A cappella | sacred |
| Laud Him | Christiansen, Olaf | 20th Century | A cappella | sacred |
| Lobet Den Herrn, Alle Heiden | Bach, J.S. | Baroque | A cappella | sacred |
| Magnificat | Hemberg, Eskil | 20th Century | A cappella | sacred |
| Mass in G Minor | Vaughn Williams, Ralph | 20th Century | A cappella | sacred |
| Nunc Dimittis | Gretchaninoff, Alexander | 20th Century | A cappella | sacred |
| O Gladsome Radiance | Gretchaninoff, Alexander | 20th Century | A cappella | sacred |
| Praise to the Lord | Christiansen, F. Melius | 20th Century | A cappella | sacred |
| Sing and Rejoice | Nystedt, Knut | 20th Century | A cappella | sacred |
| Singet Dem Herren | Distler, Hugo | 20th Century | A cappella | sacred |
| Steal Away | Simpson, Eugene Thamon | 20th Century | A cappella | sacred |
| Three Nocturnes | Lundvik, Hildor | 20th Century | A cappella | secular |

| 1984 Concert Tour Repertoire - Karle Erickson, conductor ||||||
|---|---|---|---|---|
| Ave Maris Stella | Kverno, Trond | 20th Century | A cappella | sacred |
| Beati Quorum Via | Stanford, Charles | 19th Century | A cappella | sacred |
| Crown Him King of Glory | Christiansen, Olaf | 20th Century | A cappella | sacred |
| Dalarne Lullaby | Berens/Sateren | Folk | A cappella | secular |
| Magnificat | Pachelbel, Johann | Baroque | Keyboard | sacred |
| My Soul Doth Rejoice | Homilius, G.A. | 20th Century | A cappella | sacred |
| Nocturnes | Lundvik, Hildor | 20th Century | A cappella | secular |
| O Ye People | Casals, Pablo | 20th Century | A cappella | secular |
| Praise to the Lord | Christiansen, F. Melius | 20th Century | A cappella | sacred |
| Shepherd's Pipe Carol | Rutter, John | 20th Century | Keyboard | sacred |
| Sing We Merrily Unto God Our Strength | Shaw, Martin | 20th Century | A cappella | sacred |
| Sing Ye to the Lord | Bach, J.S. | Baroque | A cappella | sacred |
| Somebody's Callin' My Name | Whalum, Wendell | 20th Century | A cappella | sacred |
| Soon-ah Will Be Done | Dawson, William | 20th Century | A cappella | sacred |
| The Path of the Just | Nystedt, Knut | 20th Century | A cappella | sacred |

## 1985 Concert Tour Repertoire - Karle Erickson, conductor

|  |  |  |  |  |
|---|---|---|---|---|
| Adoramus Te | Corsi, Giuseppi | Baroque | A cappella | sacred |
| Advent Motet | Schreck, Gustav | 19th Century | A cappella | sacred |
| Alleluia | Lekberg, Sven | 20th Century | A cappella | sacred |
| At the Round Earth's Imagined Corners | Spencer, Willametta | 20th Century | A cappella | sacred |
| Ave Maris Stella | Grieg, Edvard | 19th Century | A cappella | sacred |
| Be Not Afraid | Bach, J.S. | Baroque | A cappella | sacred |
| Bred Dina Vida Vingar | Erickson, Karle | 20th Century | Flute | sacred |
| Jubilate Deo | Lewkovitch, Bernhard | 20th Century | A cappella | sacred |
| Kyrie | Nystedt, Knut | 20th Century | A cappella | sacred |
| Praise to the Lord | Christiansen, F. Melius | 20th Century | A cappella | sacred |
| Prayer to Jesus | Oldroyd, George | 20th Century | A cappella | sacred |
| Sing to the Lord a New Song | Schutz, Heinrich | Baroque | A cappella | sacred |
| Sing Ye Merrily | Sateren, Leland | 20th Century | A cappella | sacred |
| The Earth Adorned | Ahlen, Waldemar | 20th Century | A cappella | sacred |
| Veni Sancte Spiritus | Janacek, Leos | 20th Century | A cappella | sacred |

# Appendix A

## 1986 Concert Tour Repertoire - Karle Erickson, conductor

|  |  |  |  |  |
|---|---|---|---|---|
| A Spotless Rose | Howells, Herbert | 20th Century | A cappella | sacred |
| Adoramus Te | Gasparini, Quirino | Classical | A cappella | sacred |
| All That Hath Life and Breath | Clausen, Rene | 20th Century | A cappella | sacred |
| Angels Rolled the Stone Away | Hairston, Jester | 20th Century | Keyboard | sacred |
| Benedicamus Domino | Warlock, Peter | 20th Century | A cappella | sacred |
| Day by Day Thy Mercies Lord, Attend Me | Erickson, Karle | 20th Century | A cappella | sacred |
| Get You Up | Nystedt, Knut | 20th Century | A cappella | sacred |
| Glory be to God | Berger, Jean | 20th Century | A cappella | sacred |
| God's Son Has Made Me Free | Overby, Oscar | 20th Century | A cappella | sacred |
| Hodie Christus Natus Est | Gabrielli, Giovanni | Renaissance | A cappella | sacred |
| I Am the Resurrection and the True Life | Schutz, Heinrich | Baroque | A cappella | sacred |
| I Look Not Back | Erickson, Karle | 20th Century | A cappella | sacred |
| Praise to the Lord | Christiansen, F. Melius | 20th Century | A cappella | sacred |
| Sing With Gladness | Sweelinck, Jan | Renaissance | A cappella | sacred |
| Sleep, My Young One, Gently Rest | Sateren, Leland | 20th Century | A cappella | secular |
| Thou, O Lord | Nystedt, Knut | 20th Century | A cappella | sacred |
| Tota Pulchra Es | Durufle, Maurice | 20th Century | A cappella | sacred |
| Tu Es Petrus | Durufle, Maurice | 20th Century | A cappella | sacred |
| Ubi Caritas | Durufle, Maurice | 20th Century | A cappella | sacred |
| Yea Though I Wander | Schumann, Georg | 20th Century | A cappella | sacred |

## 1987 Concert Tour Repertoire - Karle Erickson, conductor

| Title | Composer | Period | Performance | Type |
|---|---|---|---|---|
| Ain'a that Good News | Dawson, William | 20th Century | A cappella | sacred |
| Bird of Youth | Sveshnikov, A.V. | 20th Century | A cappella | secular |
| Children of the Heavenly Father | Erickson, Karle | 20th Century | A cappella | sacred |
| Help Us, O Lord | Copland, Aaron | 20th Century | A cappella | sacred |
| I Will Greatly Rejoice | Nystedt, Knut | 20th Century | A cappella | sacred |
| In the World of Nature | Dvorak, Antonin | 20th Century | A cappella | secular |
| Lark | Copland, Aaron | 20th Century | A cappella | secular |
| Let Thy Blessed Spirit | Tschesnokoff, Paul | 20th Century | A cappella | sacred |
| Lullaby, Sweet Jesu | Opheim, Vernon | 20th Century | A cappella | sacred |
| Mass in G Minor | Vaughn Williams, Ralph | 20th Century | A cappella | sacred |
| My Spirit Sang All Day | Finzi, Gerald | 20th Century | A cappella | sacred |
| Nunc Dimittis | Gretchaninoff, Alexander | 20th Century | A cappella | sacred |
| O Come, Let Us Worship | Rachmaninoff, Sergei | 19th Century | A cappella | sacred |
| O Gladsome Radiance | Gretchaninoff, Alexander | 20th Century | A cappella | sacred |
| Praise to the Lord | Christiansen, F. Melius | 20th Century | A cappella | sacred |
| Sinnuh, Please Don't Let Dis Harves' Pass | Simpson, Eugene Thamon | 20th Century | A cappella | sacred |
| Spring | Christiansen, Paul J. | 20th Century | A cappella | secular |
| The Coolin | Barber, Samuel | 20th Century | A cappella | secular |
| The Wall of Heaven | Brahms, Johannes | 19th Century | A cappella | sacred |
| Thou, O Jehovah, Abideth Forever | Copland, Aaron | 20th Century | A cappella | sacred |

# Appendix A

| 1988 Concert Tour Repertoire - Karle Erickson, conductor | | | | |
|---|---|---|---|---|
| Ain'a that Good News | Dawson, William | 20th Century | A cappella | sacred |
| Crown Him King of Glory | Christiansen, Olaf | 20th Century | A cappella | sacred |
| Der Geist Hilft Unsrer Schwachheit Auf | Bach, J.S. | Baroque | A cappella | sacred |
| Domaredansen | Hallberg, Bengt | 20th Century | keyboard | secular |
| Ecco Mormorar L'Onde | Monteverdi, Claudio | Baroque | A cappella | secular |
| Ego Sum Panis Vitae | Back, Sven-Erik | 20th Century | A cappella | sacred |
| Lost in the Night | Christiansen, F. Melius | 20th Century | A cappella | sacred |
| Magnificat | Gustafsson, Kaj-Erik | 20th Century | A cappella | sacred |
| Night / Morning | Ligeti, Gyorgy | 20th Century | A cappella | secular |
| O Day Full of Grace | Christiansen, F. Melius | 20th Century | A cappella | sacred |
| Praise to the Lord | Christiansen, F. Melius | 20th Century | A cappella | sacred |
| Song of Praise | Holmboe, Vagn | 20th Century | A cappella | sacred |
| Three Choral Ballads | Stenhammer, Wilhelm | 20th Century | A cappella | secular |
| Virga Jesse Floriut | Bruckner, Anton | 19th Century | A cappella | sacred |

| 1989 Concert Tour Repertoire - Karle Erickson, conductor | | | | |
|---|---|---|---|---|
| Benedictus | Christiansen, Olaf | 20th Century | A cappella | sacred |
| Collect for Peace | Bassett, Leslie | 20th Century | Electronic Tape | sacred |
| Create in Me a Clean Heart, O Lord | Brahms, Johannes | 19th Century | A cappella | sacred |
| Grant Unto Me the Joy of Thy Salvation | Brahms, Johannes | 19th Century | A cappella | sacred |
| Hodie Christus Natus Est | Willan, Healey | 20th Century | A cappella | sacred |
| Hymn to St. Cecilia | Britten, Benjamin | 20th Century | A cappella | sacred |
| Keep Your Lamps | Thomas, Andre | 20th Century | A cappella | sacred |
| O Beatum Et Sacrosanctum Diem | Phillips, Peter | Renaissance | A cappella | sacred |
| O Crux | Nystedt, Knut | 20th Century | A cappella | sacred |
| Praise to the Lord | Christiansen, F. Melius | 20th Century | A cappella | sacred |
| Rondes | Rabe, Folke | 20th Century | A cappella | secular |
| Sanctus from *Mass* | Martin, Frank | 20th Century | A cappella | sacred |
| Shepherd's Pipe Carol | Rutter, John | 20th Century | Keyboard | sacred |
| Signposts | Hemberg, Eskil | 20th Century | A cappella | sacred |
| Sing, O Ye Heavens | Fissinger, Edwin | 20th Century | A cappella | sacred |
| The Little Road to Bethlehem | Head, Michael | 20th Century | A cappella | sacred |
| This is the Day the Lord has Made | Peeters, Flor | 20th Century | A cappella | sacred |
| Tryggare Kan Ingen Vara | Erickson, Karle | 20th Century | A cappella | sacred |

## 1990 Concert Tour Repertoire - Karle Erickson, conductor

|  |  |  |  |  |
|---|---|---|---|---|
| Babe of Bethlehem | Fritschel, James | 20th Century | A cappella | sacred |
| Daniel, Daniel, Servant of the Lord | Moore, Undine Smith | 20th Century | A cappella | sacred |
| Die mit Tranen Saen | Schein, Johann Hermann | Renaissance | A cappella | sacred |
| Gloria | Argento, Dominick | 20th Century | keyboard | sacred |
| Gloria | Beck, John Ness | 20th Century | A cappella | sacred |
| Have Ye Not Known from *Peaceable Kingdom* | Thompson, Randall | 20th Century | A cappella | sacred |
| How Far is it to Bethlehem? | Paulus, Stephen | 20th Century | Oboe & Harp | sacred |
| Jesu, Jesu, Dulcissime | Reutter, Johann Georg | Classical | A cappella | sacred |
| Maria Magdalene et Altera Maria | Gabrielli, Andrea | Renaissance | A cappella | sacred |
| O Gud, All Sannings Kalla | Ohrwall, Anders | 20th Century | keyboard | sacred |
| O Magnum Mysterium | Victoria, Thomas Luis de | Renaissance | A cappella | sacred |
| Praise to the Lord | Christiansen, F. Melius | 20th Century | A cappella | sacred |
| Sicut Cervus | Palestrina | Renaissance | A cappella | sacred |
| Sing We Merrily | Child, William | Baroque | A cappella | sacred |
| Sing We Merrily Unto God Our Strength | Shaw, Martin | 20th Century | A cappella | sacred |
| Sitivit Anima Mea | Palestrina | Renaissance | A cappella | sacred |
| The Queen Shall Rejoice | Turner, William | Baroque | A cappella | sacred |
| Warmland | Martin, Paul I. | 20th Century | A cappella | secular |
| Ye Shall have a Song from *Peaceable Kingdom* | Thompson, Randall | 20th Century | A cappella | sacred |

## 1991 Concert Tour Repertoire - Karle Erickson, conductor

| | | | | |
|---|---|---|---|---|
| Ain'a that Good News | Dawson, William | 20th Century | A cappella | sacred |
| Ave Maris Stella | Kverno, Trond | 20th Century | A cappella | sacred |
| Exultate Deo | Scarlatti, Alessandro | Renaissance | A cappella | sacred |
| Hotaru Koi | Ogura, Ro | 20th Century | A cappella | secular |
| I Got Shoes | Parker, Alice & Shaw, Robert | 20th Century | A cappella | sacred |
| Jeanie With the Light Brown Hair | Mattson, Phil | 20th Century | A cappella | secular |
| Little Oriole | Zhang, Ning | 20th Century | A cappella | secular |
| Lux Aeterna | Fissinger, Edwin | 20th Century | A cappella | sacred |
| Muge | Xixien, Qu | 20th Century | A cappella | secular |
| My Old Kentucky Home | Moore, Donald | 20th Century | A cappella | secular |
| Nocturnes | Lundvik, Hildor | 20th Century | A cappella | secular |
| Our Father | Gretchaninoff, Alexander | 20th Century | A cappella | sacred |
| Praise to the Lord | Christiansen, F. Melius | 20th Century | A cappella | sacred |
| Shenandoah | Erb, James | 20th Century | A cappella | secular |
| Sing to the Lord a New Made Song | Distler, Hugo | 20th Century | A cappella | sacred |
| The Gift to be Simple | Chilcott, Bob | 20th Century | A cappella | secular |
| The Modern Man I Sing | Chilcott, Bob | 20th Century | A cappella | secular |
| Tjuv, Och Tjuv | Alfven, Hugo | 20th Century | A cappella | secular |
| Wake, Awake for Night is Flying | Christiansen, F. Melius | 20th Century | A cappella | sacred |
| Witness | Fissinger, Edwin | 20th Century | A cappella | sacred |

## 1992 Concert Tour Repertoire - Karle Erickson, conductor

|  |  |  |  |  |
|---|---|---|---|---|
| Advent Motet | Schreck, Gustav | 19th Century | A cappella | sacred |
| Ahrirang | DeCormier, Robert | 20th Century | A cappella | secular |
| Alleluia | Hassler, Hans Leo | Renaissance | A cappella | sacred |
| By the Waters of Babylon | Fissinger, Edwin | 20th Century | A cappella | sacred |
| Den Store, Hvide Flok | Grieg, Edvard | 19th Century | A cappella | sacred |
| Gloria | Rickard, Jerrery | 20th Century | A cappella | sacred |
| Hombe | Ekwueme, L. | 20th Century | A cappella | secular |
| I Wait for the Lord | Fritschel, James | 20th Century | A cappella | sacred |
| Joshua Fit the Battle of Jericho | Fissinger, Edwin | 20th Century | A cappella | sacred |
| Magnificat | Berger, Jean | 20th Century | Flute, Tam, Tringl | sacred |
| O Day Full of Grace | Christiansen, F. Melius | 20th Century | A cappella | sacred |
| Praise to the Lord | Christiansen, F. Melius | 20th Century | A cappella | sacred |
| The Modern Man I Sing | Chilcott, Bob | 20th Century | A cappella | secular |
| Tonerna | Sateren, Leland | Folk | A cappella | secular |
| Twelfth Night | Barber, Samuel | 20th Century | A cappella | sacred |
| Venite, Exultemus Domino | Sweelinck, Jan | Renaissance | A cappella | sacred |

| 1993 Concert Tour Repertoire - Karle Erickson, conductor ||||| 
|---|---|---|---|---|
| Aftonen | Alfven, Hugo | 20th Century | A cappella | secular |
| Gloria in Excelsis Deo | Pinkham, Daniel | 20th Century | A cappella | sacred |
| God's Son Has Made Me Free | Overby, Oscar | 20th Century | A cappella | sacred |
| Hosanna | Christiansen, F. Melius | 20th Century | A cappella | sacred |
| I Sat Down Under His Shadow | Bairstow, Edward C. | 20th Century | A cappella | sacred |
| Jesus, Come to Me | Muus, B.J. | 20th Century | A cappella | sacred |
| Mass (Three Sections) | Martin, Frank | 20th Century | A cappella | sacred |
| O Sacrum Convivium | Messiaen, Olivier | 20th Century | A cappella | sacred |
| Praise to the Lord | Christiansen, F. Melius | 20th Century | A cappella | sacred |
| Psalm 66 | Burk, Terry | 20th Century | A cappella | sacred |
| Sing With Joy, Glad Voices Lift | Distler, Hugo | 20th Century | A cappella | sacred |
| Sweet Dreams, Form a Shade | Diemer, Emma Lou | 20th Century | A cappella | sacred |
| The Gift to be Simple | Chilcott, Bob | 20th Century | A cappella | secular |
| There is No Rose of Such Virtue | Mahy, Kenneth | 20th Century | A cappella | sacred |
| Witness | Halloran, Jack | 20th Century | A cappella | sacred |

| 1994 Concert Tour Repertoire - Karle Erickson, conductor | | | | |
|---|---|---|---|---|
| A Jubilant Song | Clausen, Rene | 20th Century | A cappella | sacred |
| Ave Maria | Biebl, Franz | 20th Century | A cappella | sacred |
| Ave Verum Corpus | Raminsh, Imant | 20th Century | A cappella | sacred |
| Cantate Domino | Schutz, Heinrich | Baroque | A cappella | sacred |
| Da Droben Vom Berge | Erickson, Karle | 20th Century | A cappella | sacred |
| I'm Goin' Away | Wilberg, Mack | 20th Century | A cappella | secular |
| Let Me Fly | DeCormier, Robert | 20th Century | A cappella | sacred |
| Lo, How a Rose | Distler, Hugo | 20th Century | A cappella | sacred |
| Mass | Martin, Frank | 20th Century | A cappella | sacred |
| Praise to the Lord | Christiansen, F. Melius | 20th Century | A cappella | sacred |
| The Lord is Ris'n | Billings. William | Classical | A cappella | sacred |
| The Morning Trumpet | Fissinger, Edwin | 20th Century | A cappella | sacred |
| The Peaceable Kingdom (Second Half) | Thompson, Randall | 20th Century | A cappella | sacred |
| The Son of God | Brahms, Johannes | 19th Century | A cappella | sacred |

## Commitment to Musical Excellence

| 1995 Concert Tour Repertoire - Kenneth Jennings, conductor | | | | |
|---|---|---|---|---|
| A La Nanita Nana | Susa, Conrad | 20th Century | A cappella | sacred |
| All You Works of the Lord | Jennings, Kenneth | 20th Century | Keyboard | sacred |
| Alleluia | Thompson, Randall | 20th Century | A cappella | sacred |
| Alleluia from *Brazilian Psalm* | Berger, Jean | 20th Century | A cappella | sacred |
| As a Flower of the Field | Christiansen, Paul J. | 20th Century | A cappella | secular |
| Come, Ye That Love the Lord | Parker, Alice | 20th Century | A cappella | sacred |
| Denn er Hat Seinen Engeln Befohlen uber Dir | Mendelssohn, Felix | 19th Century | A cappella | sacred |
| Furchte dich Nicht | Bach, J.S. | Baroque | Continuo | sacred |
| Gloria ad Modum Tubae | Dufay, Guillaume | Mideivil | A cappella | sacred |
| Halle, Halle, Halle | Haugen, Marty | 20th Century | A cappella | sacred |
| Hark I Hear the Harps Eternal | Parker, Alice | 20th Century | A cappella | sacred |
| Keep Your Lamps | Thomas, Andre | 20th Century | Conga | sacred |
| Magnificat | Part, Arvo | 20th Century | A cappella | sacred |
| Motetum Archangeli Michaelis | Hambraeus, Bengt | 20th Century | Keyboard | sacred |
| O God of Mercies | Jennings, Kenneth | 20th Century | A cappella | sacred |
| Praise to the Lord | Christiansen, F. Melius | 20th Century | A cappella | sacred |
| Sanctus | Palestrina | Renaissance | A cappella | sacred |
| The Earth Adorned | Ahlen, Waldemar | 20th Century | A cappella | sacred |

| 1996 Concert Tour Repertoire - Gregory Aune, conductor ||||||
|---|---|---|---|---|
| Daniel, Daniel, Servant of the Lord | Moore, Undine Smith | 20th Century | A cappella | sacred |
| Das ist ein Kostliches Ding | Schumann, Georg | 20th Century | A cappella | sacred |
| God Is Gone Up With a Merry Noise | Hutchings, Arthur | 20th Century | A cappella | sacred |
| Hosanna to the Son of David | Gibbons, Orlando | Renaissance | A cappella | sacred |
| Ich Aber Bin Elend | Brahms, Johannes | 19th Century | A cappella | sacred |
| Lamentaciones de Jeremias Propheta | Ginastera, Alberto | 20th Century | A cappella | sacred |
| Lift Up Your Heads | Christiansen, Olaf | 20th Century | A cappella | sacred |
| Mighty River, Mighty Fire | Raminsh, Imant | 20th Century | A cappella | sacred |
| O Immanuel | Part, Arvo | 20th Century | A cappella | sacred |
| Praise to the Lord | Christiansen, F. Melius | 20th Century | A cappella | sacred |
| Virga Jesse Floriut | Bruckner, Anton | 19th Century | A cappella | sacred |
| When David Heard | Weelkes, Thomas | Renaissance | A cappella | sacred |

## 1997 Concert Tour Repertoire - Gregory Aune, conductor

| Title | Composer | Period | Style | Type |
|---|---|---|---|---|
| "Dans" Ropte Felen | Peterson-Berger, Wilhelm | 20th Century | A cappella | secular |
| Easter Morning | Christiansen, Paul J. | 20th Century | A cappella | sacred |
| Go Tell It on the Mountain | Jennings, Carolyn | 20th Century | A cappella | sacred |
| Guide Me, O Thou Great Jehovah | Welsh Hymn | Folk | A cappella | sacred |
| Haec Dies | Byrd, William | Renaissance | A cappella | sacred |
| Heilig ist Gott der Herr Zebaoth | Mendelssohn, Felix | 19th Century | A cappella | sacred |
| Jeg Horer Regnen | Norgard, Per | 20th Century | A cappella | secular |
| John Saw The Number | Parker, Alice & Shaw, Robert | 20th Century | A cappella | sacred |
| Killebukken | Peterson-Berger, Wilhelm | 20th Century | A cappella | secular |
| Mighty River, Mighty Fire | Raminsh, Imant | 20th Century | A cappella | sacred |
| Nu ar en Dag Framliden | Alf, Fredrik | 20th Century | A cappella | sacred |
| O Magnum Mysterium | Lauridsen, Morten | 20th Century | A cappella | sacred |
| Praise to the Lord | Christiansen, F. Melius | 20th Century | A cappella | sacred |
| Psalm 23 | Svedbom, Vilhelm | 19th Century | A cappella | sacred |
| Psalm 50 | Christiansen, F. Melius | 20th Century | A cappella | sacred |
| Sing to God All the Earth | Mendelssohn, Felix | 19th Century | A cappella | sacred |
| Singet Dem Herren | Bach, J.S. | Baroque | A cappella | sacred |
| Weib, was Weinest Du? | Schutz, Heinrich | Baroque | A cappella | sacred |

## 1998 Concert Tour Repertoire - Gregory Aune, conductor

| | | | | |
|---|---|---|---|---|
| Alma Dei Creatoris | Mozart, W.A. | Classical | A cappella | sacred |
| Aus der Tiefe | Haser, August | 19th Century | A cappella | sacred |
| Carol | Lawson, Phillip | 20th Century | A cappella | sacred |
| Crucifixus | Lotti, Antonio | Baroque | A cappella | sacred |
| Deep River | Barnard, John | 20th Century | A cappella | sacred |
| Exultate Deo | Palestrina | Renaissance | A cappella | sacred |
| Hail, Gladdening Light | Wood, Charles | 20th Century | A cappella | sacred |
| Jordens oro Viker | Norman, Ludwig | 19th Century | A cappella | sacred |
| Kas tie Tadi | Stametz, Steven | 20th Century | A cappella | secular |
| Lord of the Dance | Fleming, Larry | 20th Century | A cappella | sacred |
| Lord, Make Me a Instrument of Your Peace | Heitzeg, Steve | 20th Century | A cappella | sacred |
| My Song in the Night | Christiansen, Paul J. | 20th Century | A cappella | sacred |
| O Come, Little Children | Fritschel, James | 20th Century | A cappella | sacred |
| O Heiland Reiss Die Himmel Auf! | Brahms, Johannes | 19th Century | A cappella | sacred |
| Past Life Melodies | Hopkins, Sarah | 20th Century | A cappella | secular |
| Pilgrim's Hymn | Paulus, Steven | 20th Century | A cappella | sacred |
| Praise to the Lord | Christiansen, F. Melius | 20th Century | A cappella | sacred |
| Witness | Halloran, Jack | 20th Century | A cappella | sacred |

| 1999 Concert Tour Repertoire - Gregory Aune, conductor ||||| 
|---|---|---|---|---|
| Agnus Dei | Des Pres, Josquin | Renaissance | A cappella | sacred |
| Credo | Rautavaara, Einojuhani | 20th Century | A cappella | sacred |
| Deep River | Barnard, John | 20th Century | A cappella | sacred |
| Die mit Tranen Saen | Schutz, Heinrich | Baroque | A cappella | secular |
| I Will Not Leave You Comfortless | Byrd, William | Renaissance | A cappella | sacred |
| Jesus, Jesus, Rest Your Head | Nestor, Leo | 20th Century | A cappella | sacred |
| Oh Dear, What Can Be the Matter | Kubik, Gail | 20th Century | A cappella | secular |
| Praise to the Lord | Christiansen, F. Melius | 20th Century | A cappella | sacred |
| Set Down Servant | Shaw, Robert | 20th Century | A cappella | sacred |
| Shenandoah | Erb, James | 20th Century | A cappella | secular |
| Siyahumba | South African Song | Folk | A cappella | secular |
| The Earth Adorned | Ahlen, Waldemar | 20th Century | A cappella | sacred |
| The King of Love | Christiansen, Paul J. | 20th Century | A cappella | sacred |
| Thumba Mina | South African Song | Folk | A cappella | secular |
| Uyai Mose | Wesby, Roger | 20th Century | A cappella | sacred |

## 2000 Concert Tour Repertoire - Gregory Aune, conductor

|  |  |  |  |  |
|---|---|---|---|---|
| A Feast of Lanterns | Jennings, Carolyn | 20th Century | Keyboard | secular |
| A Hymne to Christ | Holst, Imogene | 20th Century | A cappella | sacred |
| A Spotless Rose | Howells, Herbert | 20th Century | A cappella | sacred |
| Ain'a that Good News | Dawson, William | 20th Century | A cappella | sacred |
| Ascendit Deus | Gallus, Jacobus | Renaissance | A cappella | sacred |
| Domino, memento mei | Back, Sven-Erik | 20th Century | A cappella | sacred |
| Durme, Durme | Parker, Alice | 20th Century | A cappella | secular |
| E'en So, Lord Jesus, Quickly Come | Manz, Paul | 20th Century | A cappella | sacred |
| From Life to Life | Eben, Peter | 20th Century | A cappella | secular |
| How Can I Keep from Singing | Stroope, Z. Randall | 20th Century | A cappella | sacred |
| Hymne au Soleil | Boulanger, Lili | 20th Century | A cappella | sacred |
| I Saw a New Heaven and a New Earth | Schalk, Carl | 20th Century | A cappella | sacred |
| My Heart is Longing to Praise My Savior | Sateren, Leland | 20th Century | A cappella | sacred |
| Praise to the Lord | Christiansen, F. Melius | 20th Century | A cappella | sacred |
| Stay With Us | Hovland, Egil | 20th Century | A cappella | sacred |
| The Woman with the Alabaster Box | Part, Arvo | 20th Century | A cappella | sacred |
| Wake, Awake for Night is Flying | Christiansen, F. Melius | 20th Century | A cappella | sacred |

| 2001 Concert Tour Repertoire - Gregory Aune, conductor | | | | |
|---|---|---|---|---|
| A Maiden is in a Ring | Alfven, Hugo | 20th Century | A cappella | secular |
| Christus Resurgens ex Mortuis | Lassus, Orlando | Renaissance | A cappella | sacred |
| For God Commanded Angels to Watch Over You | Mendelssohn, Felix | 19th Century | A cappella | sacred |
| Gardebylaten | Hahn, Gunnar | 20th Century | A cappella | secular |
| Great Day | Hogan, Moses | 20th Century | A cappella | sacred |
| How Can I Keep from Singing | Stroope, Z. Randall | 20th Century | A cappella | sacred |
| Kasar Mie la Gaji | Grau, Alberto | 20th Century | A cappella | secular |
| Laudate Dominum | Rheinberger, Josef | 19th Century | A cappella | sacred |
| Lo How a Rose e'er Blooming | Sandstrom, Jan | 20th Century | A cappella | sacred |
| Movements from Requiem | Howells, Herbert | 20th Century | A cappella | sacred |
| O Day Full of Grace | Christiansen, F. Melius | 20th Century | A cappella | sacred |
| Pater Noster | Handl, Jacob | Renaissance | A cappella | sacred |
| Praise to the Lord | Christiansen, F. Melius | 20th Century | A cappella | sacred |
| Pseudo-Yoik | Mantyjarvi, Jaakko | 20th Century | A cappella | secular |
| Salvation is Created | Tschesnokoff, Paul | 20th Century | A cappella | sacred |
| Set Me as a Seal | Clausen, Rene | 20th Century | A cappella | sacred |
| Sverige | Stenhammer, Wilhelm | 20th Century | A cappella | secular |
| The Turtle Dove | Lawson, Phillip | 20th Century | A cappella | secular |

Appendix A

| 2002 Concert Tour Repertoire - Gregory Aune, conductor ||||
|---|---|---|---|---|
| "Dans" Ropte Felen | Peterson-Berger, Wilhelm | 20th Century | A cappella | secular |
| A City Called Heaven | Poelinitz, Josephine | 20th Century | A cappella | sacred |
| Anthem | Hemberg, Eskil | 20th Century | A cappella | sacred |
| Ave Maris Stella | Kverno, Trond | 20th Century | A cappella | sacred |
| Ave Verum Corpus | Harris, Mathew | 20th Century | A cappella | sacred |
| Beati Quorum Via | Stanford, Charles | 19th Century | A cappella | sacred |
| Das ist ein Kostliches Ding | Schumann, Georg | 20th Century | A cappella | sacred |
| Die erste Elegie | Rautavaara, Einojuhani | 20th Century | A cappella | sacred |
| Give Me Jesus | Hogan, Moses | 20th Century | A cappella | sacred |
| God Is Gone Up With a Merry Noise | Hutchings, Arthur | 20th Century | A cappella | sacred |
| Hail, Gladdening Light | Wood, Charles | 20th Century | A cappella | sacred |
| How Can I Keep from Singing | Stroope, Z. Randall | 20th Century | A cappella | sacred |
| My Song in the Night | Christiansen, Paul J. | 20th Century | A cappella | sacred |
| Praise to the Lord | Christiansen, F. Melius | 20th Century | A cappella | sacred |
| Pseudo-Yoik | Mantyjarvi, Jaakko | 20th Century | A cappella | secular |
| Ride On King Jesus | Boatner, Edward | 20th Century | A cappella | sacred |
| Stay With Us | Hovland, Egil | 20th Century | A cappella | sacred |
| The Lamb | Tavener, John | 20th Century | A cappella | sacred |
| The Lightener of the Stars | Gawthrop, Daniel | 20th Century | A cappella | sacred |
| Ved Rondane | Grieg, Edvard | 19th Century | A cappella | secular |

| 2003 Concert Tour Repertoire - Gregory Aune, conductor ||||| 
|---|---|---|---|---|
| Absalom | Tomkins, Thomas | Baroque | A cappella | sacred |
| Agnus Dei | Des Pres, Josquin | Renaissance | A cappella | sacred |
| Ascendit Deus | Phillips, Peter | 20th Century | A cappella | sacred |
| Deep River | Barnard, John | 20th Century | A cappella | sacred |
| Herr wenn Ich Nur Dich Habe | Schutz, Heinrich | Baroque | A cappella | sacred |
| Hush: On the Death of a Bush Church | Grandage, Iain | 20th Century | A cappella | secular |
| I Betlehem | Leijon, Jerker | 20th Century | A cappella | sacred |
| In Remembrance | Daley, Eleanor | 20th Century | A cappella | secular |
| Lo, How a Rose e'er Blooming | Sandstrom, Jan | 20th Century | A cappella | sacred |
| Lord of the Dance | Fleming, Larry | 20th Century | A cappella | sacred |
| Past Life Melodies | Hopkins, Sarah | 20th Century | A cappella | secular |
| Praise the Lord | Johnson, Ralph | 20th Century | A cappella | sacred |
| Praise to the Lord | Christiansen, F. Melius | 20th Century | A cappella | sacred |
| Schaffe in mir Gott | Brahms, Johannes | 19th Century | A cappella | sacred |

Appendix A

| 2004 Concert Tour Repertoire - Gregory Aune, conductor ||||||
|---|---|---|---|---|
| Advent Motet | Schreck, Gustav | 19th Century | A cappella | sacred |
| Agneau de Dieu | Lang, Rupert | 20th Century | A cappella | sacred |
| All People Clap Your Hands | Weelkes, Thomas | Renaissance | A cappella | sacred |
| Betelehemu | Olatunji, Michael Babatundi | 20th Century | A cappella | sacred |
| Hymn to St. Cecilia | Britten, Benjamin | 20th Century | A cappella | sacred |
| Kasar Mie la Gaji | Grau, Alberto | 20th Century | A cappella | secular |
| O Day Full of Grace | Christiansen, F. Melius | 20th Century | A cappella | sacred |
| O Vos Omnes | Victoria, Thomas Luis de | Renaissance | A cappella | sacred |
| Praise to the Lord | Christiansen, F. Melius | 20th Century | A cappella | sacred |
| Ride On King Jesus | Boatner, Edward | 20th Century | A cappella | sacred |
| Salvation is Created | Tschesnokoff, Paul | 20th Century | A cappella | sacred |
| The Glory of the Father | Hovland, Egil | 20th Century | A cappella | sacred |
| The Lord is the Everlasting God | Jennings, Kenneth | 20th Century | A cappella | sacred |
| This Little Light of Mine | Hogan, Moses | 20th Century | A cappella | sacred |
| Thou, O Lord | Nystedt, Knut | 20th Century | A cappella | sacred |
| Through the Darkness and Fear | Rissanen, Sade | 20th Century | A cappella | sacred |
| Wana Baraka | Kirchner, Shawn | 20th Century | A cappella | sacred |

| 2005 Concert Tour Repertoire - Gregory Aune, conductor ||||||
|---|---|---|---|---|
| Daniel, Daniel, Servant of the Lord | Moore, Undine Smith | 20th Century | A cappella | sacred |
| Die mit Tranen Saen | Schein, Johann Hermann | Baroque | A cappella | sacred |
| Flower of Joy | Alfven, Hugo | 20th Century | A cappella | secular |
| Flower Songs | Britten, Benjamin | 20th Century | A cappella | secular |
| For God Commanded Angels to Watch Over You | Mendelssohn, Felix | 19th Century | A cappella | sacred |
| Gaudete Omnes | Sweelinck, Jan | Renaissance | A cappella | sacred |
| God Is Gone Up With a Merry Noise | Hutchings, Arthur | 20th Century | A cappella | sacred |
| How Can I Keep from Singing | Stroope, Z. Randall | 20th Century | A cappella | sacred |
| I Will Greatly Rejoice | Nystedt, Knut | 20th Century | A cappella | sacred |
| Lift Up Your Heads, Ye Mighty Gates | Christiansen, Olaf | 20th Century | A cappella | sacred |
| Loch Lomand | Quirk, Jonathan | 20th Century | A cappella | secular |
| Mighty River, Mighty Fire | Raminsh, Imant | 20th Century | A cappella | sacred |
| O Magnum Mysterium | Enns, Jeffery | 20th Century | A cappella | sacred |
| O Sacrum Convivium | Messiaen, Olivier | 20th Century | A cappella | sacred |
| Praise to the Lord | Christiansen, F. Melius | 20th Century | A cappella | sacred |
| Prepare the Way | Jalkeus, Margareta | 20th Century | A cappella | sacred |
| Simeon's Revolution | Jennings, Kenneth | 20th Century | A cappella | sacred |
| The Blue Bird | Stanford, Charles | 20th Century | A cappella | secular |

| 2006 Concert Tour Repertoire - Gregory Aune, conductor ||||||
|---|---|---|---|---|---|
| Agnus Dei | Vasiliauskaito, Kristina | 20th Century | A cappella | sacred |
| Antiphona de Mortz | Slogedal, Barne | 20th Century | A cappella | sacred |
| Ascendit Deus | Gallus, Jacobus | Renaissance | A cappella | sacred |
| Drei geistliche Gesange | Schumann, Georg | 20th Century | A cappella | sacred |
| El Hambo | Mantyjarvi, Jaakko | 20th Century | A cappella | secular |
| Ezekiel Saw de Wheel | Dawson, William | 20th Century | A cappella | sacred |
| Hear My Prayer, O Lord | Purcell, Henry | Baroque | A cappella | sacred |
| Heilig | Mendelssohn, Felix | 19th Century | A cappella | sacred |
| Hodie Christus Natus Est | Willan, Healey | 20th Century | A cappella | sacred |
| I Will Be with You | Paulus, Steven | 20th Century | A cappella | sacred |
| Ich Aber Bin Elend | Brahms, Johannes | 19th Century | A cappella | sacred |
| Lux Aurumque | Whitacre, Eric | 20th Century | A cappella | sacred |
| Magna Est Vis Veritas | Lukas, Zdenek | 20th Century | A cappella | sacred |
| My Song in the Night | Christiansen, Paul J. | 20th Century | A cappella | sacred |
| O Ye People | Casals, Pablo | 20th Century | A cappella | secular |
| Praise to the Lord | Christiansen, F. Melius | 20th Century | A cappella | sacred |
| Sing Ye to the Lord | Bach, J.S. | Baroque | A cappella | sacred |
| The Best of Rooms | Thompson, Randall | 20th Century | A cappella | sacred |
| Vem Kan Segla Forutan Vind? | Rathbone, Jonathan | 20th Century | A cappella | secular |

## 2007 Concert Tour Repertoire - Gregory Aune, conductor

| | | | | |
|---|---|---|---|---|
| Alleluia | Manuel, Ralph | 20th Century | A cappella | sacred |
| Beautiful River | Hawley, William | 20th Century | A cappella | sacred |
| Have Mercy on Us | Copland, Aaron | 20th Century | A cappella | sacred |
| Have Ye Not Known from *Peaceable Kingdom* | Thompson, Randall | 20th Century | A cappella | sacred |
| Homeward Bound | Keen, Marta | 20th Century | A cappella | sacred |
| Hope in God | Cherwien, David | 20th Century | A cappella | sacred |
| I Will be With You | Paulus, Stephen | 20th Century | A cappella | sacred |
| Laudate | Clausen, Rene | 20th Century | A cappella | sacred |
| Laudate Dominum | Rheinberger, Josef | 19th Century | A cappella | sacred |
| O Magnum Mysterium | Lauridsen, Morten | 20th Century | A cappella | sacred |
| O Vos Omnes | Victoria, Thomas Luis de | Renaissance | A cappella | sacred |
| Praise to the Lord | Christiansen, F. Melius | 20th Century | A cappella | sacred |
| Rockin' for the World | Saylor, Bruce | 20th Century | A cappella | sacred |
| Set Down Servant | Shaw, Robert | 20th Century | A cappella | sacred |
| Sing Ye Praises to Our King | Copland, Aaron | 20th Century | A cappella | sacred |
| Vidi Aquam | Christiansen, Paul J. | 20th Century | A cappella | sacred |
| Wake, Awake for Night is Flying | Christiansen, F. Melius | 20th Century | A cappella | sacred |
| Ye Shall have a Song from *Peaceable Kingdom* | Thompson, Randall | 20th Century | A cappella | sacred |

# APPENDIX B

## CONCERT LOCATIONS FOR THE GUSTAVUS CHOIR ON EXTENDED CONCERT TOURS

**1933 Concert Tour**
| | |
|---|---|
| Minneapolis | Minnesota |
| Red Wing | Minnesota |
| Litchfield | Minnesota |
| Duluth | Minnesota |
| Stillwater | Minnesota |
| Scandia | Minnesota |
| St. Paul | Minnesota |

**1934 Concert Tour**
| | |
|---|---|
| St. James | Minnesota |
| Guckeen | Minnesota |
| Worthington | Minnesota |
| Vermillion | South Dakota |
| Sioux City | Iowa |
| Omaha | Nebraska |
| Wahoo | Nebraska |
| Stanton | Iowa |
| Rock Island | Illinois |
| Chicago | Illinois |
| DeKalb | Illinois |
| Rockford | Illinois |
| Madrid | Iowa |
| Gowrie | Iowa |
| Swea City | Iowa |
| Forest City | Iowa |
| Lake City | Minnesota |

## 1935 Concert Tour

| | |
|---|---|
| Stillwater | Minnesota |
| Ashland | Wisconsin |
| Marquette | Michigan |
| Escanaba | Michigan |
| Manistique | Michigan |
| St. Ignace | Michigan |
| Flint | Michigan |
| Detroit | Michigan |
| Ashtabula | Ohio |
| Jamestown | New York |
| Warren | Pennsylvania |
| Kane | Pennsylvania |
| Pittsburgh | Pennsylvania |
| Youngstown | Ohio |
| Elkhart | Indiana |
| LaPorte | Indiana |
| Rockford | Illinois |
| Red Wing | Minnesota |

## 1936 Concert Tour

| | |
|---|---|
| Minneapolis | Minnesota |
| Hopkins | Minnesota |
| Braham | Minnesota |
| Duluth | Minnesota |
| St. Paul | Minnesota |
| Willmar | Minnesota |
| Fargo | North Dakota |
| Wheaton | Minnesota |
| Milbank | South Dakota |
| Ortonville | Minnesota |
| Worthington | Minnesota |
| Mitchell | South Dakota |
| Vermillion | South Dakota |
| Fremont | Nebraska |
| Wahoo | Nebraska |
| Omaha | Nebraska |
| Dayton | Iowa |
| St. James | Minnesota |

## 1937 Concert Tour

| | |
|---|---|
| St. James | Minnesota |
| Dunnell | Minnesota |
| Marathan | Iowa |
| Davenport | Iowa |
| Galva | Illinois |
| Galesburg | Illinois |
| Kane | Pennsylvania |
| Houtzdale | Pennsylvania |
| Staten Island | New York |
| Brooklyn | New York |
| Cambridge | Massachusetts |
| Worchester | Massachusetts |
| Springfield | Massachusetts |
| Schenectady | New York |
| Jamestown | New York |
| Akron | Ohio |
| Chicago | Illinois |
| Rockford | Illinois |
| Wisconsin Rapids | Wisconsin |
| St. Paul | Minnesota |
| Minneapolis | Minnesota |

## 1938 Concert Tour

| | |
|---|---|
| Center City | Minnesota |
| Rush City | Minnesota |
| Cloquet | Minnesota |
| Duluth | Minnesota |
| Superior | Wisconsin |
| Ironwood | Michigan |
| Manistique | Michigan |
| Escanaba | Michigan |
| Kenosha | Wisconsin |
| Evanston | Illinois |
| Chicago | Illinois |
| Rockford | Illinois |
| Rock Island | Illinois |
| Swea City | Iowa |
| Sioux Falls | South Dakota |
| Waseca | Minnesota |
| Minneapolis | Minnesota |

**1939 Concert Tour**

| | |
|---|---|
| Minneapolis | Minnesota |
| Marinette | Wisconsin |
| Madison | Wisconsin |
| Gary | Indiana |
| Chicago | Illinois |
| South Bend | Indiana |
| Altoona | Illinois |
| Des Moines | Iowa |
| St. James | Minnesota |
| Mankato | Minnesota |
| Cokato | Minnesota |
| Willmar | Minnesota |
| Bemidji | Minnesota |
| Warren | Minnesota |
| Fargo | North Dakota |
| Cloquet | Minnesota |

**1940 Concert Tour**

| | |
|---|---|
| Minneapolis | Minnesota |
| Two Harbors | Minnesota |
| Thief River Falls | Minnesota |
| Winthrop | Minnesota |
| Alexandria | Minnesota |
| Litchfield | Minnesota |
| Upsala | Minnesota |
| St. Cloud | Minnesota |

**1941 Concert Tour**

| | |
|---|---|
| Stillwater | Minnesota |
| Rush City | Minnesota |
| Hibbing | Minnesota |
| Superior | Wisconsin |
| Centuria | Wisconsin |
| Milaca | Minnesota |
| Vasa | Minnesota |
| Minneapolis | Minnesota |
| St. Paul | Minnesota |

**1942 Concert Tour**

| | |
|---|---|
| Mitchell | South Dakota |
| Omaha | Nebraska |
| Des Moines | Iowa |
| Rockford | Illinois |
| Chicago | Illinois |
| Madison | Wisconsin |
| Minneapolis | Minnesota |

**1943**
No Concert Tour

**1944**
No Concert Tour

**1945**
No Concert Tour

**1946 Concert Tour**

| | |
|---|---|
| St. Paul | Minnesota |
| Minneapolis | Minnesota |
| Amery | Wisconsin |
| Duluth | Minnesota |
| Superior | Minnesota |
| Brainerd | Minnesota |
| Willmar | Minnesota |
| Mankato | Minnesota |
| Red Wing | Minnesota |
| Wheaton | Minnesota |
| Virginia | Minnesota |
| Worthington | Minnesota |
| Sioux Falls | South Dakota |

**1947 Concert Tour**

| | |
|---|---|
| Chisago City | Minnesota |
| Stillwater | Minnesota |
| St. Paul | Minnesota |
| Cambridge | Minnesota |
| Cloquet | Minnesota |
| Superior | Minnesota |
| Duluth | Minnesota |

Coleraine            Minnesota
Mora                 Minnesota
Willmar              Minnesota
Cokato               Minnesota

**1948 Concert Tour**
Mason City           Iowa
Rockford             Illinois
Batavia              Illinois
Chicago              Illinois
Columbus             Ohio
Braddock             Pennsylvania
Hagerstown           Maryland
Washington           District of Columbia
Moline               Illinois
Boxholm              Iowa

**1949 Concert Tour**
Willmar              Minnesota
Benson               Minnesota
Clinton              Minnesota
Eveieth              Minnesota
Duluth               Minnesota
Chisago              Minnesota
White Bear Lake      Minnesota
Minneapolis          Minnesota
Estherville          Minnesota
Dayton               Iowa
Swea City            Iowa

**1950 Concert Tour**
White Bear Lake      Minnesota
Braham               Minnesota
Ironwood             Michigan
Cloquet              Minnesota
Grand Rapids         Minnesota
Brainerd             Minnesota
Cokato               Minnesota
St. Cloud            Minnesota
St. Paul             Minnesota

**1951 Concert Tour**
| | |
|---|---|
| Clinton | Minnesota |
| Thief River Falls | Minnesota |
| Fergus Falls | Minnesota |
| Hallock | Minnesota |
| Hoffman | Minnesota |
| Parkers Prairie | Minnesota |
| Alexandria | Minnesota |
| Litchfield | Minnesota |
| Montevideo | Minnesota |
| Dawson | Minnesota |
| Fairmont | Minnesota |

**1952 Concert Tour**
| | |
|---|---|
| Worthington | Minnesota |
| Akron | Iowa |
| Wahoo | Nebraska |
| Omaha | Nebraska |
| Oakland | Nebraska |
| Hepburn | Iowa |
| Des Moines | Iowa |
| Kewanee | Illinois |
| Swedesburg | Iowa |
| Cedar Rapids | Iowa |
| Iowa City | Iowa |
| St. James | Minnesota |

**1953 January Concert Tour**
| | |
|---|---|
| Valley Springs | South Dakota |
| Wausa | Nebraska |
| Oakland | Nebraska |
| Lincoln | Nebraska |
| Leavenworth | Kansas |
| Topeka | Kansas |
| Salina | Kansas |
| Wichita | Kansas |
| Kansas City | Missouri |
| Nebraska City | Nebraska |
| Hull | Iowa |
| Winnebago | Minnesota |

## Appendix B

**1953 Spring Concert Tour**
| | |
|---|---|
| Hector | Minnesota |
| Willmar | Minnesota |
| Benson | Minnesota |
| Eagle Bend | Minnesota |
| Hallock | Minnesota |
| Thief River Falls | Minnesota |
| Winnipeg | Canada |
| Kenora | Canada |
| Duluth | Minnesota |

**1954 Concert Tour**
| | |
|---|---|
| Scandia Grove | Minnesota |
| Iowa City | Iowa |
| Chicago | Illinois |
| Elgin | Illinois |
| Wenona | Illinois |
| Vandalia | Illinois |
| Columbus | Ohio |
| Dayton | Ohio |
| Fort Wayne | Indiana |
| Detroit | Michigan |
| Elkhart | Indiana |
| Rock Island | Illinois |
| Red Wing | Minnesota |
| Minneapolis | Minnesota |

**1955 Concert Tour**
| | |
|---|---|
| New Prague | Minnesota |
| Norseland | Minnesota |
| Ashland | Wisconsin |
| Cumberland | Wisconsin |
| Rhinelander | Wisconsin |
| Moose Lake | Minnesota |
| Duluth | Minnesota |
| Cambridge | Minnesota |
| Milaca | Minnesota |
| Brainerd | Minnesota |
| Clinton | Minnesota |
| Center City | Minnesota |
| Cokato | Minnesota |

| | |
|---|---|
| Willmar | Minnesota |
| Cannon Falls | Minnesota |
| Mankato | Minnesota |
| Waseca | Minnesota |
| Minneapolis | Minnesota |
| St. Paul | Minnesota |

**1956 Concert Tour**

| | |
|---|---|
| St. James | Minnesota |
| Winthrop | Minnesota |
| Eagle Bend | Minnesota |
| Kintrye | North Dakota |
| Bismarck | North Dakota |
| Williston | North Dakota |
| Sheridan | Wyoming |
| Cheyenne | Wyoming |
| Denver | Colorado |
| Boulder | Colorado |
| Loveland | Colorado |
| Longmont | Colorado |
| St. Francis | Kansas |
| Stromsburg | Nebraska |
| Omaha | Nebraska |
| Gowrie | Iowa |
| Mankato | Minnesota |
| Minneapolis (2) | Minnesota |

**1957 Concert Tour**

| | |
|---|---|
| Stillwater | Minnesota |
| Cannon Falls | Minnesota |
| New Richland | Minnesota |
| Eau Claire | Wisconsin |
| Wisconsin Rapids | Wisconsin |
| Chicago | Illinois |
| Grand Rapids | Michigan |
| Flint | Michigan |
| Springfield | Ohio |
| Jamestown | New York |
| New York | New York |
| Washington | District of Columbia |
| McKeesport | Pennsylvania |

| | |
|---|---|
| Chesterton | Indiana |
| Cedar Rapids | Iowa |
| Des Moines | Iowa |
| Comfrey | Minnesota |
| Sleepy Eye | Minnesota |
| LeSeuer | Minnesota |
| Minneapolis | Minnesota |
| St. Paul | Minnesota |
| Clinton | Minnesota |
| Clarkfield | Minnesota |
| Swea City | Iowa |
| Albert Lea | Minnesota |

**1958 Concert Tour**

| | |
|---|---|
| Hector | Minnesota |
| Lafayette | Minnesota |
| Robbinsdale | Minnesota |
| Rhinelander | Wisconsin |
| Ironwood | Michigan |
| Ishpeming | Michigan |
| Superior | Wisconsin |
| Duluth | Minnesota |
| Braham | Minnesota |
| Fergus Falls | Minnesota |
| Brainerd | Minnesota |
| Bemidji | Minnesota |
| International Falls | Minnesota |
| Kenora | Canada |
| Winnipeg | Canada |
| Grand Forks | North Dakota |
| Fargo | North Dakota |
| Willmar | Minnesota |
| Hopkins | Minnesota |
| Minneapolis | Minnesota |
| White Bear Lake | Minnesota |
| St. Paul | Minnesota |
| Mankato | Minnesota |

## 1959 Concert Tour

| | |
|---|---|
| Norseland | Minnesota |
| Gibbon | Minnesota |
| Winthrop | Minnesota |
| Albert City | Iowa |
| Wahoo | Nebraska |
| Lindsborg | Kansas |
| Fort Still | Oklahoma |
| Fredericksburg | Texas |
| Seguin | Texas |
| El Campo | Texas |
| Fort Arthur | Texas |
| Fort Worth | Texas |
| Topeka | Kansas |
| Stanton | Iowa |
| Burlington | Iowa |
| Oakland | Nebraska |
| Worthington | Minnesota |
| Minneapolis | Minnesota |
| Forest Lake | Minnesota |
| St. Paul (2) | Minnesota |
| Hastings | Minnesota |

## 1960 Concert Tour

| | |
|---|---|
| LeSueur | Minnesota |
| Cokato | Minnesota |
| Montevideo | Minnesota |
| Olivia | Minnesota |
| Elbow Lake | Minnesota |
| Bismarck | North Dakota |
| Kenmare | North Dakota |
| Spokane | Washington |
| Tacoma | Washington |
| Parkland | Washington |
| Seattle | Washington |
| Astoria | Oregon |
| Portland | Oregon |
| LaGrande | Oregon |
| Boise | Idaho |
| Cheyenne | Wyoming |
| Axtell | Nebraska |

Sioux City          Iowa
Minneapolis (2)     Minnesota
Cambridge           Minnesota
St. Paul            Minnesota
Algona              Iowa
Swea City           Iowa

**1961 Concert Tour**
Lafayette           Minnesota
St. James           Minnesota
Mankato             Minnesota
Clinton             Minnesota
Minot               North Dakota
Saskatoon           Canada
Edmonton            Canada
Calgary             Canada
Regina              Canada
Winnipeg            Canada
Kenora              Canada
Port Arthur         Canada
Two Harbors         Minnesota
Hibbing             Minnesota
Cloquet             Minnesota
Brainerd            Minnesota
Minneapolis (2)     Minnesota
St. Paul            Minnesota
Cannon Falls        Minnesota
Sherburn            Minnesota

**1962 Concert Tour**
Mankato             Minnesota
Winthrop            Minnesota
LeSueur             Minnesota
Hudson              Wisconsin
Eau Claire          Wisconsin
Milwaukee           Wisconsin
Chicago             Illinois
East Lansing        Michigan
Twinsburg           Ohio
Hagerstown          Maryland
Washington          District of Columbia

| | |
|---|---|
| New York | New York |
| Jamestown | New York |
| Flint | Michigan |
| Grand Rapids | Michigan |
| Rockford | Illinois |
| Minneapolis | Minnesota |
| Hastings | Minnesota |
| St. Paul | Minnesota |

**1963 Concert Tour**

| | |
|---|---|
| Clarkfield | Minnesota |
| Olivia | Minnesota |
| Mankato | Minnesota |
| Omaha | Nebraska |
| Sidney | Nebraska |
| Denver | Colorado |
| Ogden | Utah |
| Boise | Idaho |
| Yakima | Washington |
| Portland | Oregon |
| Olympia | Washington |
| Spokane | Washington |
| Missoula | Montana |
| Billings | Montana |
| Bismarck | North Dakota |
| Alexandria | Minnesota |
| Cambridge | Minnesota |
| St. Paul | Minnesota |
| Minneapolis | Minnesota |
| Robbinsdale | Minnesota |

**1964 Concert Tour**

| | |
|---|---|
| Balsam Lake | Minnesota |
| Stillwater | Minnesota |
| Hastings | Minnesota |
| Litchfield | Minnesota |
| Willmar | Minnesota |
| Fargo | North Dakota |
| Minot | North Dakota |
| Regina | Canada |
| Winnipeg | Canada |

| | |
|---|---|
| Dryden | Canada |
| Port Arthur | Canada |
| Duluth | Minnesota |
| Cloquet | Minnesota |
| Hibbing | Minnesota |
| International Falls | Minnesota |
| Fergus Falls | Minnesota |
| St. Paul | Minnesota |
| Minneapolis (2) | Minnesota |
| Little Falls | Minnesota |
| Princeton | Minnesota |

**1965 Concert Tour**

| | |
|---|---|
| Mankato | Minnesota |
| Olivia | Minnesota |
| Minneota | Minnesota |
| Lafayette | Minnesota |
| Eau Claire | Wisconsin |
| Wauwatosa | Wisconsin |
| Pontiac | Michigan |
| Pittsburgh | Pennsylvania |
| Cumberland | Maryland |
| Washington | District of Columbia |
| New York | New York |
| Bay Village | Ohio |
| Chicago | Illinois |
| Minneapolis | Minnesota |
| St. Paul | Minnesota |
| Aitkin | Minnesota |
| Robbinsdale | Minnesota |

**1966 Concert Tour**

| | |
|---|---|
| Hector | Minnesota |
| Litchfield | Minnesota |
| Hutchinson | Minnesota |
| Austin | Minnesota |
| Mankato | Minnesota |
| Albert Lea | Minnesota |
| Fremont | Nebraska |
| Omaha | Nebraska |
| Stromsburg | Nebraska |

Englewood         Colorado
Denver            Colorado
Rapid City        South Dakota
Mitchell          South Dakota
Sioux Falls       South Dakota
LeSueur           Minnesota
St. Paul          Minnesota
Minneapolis       Minnesota

**1967 Spring Concert Tour**
Lafayette         Minnesota
Mountain Lake     Minnesota
St. James         Minnesota
Glencoe           Minnesota
Red Wing          Minnesota
Escanaba          Michigan
Ishpeming         Michigan
Houghton          Michigan
Two Harbors       Minnesota
Evelyth           Minnesota
Brainerd          Minnesota
Hallock           Minnesota
Fargo             North Dakota
Aitkin            Minnesota
Braham            Minnesota
Parkers Prairie   Minnesota
Minneapolis (2)   Minnesota
Mankato           Minnesota
Buffalo           Minnesota
St. Paul          Minnesota
Hopkins           Minnesota
Mound             Minnesota

**1967 Summer Concert Tour**
Stockholm (3)     Sweden
Uppsala           Sweden
Lund              Sweden
Gothenberg        Sweden
Halsingborg       Sweden
Oslo              Norway
Copenhagen        Denmark

## 1968 Concert Tour
| | |
|---|---|
| Amboy | Minnesota |
| New Prague | Minnesota |
| Minneapolis (2) | Minnesota |
| Spencer | Iowa |
| Parkville | Missouri |
| Lindsborg | Kansas |
| Midwest City | Oklahoma |
| Austin | Texas |
| Florcsville | Texas |
| Fredericksburg | Texas |
| Hurst | Texas |
| Lawrence | Kansas |
| Wakefield | Nebraska |

## 1969 Concert Tour
| | |
|---|---|
| Winthrop | Minnesota |
| St. Paul (2) | Minnesota |
| Deephaven | Minnesota |
| Brainerd | Minnesota |
| Willmar | Minnesota |
| Litchfield | Minnesota |
| Eau Claire | Wisconsin |
| Milwaukee | Wisconsin |
| Cleveland | Ohio |
| Springfield | Virginia |
| Washington | District of Columbia |
| New York | New York |
| Twinsburg | Ohio |
| Adrian | Michigan |
| Chicago | Illinois |
| Rockford | Illinois |
| Rochester | Minnesota |

## 1970 Concert Tour
| | |
|---|---|
| Long Lake | Minnesota |
| Renville | Minnesota |
| Arlington | Minnesota |
| Waterville | Minnesota |
| Mankato | Minnesota |
| St. Cloud | Minnesota |
| Grand Forks | Minnesota |

| | |
|---|---|
| Kenmare | North Dakota |
| Assiniboia | Canada |
| Saskatoon | Canada |
| Edmonton | Canada |
| Calgary | Canada |
| Esterhazy | Canada |
| Winnipeg | Canada |
| Thief River Falls | Minnesota |
| Detroit Lakes | Minnesota |
| Minneapolis | Minnesota |

**1971 Concert Tour**

| | |
|---|---|
| Maple Plain | Minnesota |
| Lakeville | Minnesota |
| Richfield | Minnesota |
| Stillwater (2) | Minnesota |
| Alta | Iowa |
| Omaha | Nebraska |
| York | Nebraska |
| Grand Island | Nebraska |
| Longmont | Colorado |
| Colorado Springs | Colorado |
| Denver | Colorado |
| Cheyenne | Wyoming |
| Sheridan | Wyoming |
| Mitchell | South Dakota |
| Sioux Falls | South Dakota |
| St. Paul | Minnesota |
| Minneapolis | Minnesota |

**1972 Concert Tour**

| | |
|---|---|
| Butterfield | Minnesota |
| Mankato | Minnesota |
| Monticello | Minnesota |
| Fergus Falls | Minnesota |
| Benson | Minnesota |
| New Prague | Minnesota |
| Los Altos | California |
| Oakland | California |
| San Francisco | California |
| Fort Ord | California |

| | |
|---|---|
| Garden Grove | California |
| Buena Park | California |
| Barber's Point | California |
| Honolulu | Hawaii |
| Kaneoche Bay | Hawaii |
| Kailua | Hawaii |
| St. Paul | Minnesota |
| New Brighton | Minnesota |

**1973 Concert Tour**

| | |
|---|---|
| Winthrop | Minnesota |
| Mankato | Minnesota |
| Worthington | Minnesota |
| Walnut Grove | Minnesota |
| Springfield | Minnesota |
| Cambridge | Minnesota |
| Duluth | Minnesota |
| Ironwood | Michigan |
| Marquette | Michigan |
| Sault Ste. Marie | Michigan |
| Pembroke | Canada |
| Peterborough | Canada |
| Detroit | Michigan |
| Traverse City | Michigan |
| Iron Mountain | Michigan |
| Hayward | Wisconsin |
| St. Paul | Minnesota |

**1974 Concert Tour**

| | |
|---|---|
| North Minneapolis | Minnesota |
| Parkers Prairie | Minnesota |
| Elbow Lake | Minnesota |
| Winthrop | Minnesota |
| Eau Claire | Wisconsin |
| Rockford | Illinois |
| Columbus | Ohio |
| Hagerstown | Maryland |
| Washington | District of Columbia |
| Pleasantville | New York |
| Waynesburg | Pennsylvania |
| Goshen | Indiana |

| | |
|---|---|
| Chicago | Illinois |
| Oelwein | Iowa |
| Red Wing | Minnesota |
| Minneapolis | Minnesota |

**1975 Concert Tour**

| | |
|---|---|
| Clinton | Minnesota |
| Willmar | Minnesota |
| Lafayette | Minnesota |
| St. James | Minnesota |
| Mankato | Minnesota |
| Deerfield | Florida |
| Ft. Myers | Florida |
| Clearwater | Florida |
| Tampa | Florida |
| Ocala | Florida |
| St. Petersburg | Florida |
| Spring Hill | Florida |
| Port Richey | Florida |
| Winter Park | Florida |
| Minneapolis | Minnesota |

**1976 Concert Tour**

| | |
|---|---|
| Long Lake | Minnesota |
| Cannon Falls | Minnesota |
| Mankato | Minnesota |
| St. Paul | Minnesota |
| Minneapolis | Minnesota |
| Baraboo | Wisconsin |
| Madison | Wisconsin |
| Oregon | Illinois |
| Galesburg | Illinois |
| St. Louis | Missouri |
| Iowa City | Iowa |
| Des Moines | Iowa |
| Frost | Minnesota |

**1977 Concert Tour**

| | |
|---|---|
| Cokato | Minnesota |
| Winthrop | Minnesota |
| Mankato | Minnesota |
| St. Cloud | Minnesota |

| | |
|---|---|
| Moose Lake | Minnesota |
| Center City | Minnesota |
| Waukesha | Wisconsin |
| Shelby | Ohio |
| Washington | Pennsylvania |
| Pottstown | Pennsylvania |
| Lock Haven | Pennsylvania |
| Lansing | Michigan |
| Chicago | Illinois |
| Rochester | Minnesota |
| Minneapolis | Minnesota |

**1978 Concert Tour**

| | |
|---|---|
| Mankato | Minnesota |
| Willmar | Minnesota |
| Duluth | Minnesota |
| Thunder Bay | Canada |
| International Falls | Minnesota |
| Kenora | Canada |
| Winnipeg | Canada |
| Fergus Falls | Minnesota |
| Minneapolis | Minnesota |

**1979 Concert Tour**

| | |
|---|---|
| Des Moines | Iowa |
| Fremont | Nebraska |
| McPherson | Kansas |
| Stillwater | Oklahoma |
| Austin | Texas |
| San Antonio | Texas |
| Houston | Texas |
| Plano | Texas |

**1980 Concert Tour**

| | |
|---|---|
| Mankato | Minnesota |
| Buffalo | Minnesota |
| Hastings | Minnesota |
| Richfield | Minnesota |
| St. Paul | Minnesota |
| Redondo Beach | California |
| Los Angeles | California |
| Buena Park | California |

| | |
|---|---|
| Laguna Beach | California |
| Thousand Oaks | California |
| Minneapolis | Minnesota |
| Eagan | Minnesota |

**1981 Concert Tour**

| | |
|---|---|
| Fairbault | Minnesota |
| Farmington | Minnesota |
| Glenwood | Minnesota |
| Grove City | Minnesota |
| Des Plaines | Illinois |
| St. Joseph | Michigan |
| Grand Rapids | Michigan |
| Alpena | Michigan |
| Escanaba | Michigan |
| Sheboygan | Wisconsin |
| Neenah | Wisconsin |
| Taylors Falls | Wisconsin |
| Stillwater | Minnesota |

**1982 Concert Tour**

| | |
|---|---|
| Cannon Falls | Minnesota |
| Owatonna | Minnesota |
| Sioux Falls | South Dakota |
| Holdredge | Nebraska |
| Denver | Colorado |
| Longmont | Colorado |
| Colorado Springs | Colorado |
| Pueblo | Colorado |
| Durango | Colorado |
| Fort Collins | Colorado |
| Ralston | Nebraska |
| Mankato | Minnesota |

**1983 International Concert Tour**

| | |
|---|---|
| Oslo | Norway |
| Karlstad | Sweden |
| Borlange | Sweden |
| Uppsala | Sweden |
| Malmo | Sweden |
| Berlin | West Germany |

Leipzig              East Germany
Erfurt               East Germany
Copenhagen           Denmark

**1983 Domestic Concert Tour**
Virginia             Minnesota
Duluth               Minnesota
Brainerd             Minnesota
St. Cloud (2)        Minnesota
Pine City            Minnesota
Minneapolis (2)      Minnesota

**1984 Concert Tour**
Moorhead             Minnesota
Fargo                North Dakota
Cambridge            Minnesota
St. James            Minnesota
Litchfield           Minnesota
Golden Valley        Minnesota
Minneapolis          Minnesota
Wilmette             Illinois
Valparaiso           Indiana
Cleveland Heights    Ohio
Springfield          Virginia
Steubenville         Ohio
Livonia              Michigan
Prospect Heights     Illinois
Rockford (2)         Illinois

**1985 Concert Tour**
Willmar              Minnesota
Charles City         Iowa
Mason City           Iowa
Worthington          Minnesota
Sioux Falls          South Dakota
Rochester            Minnesota
Clinton              Iowa
Davenport            Iowa
Menomonee Falls      Wisconsin
St. Charles          Illinois
Valparaiso           Indiana

| | |
|---|---|
| Manitowoc | Wisconsin |
| Appleton (2) | Wisconsin |
| Eau Claire | Wisconsin |
| Center City | Minnesota |
| Minneapolis (2) | Minnesota |
| St. Paul | Minnesota |

**1986 Concert Tour**

| | |
|---|---|
| Albert Lea | Minnesota |
| Eden Prairie | Minnesota |
| Lakeville | Minnesota |
| Stillwater | Minnesota |
| Forest Lake | Minnesota |
| New Brighton | Minnesota |
| Boca Raton | Florida |
| Deerfield Beach | Florida |
| Boynton Beach | Florida |
| Brandon | Florida |
| Lake Buena Vista | Florida |
| Winter Park | Florida |
| Savannah | Georgia |
| Atlanta | Georgia |
| Hickory | North Carolina |
| West Lafayette | Indiana |
| Madison | Wisconsin |
| Edina | Minnesota |
| Burnsville | Minnesota |
| St. Paul | Minnesota |
| Minneapolis | Minnesota |

**1987 Concert Tour**

| | |
|---|---|
| Apple Valley | Minnesota |
| Bloomington | Minnesota |
| St. Paul | Minnesota |
| Moscow | Russia |
| Tallin | Estonia |
| Leningrad | Russia |
| Czestochowa | Poland |
| Krakow | Poland |
| Wroclaw | Poland |
| Olawa | Poland |

Appendix B

| | |
|---|---|
| Prague | Czechoslovakia |
| Stockholm | Sweden |
| Warsaw | Poland |
| Golden Valley | Minnesota |
| Minneapolis (2) | Minnesota |
| Fairbault | Minnesota |

**1988 Concert Tour**

| | |
|---|---|
| Red Wing | Minnesota |
| Austin | Minnesota |
| Owatonna | Minnesota |
| Willmar | Minnesota |
| Mountain Lake | Minnesota |
| St. Cloud (2) | Minnesota |
| Minnetonka | Minnesota |
| Mankato | Minnesota |
| Northwood | Iowa |
| LeMars | Iowa |
| Prairie Village | Kansas |
| Lindsborg (2) | Kansas |
| Lincoln (2) | Nebraska |
| Blair | Nebraska |
| Iowa City | Iowa |
| Dubuque | Iowa |
| Minneapolis | Minnesota |
| Bloomington | Minnesota |

**1989 Concert Tour**

| | |
|---|---|
| Hudson | Wisconsin |
| Bloomington | Minnesota |
| Jackson | Minnesota |
| Seattle | Washington |
| Vancouver | Canada |
| Portland | Oregon |
| Walnut Creek | California |
| Redwood City | California |
| Monterey | California |
| Visalia | California |
| Thousand Oaks | California |
| Northridge | California |
| Riverside | California |
| Paradise Valley | Arizona |

| | |
|---|---|
| Flagstaff | Arizona |
| Albuquerque | New Mexico |
| Colorado Springs | Colorado |
| Denver | Colorado |
| Rapid City | South Dakota |
| Sioux Falls | South Dakota |
| St. Paul | Minnesota |

**1990 Concert Tour**

| | |
|---|---|
| Hastings | Minnesota |
| Fergus Falls | Minnesota |
| Detroit Lakes | Minnesota |
| Marshall | Minnesota |
| St. Cloud | Minnesota |
| St. Paul | Minnesota |
| Mankato | Minnesota |
| Davenport | Iowa |
| Galesburg | Illinois |
| Champaign | Illinois |
| Chicago (2) | Illinois |
| Wausau | Wisconsin |
| Appleton (2) | Wisconsin |
| Milwaukee | Wisconsin |
| St. Louis Park | Minnesota |

**1991 Spring Break Concert Tour**

| | |
|---|---|
| Burnsville (2) | Minnesota |
| Edina | Minnesota |
| Long Lake | Minnesota |
| Eau Claire | Wisconsin |
| River Falls | Wisconsin |

**1991 Summer International Concert Tour**

| | |
|---|---|
| Minneapolis | Minnesota |
| Beijing | China |
| Nanjing | China |
| Wuxi | China |
| Shanghai | China |
| Hong Kong | China |
| Hirakata City | Japan |
| Kyoto | Japan |

Kumamoto　　　　　　Japan
Hiroshima　　　　　　Japan
Honolulu　　　　　　 Hawaii

**1992 Concert Tour**
Cedar Rapids　　　　 Iowa
Duluth　　　　　　　 Minnesota
Rochester　　　　　　Minnesota
St. Joseph　　　　　　Missouri
Tulsa　　　　　　　　Oklahoma
Dallas　　　　　　　　Texas
San Antonio　　　　　Texas
Sequin　　　　　　　 Texas
Houston　　　　　　　Texas
Hutchinson　　　　　 Kansas
Nevada　　　　　　　Iowa
Mahtomedi　　　　　 Minnesota
Minneapolis (2)　　　  Minnesota

**1993 Concert Tour**
Minneapolis (3)　　　  Minnesota
Grand Rapids　　　　 Minnesota
Benson　　　　　　　 Minnesota
New Ulm　　　　　　 Minnesota
Glenwood　　　　　　Minnesota
St. James　　　　　　 Minnesota
Grand Forks　　　　　North Dakota
Bismarck　　　　　　 North Dakota
Billings　　　　　　　Montana
Missoula　　　　　　 Montana
Great Falls　　　　　　Montana
Rapid City　　　　　　South Dakota
Sioux Falls　　　　　　South Dakota
Golden Valley　　　　 Minnesota

**1994 Concert Tour**
Plymouth　　　　　　 Minnesota
Oregon　　　　　　　 Wisconsin
Madison　　　　　　　Wisconsin
River Forest　　　　　 Illinois
Sylvania　　　　　　　Ohio

| | |
|---|---|
| Columbus (2) | Ohio |
| Pittsburgh | Pennsylvania |
| Pittsfield | Massachusetts |
| Cambridge | Massachusetts |
| Manhattan | New York |
| New York | New York |
| East Orange | New Jersey |
| Cherry Hill | New Jersey |
| Fredericksburg | Virginia |
| Washington (2) | District of Columbia |
| Gettysburg | Pennsylvania |
| Richmond | Virginia |
| Apple Valley | Minnesota |
| Bloomington | Minnesota |
| Rush City | Minnesota |

**1995 Concert Tour**

| | |
|---|---|
| Minneapolis | Minnesota |
| Warsaw | Poland |
| Gdansk | Poland |
| Leipzig | Germany |
| Berlin | Germany |
| Soderakra (2) | Sweden |
| Vakjo | Sweden |
| Uppsala | Sweden |
| Stockholm (2) | Sweden |
| Helsinki | Finland |

**1996 Concert Tour**

| | |
|---|---|
| Grand Rapids | Minnesota |
| Eagan | Minnesota |
| Omaha | Nebraska |
| Des Moines | Iowa |
| Cedar Rapids | Iowa |
| Mt. Pleasant | Iowa |
| Wausau | Wisconsin |
| Appleton (2) | Wisconsin |
| Eau Claire (2) | Wisconsin |
| West St. Paul | Minnesota |

## Appendix B

**1997 Concert Tour**

| | |
|---|---|
| Plymouth | Minnesota |
| Richfield | Minnesota |
| Owatonna | Minnesota |
| Naperville | Illinois |
| Nashville | Tennessee |
| Atlanta | Georgia |
| Clearwater | Florida |
| Vero Beach | Florida |
| Hollywood | Florida |
| Naples | Florida |
| Sarasota | Florida |
| Bloomington | Minnesota |

**1998 Concert Tour**

| | |
|---|---|
| Norwood | Minnesota |
| Coon Rapids | Minnesota |
| Cambridge | Minnesota |
| Duluth (2) | Minnesota |
| Virginia | Minnesota |
| Hibbing | Minnesota |
| Moorhead | Minnesota |
| Alexandria | Minnesota |
| Fergus Falls | Minnesota |
| Marshall | Minnesota |
| Mitchell | South Dakota |
| Red Wing (2) | Minnesota |
| Apple Valley | Minnesota |
| Minneapolis | Minnesota |

**1999 Concert Tour**

| | |
|---|---|
| Plymouth | Minnesota |
| Soweta | South Africa |
| Pretoria | South Africa |
| Pietersburg | South Africa |
| Kruger National Park | South Africa |
| Mapulumo | South Africa |
| Clermont | South Africa |
| Port Elizabeth (3) | South Africa |
| Cape Town (3) | South Africa |

**2000 Concert Tour**
| | |
|---|---|
| Jackson | Minnesota |
| Topeka | Kansas |
| Overland Park | Kansas |
| Tulsa | Oklahoma |
| Austin | Texas |
| Seguin | Texas |
| Dallas | Texas |
| Lindsborg | Kansas |
| Cedar Rapids | Iowa |
| Decorah | Iowa |
| Wayzata | Minnesota |

**2001 Concert Tour**
| | |
|---|---|
| Duluth | Minnesota |
| Port Angeles | Washington |
| Issaquah | Washington |
| Seattle | Washington |
| Beaverton | Oregon |
| Sacramento | California |
| Cupertino | California |
| Carmel | California |
| Visalia | California |
| Solana Beach | California |
| North Hollywood | California |
| Riverside | California |
| Peoria | Arizona |
| Phoenix | Arizona |
| Albuquerque | New Mexico |
| Santa Fe | New Mexico |
| Highlands Ranch | Colorado |
| Wheat Ridge | Colorado |
| Rapid City | South Dakota |
| Sioux Falls | South Dakota |
| Apple Valley | Minnesota |

**2002 Concert Tour**
| | |
|---|---|
| Edina | Minnesota |
| Naperville | Illinois |
| Loves Park | Illinois |
| Wauwatosa | Wisconsin |
| Lincolnwood | Illinois |

| | |
|---|---|
| Moline | Illinois |
| La Crosse | Wisconsin |
| Madison | Wisconsin |
| West St. Paul | Minnesota |
| Des Moines | Iowa |

**2003 Concert Tour**

| | |
|---|---|
| Rome (3) | Italy |
| Sorrento | Italy |
| Assisi (2) | Italy |
| Florence (2) | Italy |
| Venice (2) | Italy |
| Minneapolis | Minnesota |

**2004 Concert Tour**

| | |
|---|---|
| St. Paul | Minnesota |
| East Grand Forks | Minnesota |
| Hillsboro | North Dakota |
| Bismarck | North Dakota |
| Colorado Springs | Colorado |
| Englewood | Colorado |
| Kearney | Nebraska |
| Lincoln | Nebraska |
| Fremont | Nebraska |

**2005 Concert Tour**

| | |
|---|---|
| Cambridge | Minnesota |
| Bloomington | Minnesota |
| Ann Arbor | Michigan |
| Jamestown | New York |
| Cambridge | Massachusetts |
| New York | New York |
| Washington (2) | District of Columbia |
| Richmond | Virginia |
| Charleston | South Carolina |
| Peachtree City | Georgia |
| St. Petersburg | Florida |
| Vero Beach | Florida |
| Marco Island | Florida |

**2006 Concert Tour**

| | |
|---|---|
| West St. Paul | Minnesota |
| Grand Rapids (2) | Minnesota |
| Duluth (2) | Minnesota |
| Bemidji (2) | Minnesota |
| Morris | Minnesota |
| Montevideo | Minnesota |
| Apple Valley | Minnesota |
| Marshfield (2) | Wisconsin |
| Brainerd | Minnesota |
| Winona (2) | Minnesota |
| Red Wing | Minnesota |

**2007 Concert Tour**

| | |
|---|---|
| Lisbon (2) | Portugal |
| Seville | Spain |
| Malaga (2) | Spain |
| Granada | Spain |
| Madrid (2) | Spain |

# APPENDIX C

# CHRISTMAS IN CHRIST CHAPEL THEMES

| Year | Theme |
|---|---|
| 1973 | Advent / Christmas Choral Vespers |
| 1974 | Lessons and Music in the Celebration of the Incarnation of Our Lord |
| 1975 | Christmas in Christ Chapel |
| 1976 | Christmas in Christ Chapel |
| 1977 | Christmas in Christ Chapel |
| 1978 | Gloria |
| 1979 | Hail the Day |
| 1980 | Advent / Christmas Choral Vespers |
| 1981 | The Nativity Angels |
| 1982 | Choral Vespers - "A Service of Light" |
| 1983 | "Unto Us… A Child" |
| 1984 | Soli Deo Gloria |
| 1985 | Service of Lessons and Carols |
| 1986 | Russian Service of Great Vespers |
| 1987 | Celebrating the Old and New Worlds from Which We Have Come |
| 1988 | The Primordial Light, that Enlightens Everyone, was Coming Into the World |
| 1989 | ChristMass For The Animals |
| 1990 | A Rose in Winter: The Life of Mary |
| 1991 | Of the Father's Love Begotten |
| 1992 | Christmas in Christ Chapel |
| 1993 | A German Christmas: A Celebration of the Nativity of our Lord with a Salute to Old and New Leipzig |
| 1994 | Old and New Spain: Prepare for an Age of Abundance |
| 1995 | The Tree of Life |
| 1996 | Child of Light |
| 1997 | Portals of Prophesy and Promise |
| 1998 | The Holy Family |
| 1999 | Even So, Come, Lord Jesus: Scenes From The Revelation |
| 2000 | Heaven and Nature Sing |

| | |
|---|---|
| 2001 | A Celtic Pilgrimage |
| 2002 | Julbon Christmas Prayer |
| 2003 | Some Children See Him |
| 2004 | Seasons of Promise |
| 2005 | Ageless Visions of a Timeless Moment |
| 2006 | An American Odyssey |

# BIBLIOGRAPHY

"'56 Choir Purchases New Robes," in *The Gustavian*, 75. St. Peter, MN: Gustavus Adolphus College, 1956.

"60 Voice Gustavus Choir Prepares for NW Journey." *The Gustavian Weekly*, 11 March 1947.

"500 Applaud A Capella Choir in Homecoming Concert Sunday." *The Gustavian Weekly*, 8 May 1934, 1.

"800 Guest Singers Coming to Gustavus May Festival." *The Gustavian Weekly*, 23 April 1947, 1.

"1989 Gustavus Choir and Gustavus Band Tours are Westward Bound." *Greater Gustavus Quarterly 45*, no. 3 (1988): 12.

"A Cappella Appears on Chapel Program." *The Gustavian Weekly*, 24 March 1931, 1.

"A Capella Choir is Organized at Meet." *The Gustavian Weekly*, 13 January 1931, 1.

"A Capella Choir, Symphonic Band, Music Faculty Give Annual Concert." *The Gustavian Weekly*, 19 December 1945, 1 & 3.

"A Capella Choir to Begin Concert Tour Sunday Afternoon." *The Gustavian Weekly*, 28 March 1933, 1.

"A Capella Chorus Presents Concert Saturday Evening." *The Gustavian Weekly*, 6 June 1933, 1.

"A Capella Concert Given at Minnesota Conference Meeting." *The Gustavian Weekly*, 21 March 1933, 1.

"A Capella Tryouts are Completed Today." *The Gustavian Weekly*, 12 October 1926, 1 & 3.

"Acapella Chorus Sings." *The Gustavian Weekly*, 27 February 1923, 2.

American Choral Directors Association of Minnesota. *We Sing the Year Round – A Celebration in Song*. Concert Program. 21 November 1981.

Armstrong, Anton. "The Musical Legacy of F. Melius Christiansen." *Choral Journal* 37, no. 4 (1996): 9-13.

Arwidson, Carole. "Swedish Majesties Pay Visit to Gustavus Campus." *The Gustavian Weekly*, 16 November 1982, 1-2

Aune, Gregory. "Conductor's Column." *Echoes & Overtones 2*, no. 2 (2001): 2.

—. "Conductor's Column." *Echoes and Overtones 5*, no. 2 (2004): 2.

—. Phone interview by author, 5 October 2006, Tape Recording.

Aune, Gregory J. "The Choral Methodology and Philosophy of F. Melius Christiansen: A Tradition Continues." *Choral Journal* 37, no. 4 (1996): 15-17.
"Bach's Birthday Commemorated by Singers, Organist." *The Gustavian Weekly*, 26 February 1935, 1.
"Band and Choir Return for Concerts." *The Gustavian Weekly*, 11 February 1977, 3.
"Band and Choir to Tour in California." *Great Gustavus Quarterly 44*, no. 1 (1979): 13.
"Band-Choir Concert to be Given Sunday." *The Gustavian Weekly*, 9 April 1954, 1
"Band and Chorus Return in Midst of Snowstorm." *The Gustavian Weekly*, 25 February 1955, 1.
Behrends, Al. Interview by author, 15 June 2006, St. Peter, MN. Tape Recording. Gustavus Adolphus College, St. Peter, MN.
Beissel, Michelle. "Choir Ends Successful Tour." *The Gustavian Weekly*, 13 February 1998, 7.
—. "Gustavus Choir to Perform Combination of Organ and Choral Music." *The Gustavian Weekly*, 26 April 1996, 7.
Bergman, Denny. "'Prof' Casselman Build GA Choir in Short Stay." *The Gustavian Weekly*, 14 May 1954, 4.
Bloomquist, Aldrich. "Gustavus at War." *Greater Gustavus Association Quarterly* (31 October 1944), 11.
Boelter, Deb. "Christmas in Christ Chapel Celebrates 20th Year of Worshipping Through Musical Talent." *The Gustavian Weekly*, 4 December 1992, 5.
—. "Musicians Travel Throughout the Country Performing Concerts During Touring Week." *The Gustavian Weekly*, 22 January 1993, 4.
—. "Gustavus Commissions Composer to Finish 'Easter Symphony.'" *The Gustavian Weekly*, 28 February 1992, 5.
Bukowski, Michael R. "Choir Learns Music and More for South Africa Tour." *The Gustavian Weekly*, 27 January 1999, 5.
*Bulletin of Gustavus Adolphus College Cataloge, 1945-1946*. St. Peter, MN: Gustavus Adolphus College, [1946].
*Bulletin of Gustavus Adolphus College Cataloge, 1947-1948*. St. Peter, MN: Gustavus Adolphus College, [1948].
*Bulletin of Gustavus Adolphus College 1958-1960 Catalog*. St. Peter, MN: Gustavus Adolphus College, [1946].
*Bulletin of Gustavus Adolphus College Catalog Issue 1974-75*. St. Peter, MN: Gustavus Adolphus College, [1974].

"Calendar Upcoming Events." *Greater Gustavus Quarterly 51*, no. 2 (1994): 83.
"Calgary and Regina Critics Laud Choir's Performance." *The Gustavian Weekly*, 17 February 1961, 2.
Carlson, Edgar M. "The Chapel – Now it is Finished and Dedicated," *The Gustavian Weekly*, 12 January 1962, 2.
*Catalogue of Gustavus Adolphus College for the academic year 1900-1901*. St. Peter, MN: Gustavus Adolphus College, [1901].
*Catalogue of Gustavus Adolphus College for the academic year 1901-1902*. St. Peter, MN: Gustavus Adolphus College, [1902].
*Catalogue of Gustavus Adolphus College at St. Peter, Minnesota, for 1887-1888*. Rock Island, IL: Augustana Book Concern, [1888].
*Catalogue of Gustavus Adolphus College, at St. Peter, Minnesota, for 1888-1889*. St. Peter, MN: Tribune Steam Print, [1889].
*Catalogue of Gustavus Adolphus College, at St. Peter, Minnesota, for 1889-1890*. St. Peter, MN: The Herald Book Print, [1890].
"Chapel Dedication Begins '62 Centennial." *The Gustavian Weekly*, 12 January 1962, 1.
"Chapel Carol Services to Open Holiday Festivities at Gustavus." *The Gustavian Weekly*, 6 December 1963, 1.
"Choir and Band Begin Hawaii Tour." *Junction*, 28 January 1972, 1.
"Choir and Band Prepare for Tours." *The Gustavian Weekly*, 20 January 1961, 1.
"Choir and Band to Tour in Colorado and Canada Respectively." *Greater Gustavus Quarterly 46*, no. 3 (1981): 7.
"Choir and Band Tours." *Greater Gustavus Quarterly 41*, no. 1 (1977): 13.
"Choir and Orchestra Perform in Harmony." *The Gustavian Weekly*, 10 May 1983, 5.
"Choir Appears at L.L. Conference." *The Gustavian Weekly*, 17 December 1943, 1.
"Choir, Bands Travel 8,000 Miles on 1972 Winter Tour to Hawaii." *Greater Gustavus Quarterly*, February 1972, 12.
"Choir Director Prepares Singers for Spring Tour." *The Gustavian Weekly*, 12 March 1940, 1.
"Choir Divides in Two Units." *The Gustavian Weekly*, 21 July 1943, 1.
"Choir, Eisenhower Highlight JC Meet," *The Gustavian Weekly*, 14 November 1958, 1
"Choir Leaves Sunday on Tour of Eastern United States." *The Gustavian Weekly*, 19 March 1935, 1 & 3.

"Choir Opens Yuletide Season with 'Vespers of Christmas.'" *The Gustavian Weekly*, 17 December 1935, 1.
"Choirs, Orchestra Go for Baroque." *The Gustavian Weekly*, 11 May 1982, 10.
"Choir Organization by Prof G. A. Nelson to Begin this Week." *The Gustavian Weekly*, 19 September 1933, 1.
"Choir Plans Pre-Tour Bernadotte Concert." *The Gustavian Weekly*, 13 January 1950, 1.
"Choir Practicing for Concert Tour." *The Gustavian Weekly*, 5 December 1945, 1.
"Choir Presents Homecoming Concert Sunday Night." *The Gustavian Weekly*, 4 March 1955, 1.
"Choir Ready for Tour April 26." *The Gustavian Weekly*, 17 April 1946, 1.
"Choir Records New Songs at Request of Columbia Co." *The Gustavian Weekly*, 30 September 1960, 4.
"Choir Returns from Sixteen Day Schedule." *The Gustavian Weekly*, 24 April 1934, 1.
"Choir Season Climaxed by Midwest Appearances on Extensive Tour," *The Gustavian Weekly*, 7 June 1938, 5.
"Choir Sings Bach's Cantata in Broadcasts." *The Gustavian Weekly*, 4 November 1941, 3.
"Choir Sings Oratorio Sunday, December 13." *The Gustavian Weekly*, 25 November 1942, 1.
"Choir to Appear at Christiansen Festival." *Echoes & Overtones* 7, no. 1 (2006): 6.
"Choir to Embark Feb. 6 on Six-State Venture." *The Gustavian Weekly*, 23 January 1959, 1.
"Choir to Present Afternoon Concert." *The Gustavian Weekly*, 4 April 1952, 1.
"Choir to Sing for Alumni Service Sat." *The Gustavian Weekly*, 23 October 1946, 1.
"Choir to Sing King's Birthday Salute at Ordway Music Theatre." *Greater Gustavus Quarterly 49*, no. 4 (1985): 3.
"Choir Tour of Four states Slated to Begin January 31." *The Gustavian Weekly*, 18 January 1952, 1-2.
"Choir Will Sponsor Big Christmas Party." *The Gustavian Weekly*, 21 November 1933, 1.
"Choir Winds Up Successful Tour of Twenty Days." *The Gustavian Weekly*, 16 April 1935, 1 & 3.
"Choir's Soviet Union Tour Opens 125th Anniversary Year." *Greater Gustavus Quarterly 53*, no. 2 (1986): 1.

"Choristers Finally Return: Now They Reveal Hardships," *The Gustavian Weekly*, 20 April 1937, 1.
"Choruses to Give Concert Here." *The Gustavian Weekly*, 2 February 1951, 1.
Christensen, Carol. "Choir Home from Travels." *The Gustavian Weekly*, 13 February 1953, 2.
"Christmas Music Keynotes Yule Spirit." *The Gustavian Weekly*, 10 December 1954, 2.
"College Choir," In *The Gustavian*, 132-133. St. Peter, MN: Gustavus Adolphus College, 1949.
"College Choir Acclaimed During Annual Concert Tour," *The Gustavian Weekly*, 6 June 1939, 1.
"College Choir Begins Tour of Five States." *The Gustavian Weekly*, 10 April 1934, 1 & 3.
"College Choir of 41 Voices Begins Work." *The Gustavian Weekly*, 3 October 1933, 1.
"College Choir Sings Story of Christmas." *The Gustavian Weekly*, 11 December 1934, 1 & 3.
"College Choir to Go on Tour to Canada." *The Gustavian Weekly*, 10 April 1953, 3.
*Commencement Program.* St. Peter, MN: Gustavus Adolphus College, 1883.
*Commencement Program.* St. Peter, MN: Gustavus Adolphus College, 1885.
*Commencement Program.* St. Peter, MN: Gustavus Adolphus College, 1887.
*Commencement Program.* St. Peter, MN: Gustavus Adolphus College, 1888.
"Conservatory of Music." In *Breidablick*, 124-133. St. Peter, MN: Gustavus Adolphus College, 1912.
Davis, Elena. "Lawsuit Against Gustavus Settled Out of Court." *The Gustavian Weekly*, 30 January 1998, 1.
Davis, Janey. "Choir to Repeat Guthrie Program." *The Gustavian Weekly*, 3 December 1965, 4.
Day, Lori. "Choir Incur Lenin's Revenge." *The Gustavian Weekly*, 12 March 1987, 3
De Remee, Richard. "Ambassadors of Song: Gustavus Choir Goes on Winter Tour." *The Lutheran Companion* (4 February 1953): 8 & 23.
Detisch, Doug. "Swedish Opera Premieres." *The Gustavian Weekly*, 28 April 1988, 8.

Dietrich, Clinton. "Musicians Anticipating *Easter* Premiere." *The Gustavian Weekly*, 24 March 1995, 1.
Douma, Kathie. Interview by author, 2 November 2006. Phone interview.
"Dr. Carlson, Choir at 90$^{th}$ Synod Meet." *The Gustavian Weekly*, 4 May 1948, 1.
"Dr. Lundquist Proposes Occopello Chorus." *The Gustavian Weekly*, 3 October 1922, 1-2.
"Dynamic Pianist Performs and Directs Choir." *The Gustavian Weekly*, 2 December 1941, 4.
Eckberg, Samuel. "The New Commission." *Echoes & Overtones 7*, no. 1 (2006): 1-2.
Eggers, Amanda. "Ericson Communicates with Unique Conducting Style." *The Gustavian Weekly*, 26 February 1988, 7.
"Eight New Instructors are Added to the Gustavus Adolphus Faculty." *The Gustavian Weekly*, 12 September 1945, 1.
Elvee, Richard. Interview by author, 6 June 2006, St. Peter, MN. Tape Recording. Gustavus Adolphus College, St. Peter, MN.
Erickson, June. "The Music Box." *The Gustavian Weekly*, 21 October 1947, 2.
Erickson, Karle. Interview by author, 13 June 2006, Eden Prairie, MN. Tape Recording. Erickson Home, Eden Prairie, MN.
—. *The Gustavus Choir Handbook*. St. Peter, MN: Gustavus Adolphus College. Gustavus Adolphus College Archives, Box 16.1.2.2, "Gustavus Choir 1980-81 – 1986-87." Folder 2, "Gustavus Choir, 1981-82."
"Falck-Knautz to Direct GA Band-Choir Production." *The Gustavian Weekly*, 6 April 1956, 1.
"Famous Composers Tour with Band and Choir." *The Gustavian Weekly*, 23 September 1941, 5.
Felkey, Anna. "Concerto Inaugurale: Millennium in Musica." *Echoes & Overtones 4*, no. 2 (2003): 1.
Fenton, Kevin. "Friends University's Singing Quakers: The Development of a Tradition." Ph.D. diss., Florida State University, 1994.
Fienen, David. Interview by author, 12 June 2006, St. Peter, MN. Tape Recording. Gustavus Adolphus College, St. Peter, MN.
"Final SPCO Concert Slated for Tonight." *The Gustavian Weekly*, 20 April 1982, 11.
"First Choir Reunion Attracts Many Alumni." *The Gustavian Weekly*, 8 October 1935, 3.
"G. A. Choir Meets with Big Welcome." *The Gustavian Weekly*, 17 April 1934, 1.

"GA College Choir Presents Concerts in Eight States During Two Week Tour." *The Gustavian Weekly*, 20 January 1956, 1.
"GAC band and Choir Tours Cover Midwest." *The Gustavian Weekly*, 23 January 1976, 6.
"Gustav Adolph Nelson, " *St. Peter Herald*, 17 May 1979
Gustavus Adolphus College. *Gustavus Adolphus College Choir 10$^{th}$ Annual Concert Tour*. Concert Program, 1942.
—. *Gustavus Adolphus Choir Season of 1951-52*. Concert Program Notes, 1952.
—. *Gustavus Music Showcase*. Concert Program Notes. March 20, 2005.
—. *Parent's Day Concert*. Concert Program. 5 October 1980.
—. *President's Day Concert*. Concert Program. 4 May 1975.
—. *Requiem*. Concert Program. 1981.
—. *Songs of Victory Spring Benefit Concert*. Concert Program. 17 May 1998.
—. *The Gustavus Choir*. Concert Program. 1955.
—. *The Gustavus Choir*. Concert Program. 1973.
—. *The Gustavus Choir*. Concert Program. 1981.
—. *The Gustavus Choir*. Concert Program. 1997.
—. *The Gustavus Choir Winter Concerts – 1979*. Concert Program. 1979.
—. *The Gustavus Choir in Concert, 1993*. Concert Program Notes. 1993.
—. *The Gustavus Choir in Concert*. Concert Program Notes. 2006.
—. *The Gustavus Symphony Band and The Gustavus Choir*. Concert Program. 24 May 1953.
—. *The Messiah*. Concert Program. 7 December 1952.
—. *The Messiah*. Concert Program. 6 December 1953.
*Gustavus Adolphus College Academic Catalog, 2006-2007*. St. Peter, MN: Gustavus Adolphus College, [2006].
*Gustavus Adolphus College Catalogue for the year 1892-1893*. St. Peter, MN: Herald Power Print, [1893].
*Gustavus Adolphus College Catalogue for the year 1894-1895*. St. Peter, MN: Herald Power Print, [1895].
*Gustavus Adolphus College Catalog of the academic year 1910-1911*. St. Peter, MN: Gustavus Adolphus College, [1911].
*Gustavus Adolphus College Catalog for the academic year 1912-1913*. St. Peter, MN: Gustavus Adolphus College, [1913].
*Gustavus Adolphus College Catalog for the academic year 1913-1914*. St. Peter, MN: Gustavus Adolphus College, [1914].
*Gustavus Adolphus College Catalog for the academic year 1914-1915*. St. Peter, MN: Gustavus Adolphus College, [1915].

*Gustavus Adolphus College Catalog for the academic year 1916-1917.* St. Peter, MN: Gustavus Adolphus College, [1917].
*Gustavus Adolphus College Catalog for the Academic Year 1921-1922.* St. Peter, MN: Gustavus Adolphus College, [1922].
*Gustavus Adolphus College Catalog for the academic year 1926-1927.* St. Peter, MN: Gustavus Adolphus College, [1927].
*Gustavus Adolphus College Catalog for the academic year 1928-1929.* St. Peter, MN: Gustavus Adolphus College, [1929].
*Gustavus Adolphus College Catalog for the academic year 1931-1932.* St. Peter, MN: Gustavus Adolphus College [1932].
"Gustavus Band, Choir Return from Successful Tours." *Greater Gustavus Quarterly 36*, no. 4 (1975): 15.
"Gustavus Band and Choir Tours Scheduled West and East." *Greater Gustavus Quarterly 48*, no. 3 (1983): 9.
"Gustavus Band, Choir Schedule Annual Winter Concert Tours." *The Gustavian Weekly*, 19 January 1968, 6.
"Gustavus Choir: Chamber Singers Add to Sacred Music." In *The 1966 Gustavian*, 74-75. St. Peter, MN: Gustavus Adolphus College, 1966).
"Gustavus Choir Director Eugene Casselman Resigns." *Greater Gustavus Quarterly 10*, no. 2 (1954): 4.
"Gustavus Choir Gives Concert February 18." *The Gustavian Weekly*, 16 February 1962, 6.
"Gustavus Choir Plans Concert on Sunday." *Mankato Free Press*, 16 February 1957, 6.
"Gustavus Choir Records Album." *The Gustavus Weekly*, 12 April 1983, 7.
"Gustavus Choir Returns After Concert Tour Acclaimed Most Successful in History," *The Gustavian Weekly*, 5 April 1938, 1.
"Gustavus Choir Returns from Scandinavian Tour." *St. Peter Herald*, 13 July 1967, 4.
"Gustavus Choir to Go East for Annual Tour." *The Gustavian Weekly*, 18 January 1957, 1.
"Gustavus Musicians Slate Tours." *The Gustavian Weekly*, 22 January 1960, 1.
"Gustie Choristers Lay Season Plans." *The Gustavian Weekly*, 26 September 1958, 4.
Haeuser, Michael. Interview by author, 12 June 2006, St. Peter, MN. Tape Recording. Gustavus Adolphus College, St. Peter, MN.
Herzog, Linda. "Band and Choir Tours End in Home Concerts." *The Gustavian Weekly*, 19 February 1987, 11.
Holcomb, Howard. "2 Choir Recordings Made Last Spring Now on Sale at Bookstore." *The Gustavian Weekly*, 18 November 1947, 1.

Holm, Bill. "A Note to Parents and Sponsors: What Really Happened to Your Children in Asia?" *Greater Gustavus Quarterly 48*, no. 1 (1991): 10-12.
Howe, Katie. "Tour 2000: Texas or Bust!" *Echoes & Overtones 1*, no. 1 (2000): 3.
*The Holy* City. Concert Program. Gustavus Adolphus College Archives. St. Peter, MN, 1898.
"Intensive drill for the Gustavian Choir." *The Gustavian Weekly*, 25 September 1923, 1.
Johnson, Albert Rykken. "The Christiansen Choral Tradition: F. Melius Christiansen, Olaf C. Christiansen, and Paul J. Christiansen." Ph. D. diss, University of Iowa, 1973.
Johnson, Dennis. "The Gustavus Choir 'Sings South Africa.'" *Greater Gustavus Quarterly 55*, no. 3 (1999): 5-9.
Jones, Jeremy. "Erickson Sues College, President." *The Gustavian Weekly*, 30 September 1994, 1.
Jones, William Darryl. "An Index of Choral Music Performed During National Conventions of the American Choral Directors Association." Ph.D. diss., Florida State University, 1988.
Jorgensen, Michael. Interview by author, 12 June 2006, St. Peter, MN. Tape Recording. Gustavus Adolphus College, St. Peter, MN.
"Karle Erickson Named Director of Concert Choir." *Greater Gustavus Quarterly 44*, no. 3 (1980): 11.
Knautz, Philip. Interview by author, 9 June 2006, St. Peter, MN, Tape Recording. Gustavus Adolphus College, St. Peter, MN.
—. "Choir Concert Season Record." Personal File.
Kolich, Kristin. "Nobel Concert: Mozart for the Masses." *The Gustavian Weekly*, 27 September 2002, 5.
Lammers, Mark to Music Faculty, 11 September 1980. Memo: "Music for 1980 Nobel Conference." Archives, Folk Bernadotte Library, Gustavus Adolphus College, St. Peter, Minnesota.
"Large Crowds Hear Choir in the Twin Cities." *The Gustavian Weekly*, 26 March 1935, 1.
"Large Frosh Turnout for Choir Announced." *The Gustavian Weekly*, 23 September 1942, 1.
Lenius, Kathy. "GOY2UK International Tour a New Tradition for Orchestra." *The Gustavian Weekly*, 14 April 2000, 5 & 7.
Levithan, Wendy. "Choir Stays Close to Home." *The Gustavian Weekly*, 28 January 1988, 2.
Lund, Doniver A. *Gustavus Adolphus College: a Centennial History, 1862-1962*. St. Peter, MN: Gustavus Adolphus College Press, 1963.

"Lutheran Choir from Texas to Appear at GA Tuesday." *The Gustavian Weekly*, 10 April 1953, 3.

"Lyric Male Chorus." In *The Gustavian*, 142. St. Peter, MN: Gustavus Adolphus College, 1932.

"Mass in B Minor on May 4." *Greater Gustavus Quarterly 43*, no. 1 (1979): 5.

"Manager Charts Six-State Tour." *The Gustavian Weekly*, 2 December 1941, 3.

"Mankato concert postponed because of director's illness." *The Gustavian Weekly*, 12 March 1935, 1 & 3.

Mark, Michael L. "Unique Aspects of Historical Research in Music Education." *The Bulletin of Historical Research in Music Education* 6, no. 1 (1985): 29-33.

McCormick, Sarah. "Faculty has Conquered a Whirlwind of Problems." *The Gustavian Weekly*, 28 April 1998, 1.

"Memorable Experiences Fill Minds of Gustavus Songsters." *The Gustavian Weekly*, 16 Febraury 1962, 6.

"Minneapolis Concert Ends '42 Choir Tour." *The Gustavian Weekly*, 10 December 1942, 3.

"More Men Needed for A Capella Choir." *The Gustavian Weekly*, 19 September 1945, 1.

"Mrs. Myrum Starts New Choir Duties." *The Gustavian Weekly*, 5 October 1937, 1.

"Music Department Moves Into New Fine Arts Center." *Greater Gustavus Quarterly 31*, no. 1 (1971): 12-13.

"Music Faculty Revamped; Swanson on U Tour Slate." *The Gustavian Weekly*, 15 March 1949, 1.

"Music Groups Prepare to Tour." *The Gustavian Weekly*, 23 January 1981, 2.

"Music Head Plans Organization of A Capella Choir." *The Gustavian Weekly*, 25 September 1926, 1 & 4.

"Music Panorama of 800 Years: A Choral Achievement." (1942). *The Lutheran Companion* (5 February 1942): 172.

"Musical Organizations." In *The Gustavian*, 165. St. Peter, MN: Gustavus Adolphus College, 1917.

"Musicians Serenade World." *The Gustavian Weekly*, 11 March 1960, 1.

"Nat'l Music Group Accepts G. A." *The Gustavian Weekly*, 25 March 1947, 1.

"Nelson Announces Choir in Concert Thursday Evening." *The Gustavus Weekly*, 7 April 1943, 1.

"Nelson Resigns as College Music Head," *Gustavus Adolphus College Archives; Faculty Staff Clippings*: Nelson, G. Adolph.

"Nelson Selects Forty-Five for A Cappella Choir." *The Gustavian Weekly*, 26 September 1939, 1 & 3.

Neuleib, Charles. "Students Sing for King of Sweden During Concert Tour of Europe." *The Gustavian Weekly*, 15 September 1967, 1.

"New Music Comes in Under Wire for Nobel." *The Gustavian Weekly*, 5 October 1982, 7.

Nimmo, Doug. Interview by author, 14 June 2006, St. Peter, MN. Tape Recording. Nimmo Home, St. Peter, MN.

"No Coughing Please!" *St. Peter Herald*, 6 March 1958, 8.

"O'Hara 'Joins' Choir Greets Choirsters with Swede Escort." *The Gustavian Weekly*, 7 December 1948, 1.

"Olson Books Three State Appearances for the College Choir." *The Gustavian Weekly*, 8 December 1936, 1.

"Personnel of College Choir Includes 47." *The Gustavian Weekly*, 9 October 1934, 1.

Peterson, Conrad. *Remember Thy Past: A History of Gustavus Adolphus College 1862-1952*. St. Peter, MN: Gustavus Adolphus College Press, 1953.

Peterson, Megan. "Christmas is Christ Chapel Goes Swedish." *The Gustavian Weekly*, 13 December 2002, 1.

—. "Gustavus Choir Departs on International Tour." *The Gustavian Weekly*, 17 January 2003, 3.

Pittack, Mary Lou. "Gustavus Choir to Leave on Two Weeks Tour." *The Gustavian Weekly*, 8 January 1954, 1.

"Philip Knautz to Direct G.A. Fine Arts Programs." *Greater Gustavus Quarterly 44*, no. 2 (1980): 8.

"Post-Tour Choir Concert Tuesday." *The Gustavian Weekly*, 16 February 1951, 1.

"Press Comment Cites Concerts of A Cappella" *The Gustavian Weekly*, 11 May 1937, 1.

"Prof. Nelson Leads Busy Life Guiding Music Dept." *The Gustavian Weekly*, 3 19 1940, 3.

"Prof. Swanson Picks Choir." *The Gustavian Weekly*, 2 October 1946, 1.

*Program for the Pipe Organ Concert, in the Swedish Lutheran Church*. Gustavus Adolphus College Archives. St. Peter, MN, 1893.

*Programme of Jubilee Festival of Gustavus Adolphus College at Swedish Lutheran Church, St. Peter, Minn*. Gustavus Adolphus College Archives. St. Peter, MN, 1885.

"Recording Artists Abound at Gustavus." *The Gustavian Weekly*, 1 October 1985, 9.
Regier, Bernard. "The Development of Choral Music in Higher Education." D.M.A. diss., University of Southern California, 1963.
Risco, Jessica. "'The Easter Symphony' in its Second Performance." *The Gustavian Weekly*, 30 April 1999, 5.
Roeder, Dan, and Paul Miller. "Nobel Symphony Generates Excitement." *Echoes & Overtones 3*, no. 1 (2001): 3.
Rosell, Erland. "Noteworthy Encounter with Swedish-America." Translated from Swedish by Martha Lundholm Jansson. Karlstad Newpaper, photocopy located in Gustavus Adolphus College Archives. Box 16.1.2.2, "Gustavus Choir 1980-81 – 1986-87," Folder 4, "Gustavus Choir, Tour 1983."
Rundle, Amber. "Nimmo, Aune Take Groups on the Road." *The Gustavian Weekly*, 19 January 1996, 5.
Russell, Beth. "125th Anniversary Celebration of F. Melius Christiansen Underway." *The Gustavian Weekly*, 15 November 1996, 8.
—. "G-Choir Celebrates Christianity in Europe." *The Gustavian Weekly*, 13 January 1995, 4.
—. "Perserverance and Hard Work are Lessons New Choral Director Aune Hopes Students Will Learn." *The Gustavian Weekly*, 15 September 1995, 5.
"Schumann Laides Chorus." In *The Gustavian, 143*. St. Peter, MN: Gustavus Adolphus College, 1932.
"Schumann, Lyric Groups Unite in Acapella Chorus." *The Gustavian Weekly*, 18 November 1930, 1.
*Schumann – Lyric Home Concert*. Concert Program. Gustavus Adolphus College Archives, St. Peter, MN, 1916.
*Schumann – Lyric Home Concert*. Concert Program. Gustavus Adolphus College Archives, St. Peter, MN, 1917.
"Schumann – Male Choruses." In *The Gustavian*, 50. St. Peter, MN: Gustavus Adolphus College, 1944.
"Senior Class Observes Cap and Gown Day in Presence of Board." *The Gustavian Weekly*, 10 April 1923, 1 & 4.
"Services Feature Hall Sermon, Bach Cantata." *The Gustavian Weekly*, 15 October 1949, 1-2.
"Seventy Voices Try Out for A Capella." *The Gustavian Weekly*, 26 September 1933, 1.
Simonsen, Jane. "Choir's Music Reaches Across the Globe." *The Gustavian Weekly*, 6 September 1991, 3.

"St. Olaf Choir Will Sing Here Friday Evening." *The Gustavian Weekly*, 12 May 1936, 1.
Stalter, Tobias. "Gustavus Choir Accepts Historic Invitation." *Echoes & Overtones 3*, no. 1 (2001): 1.
"Stormy Weather Halts College Choir." *The Gustavian Weekly*, 28 March 1952, 2.
Stottrup, Joel. "European Choir Tour has Images of Horror, Beauty." *Princeton Union-Eagle*, 24 February 1983, 10.
"Success Crowns Choir Concerts on Annual Tour." *The Gustavian Weekly*, 24 March 1936, 1.
"Sunday Finishes Big Tour." *The Gustavian Weekly*, 19 February 1960, 5.
"Superb Gustavus Choir Brings Wide Acclaim." In *The Gustavian*, 71-72. St. Peter, MN: Gustavus Adolphus College, 1960.
Swan, Howard. "The Development of a Choral Instrument" in *Choral Conducting Symposium*. Upper Saddle River, NJ: Prentice Hall, 1988.
"Swanson Announces Choir Personnel." *The Gustavian Weekly*, 26 September 1945, 1.
"Swanson Directs Choir in Benefit Concert Tonight." *The Gustavian Weekly*, 22 May 1946, 1.
"Swanson to Conduct A Capella Tryouts." *The Gustavian Weekly*, 12 September 1945, 1.
*Tenth annual catalogue of Gustavus Adolphus College at St. Peter, Minnesota, for 1885-1886.* Rock Island, IL: Augustana Book Concern, 1886.
"Texas Sun Awaits GAC Band & Choir." *The Gustavian Weekly*, 31 January 1979, 2.
"The A Capella Chorus." In *The Gustavian*, 146. St. Peter, MN: Gustavus Adolphus College, 1932.
"The A Capella Choir." In *The Gustavian*, 148. St. Peter, MN: Gustavus Adolphus College, 1936.
"The College Choir." In *The Gustavian*, 138-139. St. Peter, MN: Gustavus Adolphus College, 1948.
"The Gustavus Choir 1991-92." In *The 1991-92 Gustavian*, 60. St. Peter, MN: Gustavus Adolphus College, 1992.
"The Lyric." In *Breidablick*, 134-135. St. Peter, MN: Gustavus Adolphus College, 1912.
*The Lyric Concert Co. The Lyric Quartette.* Gustavus Adolphus College Archives. St. Peter, MN, 1893.
*The Lyric Male Quartet and The Gounod Ladies Quartet Assisted by Mr. Leonard N. Pehrson, the Popular Trombone Soloist, Will Give a Select*

*Concert.* Concert Program. Gustavus Adolphus College Archives. St. Peter, MN, 1895.

"The Past, Present and Future." In *The Gustavian*, 80-81. St. Peter, MN: Gustavus Adolphus College, 1920.

Tollefson, Sara. "Gustavus Choir Croons in the Big Apple." *The Gustavian Weekly*, 14 January 1994, 7.

"Tour Prospects for College Singers Very Encouraging." *The Gustavian Weekly*, 13 February 1923, 1.

"Touring Week Lasted 17 Days for Choir." *The Gustavian Weekly*, 20 February 1986, 7.

Tourtelot, Bea. "GA Choir Presents TV Show." *The Gustavian Weekly*, 14 December 1962, 3.

"Unrestrained Recognition Meets Choir." *The Gustavian Weekly*, 23 March 1948, 1-2.

"Unseasonable Tornado Redefines Community, Brings Gusties Together Despite Tearing Apart the Campus." *The Gustavian Weekly*, 28 April 1998, 8-9.

Van Camp, Leonard. "The Development and Present Status of A Cappella Singing in the United States Colleges and Universities." D.M.A. diss., University of Missouri-Kansas City, 1964.

Wager, W. J. & McGrath, E. J. *Liberal Education and Music*. New York, NY: Columbia University, 1962.

Wahlund, Dean. Interview by author, 12 June 2006, St. Peter, MN. Tape Recording. Gustavus Adolphus College, St. Peter, MN.

—. "The Gustavus Choir Will Reign in Spain (and Not Only on the Plane)." *Echoes and Overtones 7*, no. 1 (2006): 5.

Williams, Josh. "Gusties Truly Shine." *The Gustavian Weekly*, 20 February 2004, 5.

"Worship Service, Oratorio, Dorm Open House Highlight Program for Parent's Day." *The Gustavian Weekly*, 2 May 1958, 1.

Ziebarth, Angela. "Taking the West by Storm." *Echoes & Overtones 2*, no. 1 (2000): 1.

# INDEX

75th Anniversary Celebration, 122, 123
A Cappella Choir, 14, 15, 16, 18, 19, 20, 21, 25, 26, 33, 34
A Cappella Chorus. *See* A Cappella Choir,
Adolph VI, Gustav, 64, 65
Allen, O. A., 8
Allwardt, Paul, 53, 56, 61, 63, 68, 69
American Choral Directors Association, 85, 92, 106, 112, 118, 121
Anderson, A. Waldemar, 11
Augustana College, 3, 35, 37,
Augustana Synod, 3, 39
Aune, Gregory, 104-124
Barth, Frank, 72
Bethany College, 106, 107, 110
Bjorling Concert Hall, 65, 66, 94
Bjorling, Ann Charlotte, 90
Bjorling, Jussi, 64, 65
Brunelle, Phillip, 93
Byrne, Kevin, 99
Caliope, 8
Carlson, Edgar, 32, 39, 51, 59, 61
Casselman, Eugene, 41-45
Cathedral Choir of the Augustana Synod, 27
Chapel Choir, 37, 43, 52, 53, 56, 64, 68, 69, 70, 74, 75, 85, 88, 103, 104, 117, 118
Christ Chapel, 58, 59-62, 63, 66, 68, 69, 72, 74, 75, 84, 85, 86, 88, 93, 94, 95, 104, 111, 112, 113, 118, 121
Christiansen, F. Melius, 1, 4, 5, 6, 14, 16, 18, 19, 27, 34, 36, 38, 45, 67, 73, 74, 79, 81, 84, 99, 101, 109, 112, 113, 121, 123, 125
Christiansen, Olaf, 73, 78
Christiansen, Paul J., 47, 49, 50, 105, 106, 108, 112
Christmas in Christ Chapel, 36, 67, 68-72, 75, 84, 85, 88, 98, 100, 101, 111, 119, 121, 126
Concordia College, 47, 104, 105, 106, 112
Conservatory Chorus, 9, 10, 11, 12
Dakota Wesleyan University, 106
East Union, 3
Echoes Ladies' Chorus, 11
Eisenhower, Dwight D., 56
Elvee, Richard, 59, 61, 67, 68, 69, 70, 71, 72
Engen, David, 74
Erickson, Karle, 5, 77-100, 101, 111, 112, 114, 118
Ericson, Eric, 92, 93
Festival Orchestra, 85, 88
Fienen, David, 69, 88
Fine Arts Building, 67, 114
Gibson, Daryl, 40, 41
Gounod Ladies Quartet, 10
Grainger, Percy, 29, 30
Gustav Adolf II, 4
Gustavian Male Chorus, 41, 42, 43, 45
Gustavus Band, 29, 52, 53, 66, 74, 103, 105, 116, 121
Gustavus Music Showcase, 121
Gustavus Singers, 51, 52
Guthrie Theater, 64
Hilary, Frederic, 28, 29, 32
Holm, Bill, 95
Jennings, Kenneth, 101, 102, 103, 104, 112, 121

Johnson, Dennis, 101, 115
Jussi Bjorling Memorial Concert, 64
Karvonen, Paul, 40
King's Singers, 94, 98
Knautz, Philip, 39, 47-76, 80
Knock, C. J., 11
Lagerstrom, Reinhold, 8, 9, 11
Lawrence University, 79
Lundeen, Malvin, 59
Lundquist, Matthew, 12, 13
Lutheran Choral School, 1, 36, 75, 77, 79, 81, 104, 109, 125
Lyric, 8, 9, 10, 11, 12, 13, 14, 15, 16, 17, 18, 19, 20, 23
Mandela, Nelson, 114, 115, 118
Minnesota Elementary School, 3
Moline, Robert, 94, 1117
Moses, Don, 106
National Association of Schools of Music, 37
Nelson, G. Adolph, 16-35, 41
Nielsen, Waldo, 15
Nimmo, Douglas, 103, 104, 116
Nixon, Richard, 54
Nobel Conference, 84, 86, 118
Norelius, Erik, 3, 125
*O God Our Help in Ages Past*, 82
O'Hara, Joseph, 39, 54, 55
Olsen, Per, 11
Oratorio Chorus, 12, 15, 16, 18, 23
Peterson, Albin O., 15, 16

Peterson, Gregory, 115
*Praise to the Lord*, 2, 5, 14, 15, 18, 73, 81, 84, 99, 112, 123
*Saint Erik's Crown*, 93
Sappho, 8
Schumann Ladies Chorus, 11, 12, 13, 14, 15, 16, 17, 18, 19, 20, 23, 26, 31, 32, 35, 36, 42, 43, 45
Seashore, Carl, 8
Seeley, Rachael, 120
Shaw, Robert, 5, 106, 107, 108
St. Ansgar's Academy, 3
St. Olaf Choir, 6, 22, 25, 73, 78, 82, 101, 112
St. Olaf College, 5, 33, 70, 78, 79, 112
St. Paul Chamber Orchestra, 64, 85
Stromgren, June, 32, 35
Sutphen, Joyce, 119
Swanson, Wilbur, 33-40, 44
Texas Lutheran College, 47, 49, 56
Thalia, 8
*The Easter Symphony*, 103, 104, 116
tornado, 61, 113, 116
University of Illinois, 79
University of Iowa, 34, 106
V-12 Program, 31
Wahlund, Dean, 83, 102
Walker, Courtney, 120
Westminster Choir College, 41

**DATE DUE**

DEMCO 38-296